LIVE
NAKED
AF

LIVE NAKED AF

A Joyful Approach to
Living Alcohol Free

ANNIE GRACE

AVERY
an imprint of Penguin Random House
New York

AVERY

an imprint of Penguin Random House LLC
1745 Broadway, New York, NY 10019
penguinrandomhouse.com

Most Avery books are available at a discount when purchased in quantity for sales promotions or corporate use. Special editions, which include personalized covers, excerpts, and corporate imprints, can be created when purchased in large quantities. For more information, please e-mail specialmarkets@penguinrandomhouse.com. Your local bookstore can also assist with discounted bulk purchases using the Penguin Random House corporate Business-to-Business program. For assistance in locating a participating retailer, e-mail B2B@penguinrandomhouse.com.

Book design by Ashley Tucker

Library of Congress Cataloging-in-Publication Data

Names: Grace, Annie, 1978– author
Title: Live naked AF: a joyful approach to living alcohol free / Annie Grace.
Description: New York: Avery, an imprint of Penguin Random House, [2025] | Includes index.
Identifiers: LCCN 2025030682 (print) | LCCN 2025030683 (ebook) |
ISBN 9780593853221 paperback | ISBN 9780593853238 ebook
Subjects: LCSH: Temperance | Drinking of alcoholic beverages—Social aspects |
Alcohol | Alcoholism
Classification: LCC HV5060 .G67 2025 (print) | LCC HV5060 (ebook)
LC record available at https://lccn.loc.gov/2025030682
LC ebook record available at https://lccn.loc.gov/2025030683

Printed in the United States of America
1st Printing

The authorized representative in the EU for product safety and compliance is Penguin Random House Ireland, Morrison Chambers, 32 Nassau Street, Dublin D02 YH68, Ireland, https://eu-contact.penguin.ie.

To my dad.

Who I lost forty-four days before the final draft of this book was due.

And who, in both life and death, helped me bring it into the world.

I love you, Daddy.

CONTENTS

Introduction ix

CHAPTER 1
We Follow the Worse 1

CHAPTER 2
We've Been Programmed 12

CHAPTER 3
The Internal Battle 30

CHAPTER 4
The Brain's Default Mode 44

CHAPTER 5
Rewrite the Code 58

CHAPTER 6
Normal AF 71

CHAPTER 7
Awareness, Clarity, and Transformation 82

CHAPTER 8
How to Navigate AF Firsts 97

CHAPTER 9
How to Escape Dangerous Cultural Programming 107

CHAPTER 10
How to Say No to a Drink 120

CHAPTER 11
How to Overcome a Craving 131

CHAPTER 12
How to Build Strong AF Relationships 149

CHAPTER 13
How to Enjoy Sex Alcohol Free **164**

CHAPTER 14
How to Find Happiness Without Alcohol **173**

CHAPTER 15
How to Handle "Relapse" **184**

CHAPTER 16
Building a Joyful AF Life, Part 1: Switches **201**

CHAPTER 17
Building a Joyful AF Life, Part 2: Seeds **215**

CHAPTER 18
How to Authentically Influence Others **231**

CHAPTER 19
How to Get Your Power Back **250**

CHAPTER 20
How to Shift Your Animating Energy **260**

CHAPTER 21
Grace First: A New Order of Operations **272**

APPENDIX 1
Affective Liminal Psychology **283**

APPENDIX 2
Filters for Truth **293**

APPENDIX 3
ACT Questions **295**

Acknowledgments **299**
Index **303**

INTRODUCTION

The only way to deal with an unfree world is to become so absolutely free that your very existence is an act of rebellion.
—Albert Camus

I've struggled with anxiety for as long as I can remember. Most of my childhood memories carry a quiet, constant sense of dread. And because no one else seemed to feel the same way, I wondered why the *inside of me* felt so different from the *outside of everyone else.*

Enter alcohol.

Alcohol took the edge off, making the ever-present pit in my stomach less deep. If I drank enough, the pit might even disappear—at least for a while. But when it came back, usually deeper than before, another drink always felt like the answer. Alcohol seemed to fix everything. It felt like the glue holding my entire life together.

Cracks started to appear. And in a painful moment of realization, I understood something terrifying: Maybe alcohol wasn't the solution. Maybe it was the problem. That thought shook me because I didn't know how to live without it. I didn't know how to have fun, how to relax, *how to function.* And if I'm brutally honest, life without alcohol almost didn't seem worth living.

The cracks grew.

What I'd once believed was holding my life together was quietly pulling it apart. Instead of strengthening my marriage or helping me have better sex, alcohol was creating distance between my husband and me, a subtle, brewing conflict that threatened our entire foundation. *Crack.*

Instead of a social lubricant making me great at networking, my drinking was brought up in my performance review. *Crack.*

The costs of drinking began to outpace the benefits. But I didn't want to be one of *those people.* I didn't want to admit I had *that problem.*

I was so attached to alcohol that quitting wasn't an option. I did the sensible, less drastic thing and decided to cut back. A friend who attended Alcoholics Anonymous (AA) told me I wasn't an alcoholic, and I certainly didn't *feel like one*, so I assumed that surely I couldn't be addicted. I just needed to get back in control and drink less. I thought it would be easy.

I made endless deals with myself: *No drinking until the weekend.* Or *Just two glasses of wine—okay, maybe three.* Nothing worked.

In an unexpected plot twist, the more I tried to control my drinking, the more alcohol began to control me. I felt trapped. My inner voices, all with seemingly different agendas, got loud and argumentative. I was constantly thinking about drinking: *Would I drink today? Would I overdo it? Could I stick to my limits? Why was this so hard?*

I was in a battle with myself—alone, afraid, and broken.

I imagined that if I could just get some alcohol-free (AF) time under my belt, *then* I would feel good again—then I would laugh again. If enough time passed, it would get easier. Life wouldn't feel so flat. I never found out what a year or even a month felt like. I never made it that far. The more I tried to get a handle on my drinking, *the worse my drinking got.*

It made no sense.

This went on for years. I was hurting myself, my family, and even my career. Like struggling in quicksand, the more I tried to escape the hold alcohol had on my life, the faster I sank. It was terrifying. And this isn't just my story—it's the story of thousands.

It Doesn't Add Up

No one would knowingly choose a drink that makes them feel miserable over the people they love. And yet we do. That contradiction lies at the heart of one of the most important questions we must answer if we want to live joyfully alcohol free.

After more than a decade of living AF, I've learned that putting down the bottle is just the beginning. The first step toward a deeper journey—a journey of self-discovery, peace, and living fully awake.

So how can living alcohol free become truly joyful, so that your chances of long-term success skyrocket? We need to understand—*what's really going on here?*

Let's begin with this fundamental truth:

The harder it feels to be AF, the more likely you are to go back to drinking.

This is a harsh reality when we live in a culture that treats sobriety like a social death sentence. There was a time when I would have rather drunk myself into an early grave than suffer the misery of giving up my beloved alcohol.

Feeling good while living AF has very little to do with not drinking. It's really about the kind of life you're living, what you are thinking and believing—and your relationship with alcohol—after you've put down the bottle. One of the most important things you can do to stay free from alcohol is to learn how to build a joyful life, one you genuinely don't want to escape.

What if you could take out an insurance policy against falling back into the alcohol trap? That would be great, considering how rare lasting success is. According to an article published by the University of New Hampshire, 90 percent of people who try to stop drinking eventually relapse. That's a staggering number, especially when so many of those people are deeply committed to change. The best way to permanently escape the trap is to learn how it works. And through education, this book is that insurance policy.

Right now, there are subconscious programs running in your mind—programs that, despite your best intentions, threaten to derail your progress. This book will free you, helping you rewrite those programs so alcohol becomes truly small and irrelevant—*you just won't want it.*

The path from being stuck in a vicious alcohol cycle to feeling at home, at peace, and even joyful in my life has been incredible. And the single most important part of that journey is a new understanding of what is going on in my mind, and why, *despite my best efforts*, I do things that I know are bad for me.

When you start to understand how to change from the inside out, life no longer feels like something to endure or escape. Instead, you wake up excited for what's ahead.

You're making—or have already made—one of the most badass, life-giving, and health-conscious decisions a person can make: leaving alcohol behind. It's a revolutionary act, a subversive choice where you stand up to the status quo and take your life back from a toxic substance that numbs your mind and pollutes your body.

The latest research confirms what many of us have come to know personally: No amount of alcohol is safe for the human body. Choosing to live alcohol free is like recovering from a life-threatening illness. It is a second chance—quite literally a new lease on life. Given the extensive health benefits of life beyond alcohol, many experts suggest that going alcohol free may be the closest we can get to a real fountain of youth.

Your decision to stop drinking is incredible, but maybe it doesn't feel that way yet. Maybe you feel more like Jess, who told me:

"Annie, I stopped drinking, and I know I should feel great, but I'm miserable. Why?"

Jess was constantly on a diet from alcohol. She wasn't drinking, but she still wanted to. Every day felt like an uphill battle. She was thinking about alcohol more than ever, even though she wasn't touching it. I'll share with you what helped Jess move from struggle to freedom: why you might not feel great right now, and more important, how to start feeling better than ever.

Interestingly, putting down the bottle is only the first step. The real transformation begins when you discover who you are and *why you were drinking in the first place*. It's not just about a life without alcohol—it's about a life that's fuller, freer, and entirely your own.

I've spoken with countless people who've left alcohol behind, finding true freedom. The most common thing they share about the AF life is how they rediscovered *themselves*. This is profound because I believe the deepest wisdom available for your specific life path is the wisdom you hold within.

This book is an invitation to a new way of living—one that is joyful, playful, and authentic. A life in which your relationships deepen, your heart finds peace, and you finally feel at home.

Imagine a life in which you don't feel deprived or like you're missing out. Where you're having so much fun, you can't imagine allowing a drink to steal that joy from you.

That might sound impossible, especially if, like Jess, you've been alcohol free for a while and still feel miserable. But here's what the latest research shows: The amount of time you've been alcohol free has very little to do with how likely you are to *stay* free, and even less to do with how happy you are. There are people who've been sober for years and still quietly mourn the fact that they no longer drink.

This book will help you understand what's going on beneath the surface. It is designed to help shift your mindset and rewire your psychology so you don't just tolerate life without alcohol—you love it.

You'll find answers to the most important questions:

- How do you stay free from alcohol?

- How do you build a life you don't want to escape?

- How can you understand why you were drinking in the first place, so you don't replace alcohol with something else?

Neurosurgeon Dr. Lee Warren tells me that my work is like brain surgery. He explains how this process can change the gray matter in your brain—the actual cells. It's like removing harmful patterns and beliefs and replacing them with new, empowering ones. Gently, and in the most accessible way possible, we will run a few updates to your internal programming—the subconscious drivers behind your behavior.

The promise of this book is bold: *It will help rewire your brain.* I know it's a big one, but I stand by it. However, if you want to rewire your brain—so that you no longer *desire* a drink—you have to do your part. That means reading *all of it*. A study of twenty-seven million readers showed that only 44 percent finish the books they start. Don't be part of that statistic.

You don't have to rush. In fact, reading slowly is often better. Maybe a chapter a day. Or start a book club with friends so you can read and reflect together. If you stick with it, by the end of this book, you'll discover a version of yourself that's not just free from alcohol but also genuinely excited about what's ahead.

This book is for you if . . .

. . . you've been alcohol free for years—or even decades—but still find yourself missing a drink.

. . . you're just starting your AF journey and want to make the next part of your life the best one yet.

. . . you're not feeling as good as you'd hoped living alcohol free and are considering drinking again.

. . . you're feeling okay alcohol free, but it also feels like something's missing—and you're not quite sure what that is.

. . . you're sober-curious and wondering what life might be like with less alcohol.

. . . you want to change another bad habit or addiction—the principles in this book can work for *anything*.

———

In this book, you'll find a fresh, science-backed, empowered approach to your first—or next—year of living alcohol free. It blends real-life experience, science, ancient wisdom, and just a touch of woo-woo. Along with tips on shifting your mindset, it's packed with practical how-to strategies. Since publishing *This Naked Mind*, I've received and responded to hundreds of questions like these:

- How do I loosen up for sex without a drink?

- How can I enjoy my vacation without drinking?

- What are the ways—*that actually work*—to relax without alcohol?

- How can I keep my friendships when they've always revolved around drinking?

- What will a first date be like?

- How do I tell my friends?

- How will I have fun without alcohol?

- How do I inspire my friends and family to join me?

This book contains the answers, gathered during more than ten years of research, and by the time you reach the end, you'll see your first—or next—year alcohol free through an entirely new lens. You'll have a new perspective that feels empowering and uplifting. One that leaves you feeling proud and deeply grateful for the brave, powerful decision you've made to live alcohol free.

First, we're going to explore, in detail, why we stay stuck—locked in behaviors we no longer want or craving alcohol long after we've stopped drinking. We'll take a deep dive into how the brain functions when it comes to habits, behavior change, and addiction—not just with alcohol, but beyond.

Next, we'll walk through the processes that create effortless behavior change, using fresh, often counterintuitive perspectives. We'll blend science with practical tools to equip you to live happily—and even joyfully—alcohol free.

This book is built on the science-based tenets of Affective Liminal Psychology (ALP). Once you've had an experience of how ALP works, you can turn to appendix 1 for a deeper dive into the theory behind it. I recommend reading the main text first and letting yourself experience the process. That will set you up to better understand the theory that follows.

I filled this book with unique, scientific insights to help make living AF feel joyful—rather than a daily struggle. Living without alcohol doesn't have to be exhausting or filled with effort. It can feel light, even exciting. You can have a truly happy first—or next—year AF, where life becomes more than you ever imagined.

You can think of this book as your best friend—the one who always gives honest, helpful advice. It's also like a therapist, offering practical tools to help you navigate life. And it's like an ancient sage, constantly guiding you back to the most valuable wisdom of all: the wisdom found within.

If you want help finding freedom from alcohol, read my first book, *This Naked Mind*.

This book is about everything that happens next.

Love,
Annie Grace

LIVE
NAKED
AF

CHAPTER 1

WE FOLLOW THE WORSE

I see the better way and approve it, but I follow the worse.
—Ovid

I could barely move. My whole body felt like lead—thick and heavy, as if sludge were running through my veins. My alarm was blaring as I looked around, disoriented. It took me a full minute to remember—I was in London, in a hotel room. I had set my alarm for an early wake-up to catch my flight home to Colorado, where my husband and two young boys were waiting.

That thought made me sad. They were excited for my return and didn't yet know how much of a mess I was, how I was barely holding it together. A surge of shame rose up in my chest, sharp and sudden, tightening around my heart and threatening tears. I pushed it down.

What had happened last night?

I remembered being in a hotel room that wasn't mine. There were about six of us, mostly colleagues from our Australian team. We were all in London for a leadership meeting. At the time, I was the global head of marketing, responsible for twenty-eight countries, and this was one of the rare times we were all together in person.

We were loud, drunk, and out of control. There was an Australian football game on TV, and because of the time difference, it ended at three a.m. In hindsight, I'm surprised we didn't get a visit from the hotel manager. I probably made it back to my room around four. The clock now read 5:30 a.m.—*brutal*.

I dragged myself down to the hotel restaurant, my head pounding, desperate for something greasy—fried potatoes—and a mimosa to take the edge off. A thought flickered: *Should I really be drinking at six in the morning?* I pushed it away. A mimosa is a breakfast drink, after all.

The waitress told me it was too early to open the champagne, saying the rest of the bottle would go flat before anyone else ordered. Panic—I needed that drink. She noticed my disappointment and tried to help, offering a screwdriver instead—vodka and orange juice.

Vodka—at six a.m.—*yikes*.

My internal alarm bells rang. Hard alcohol in the morning had always been one of my lines. Those invisible, self-imposed lines that told me I was still a *normal* drinker. As long as I didn't cross them, I could convince myself I was okay.

That morning was full of pain. I felt the weight of shame from the night before, the regret from the entire booze-filled week, and the physical pain of the hangover, but worse was the guilt, knowing I was bringing home the worst version of myself to my family when they deserved the best. It hurt so much that I didn't stop at one screwdriver. I drank three.

By then I was blacking out regularly. I'd be fully conscious and awake, but later I'd have no memory of what had happened. I must have blacked out again because I didn't remember taking the train from Paddington Station to Heathrow. The next thing I knew, I was sitting in a deserted tunnel deep in the airport, feeling lost. A wave of dread swept over me. I could see that my drinking wasn't just problematic—it was dangerous.

I looked down and found my journal open on my lap, where I'd been writing. I'll never forget the words I scribbled on the page:

I am an alcoholic. Those four words broke me.

I remember my thoughts as clearly as if they had been shouted inside my head: *This is all wrong. This isn't who I'm supposed to be.*

The last thing I wanted to be was an alcoholic. Shame and fear flooded me, and I started to cry so hard I could barely breathe. I was desperate, alone, and afraid.

Eventually I found the calm that is on the other side of a good cry, a sense of peace that I now believe is ever present but hidden below so many of our unfelt and unexpressed emotions. As my tears dried, I scratched out the hateful words and turned the page. On the blank page I wrote:

Why?

I started to wonder: Why did alcohol control my entire life when I used to be able to take it or leave it? Why was I desperate for a drink when I used to hate the taste? Why did I crave alcohol even as it made me miserable? Why was it that the more I tried to control my drinking, the worse it got?

Why?

———

That single word opened an entire world. It was a sliver of compassion and curiosity. What if I wasn't an awful person, or broken and diseased? What if I wasn't an alcoholic?

I made myself a promise. Not a promise to stop drinking—I'd made that promise dozens, maybe hundreds, of times and broken every single one. This promise had to be different; it had to be a promise I could keep. I promised myself I would find out *why*.

In that moment, drunk at six in the morning with those four awful words voiced on the page, I had nothing left to lose. Why not try something new? Why not try to understand?

What I did next felt simple and obvious, but I now know how radical it was. I decided that I would stop trying to stop drinking while I searched for answers. I let go of the shame, the guilt, and the pressure.

I gave myself a year to figure out why I drank, and why I couldn't stop. I stopped fighting myself and instead observed what was happening with honesty and curiosity. And if I wanted to drink, I would. I didn't realize it then, but that was my first true step toward freedom.

Suddenly hopeful, I left the maze of tunnels and found my gate. Instead of ordering wine like I always did at the airport, no matter the time of day, I ordered water and wrote a list of every reason I drank. My list was long, including things like the following:

- Alcohol relaxes me.

- Drinking is fun.

- Alcohol helps me loosen up for sex.

- I love the taste.

- I won't get invited if I'm not drinking.

- Alcohol relieves boredom and makes certain people more tolerable.

I had dozens of reasons. During the next few weeks, I started asking everyone I knew why they drank. The list kept growing. I got to work. But I didn't do just any research; I wanted real answers, so I focused on information from published, scientific, peer-reviewed studies. (You can find each study referenced in this book in the extensive online footnotes at LiveNakedAF.com.)

I went through each reason on my list, methodically and honestly. I searched for the truth behind each belief, and little by little, I started to see things differently:

Did alcohol relax me?

Not really. Even a single drink triggers a stress response. The body reacts to alcohol by releasing both cortisol (the stress hormone) and adrenaline—two chemicals that increase stress, not reduce it.

Did alcohol make things more fun?

No. But it feels like it does because it overstimulates the brain's pleasure center, which might sound good—but it backfires. The brain compensates by turning down our ability to feel pleasure, not just by building a tolerance to alcohol, where alcohol feels less and less fun, but by sucking the joy out of everything else—without regard for what it is. Life without alcohol begins feeling flat, so a drink appears to feel good—whereas the previous drinks were responsible for making the world feel lifeless in the first place.

Did alcohol help me enjoy sex?

No, alcohol dulls our sense of touch and makes it harder to climax. Drinking disconnects us from the physical sensations that make sex enjoyable.

What I was learning blew my mind. And interestingly, as I learned more, my recycling bin—which used to be full of my empty alcohol bottles—got lighter. This shift happened *without my noticing*. It was my husband, Brian, who noticed the bin was lighter. He trekked it out to the curb and commented on how much less we were spending on wine. As I learned new things, my drinking was changing—even though I wasn't trying to change. I wasn't even aware it was happening. Something started to shift, way below my conscious awareness—something in my *subconscious*.

Almost a year after I began, I walked out of my office and said to Brian, "If you want to get drunk with me, tonight is the night, because I think I'm done drinking."

He was skeptical. After everything we'd been through together, it was hard for him to believe I was serious. That moment was more than a decade ago.

What neither of us realized then was that something deep inside me had changed. My desire to drink was gone. I didn't have to force it—not drinking felt completely natural. It was effortless. As easy as not drinking milk. (I hate milk.)

I finally understood *why*. And once my mind—specifically my unconscious mind—saw the full truth about alcohol, when it understood the trap, it quite literally rewired itself. My drinking habit broke.

I started sharing my research on a blog. People who had spent years, even decades, trying to change their drinking read what I had discovered—and found freedom.

One man who effortlessly let go of alcohol, after trying for half of his life, encouraged me to turn my research into a book. I took his advice seriously. I figured out how to self-publish my first book, *This Naked Mind*. That book, which began as a passion project, went on to sell millions of copies.

I started receiving letters from all over the world, often from people who had struggled deeply. One woman had gone to rehab fourteen times before finally finding freedom through *This Naked Mind*. Others found freedom unexpectedly, like this Amazon reviewer:

> *I read this book for my sister who has been struggling with alcohol. Now I don't even like beer and will probably never drink again. Thanks a lot—5 stars.*

Encouraged, I hired a research PhD to evaluate the effectiveness of *This Naked Mind*. We asked thousands of people one simple question:

> *How has your drinking changed since you came into contact with* This Naked Mind?

The results stunned even the researcher:

- Fifty-four percent of respondents said they no longer drank alcohol.

- Thirty-six percent said they now drank less.

That means 90 percent of people reported a healthier relationship with alcohol.

These results were remarkable, especially when compared to the effectiveness of traditional methods of change. As word spread, people began to take notice. I was soon invited to speak on multiple national mainstream news channels about the method I'd developed. And almost every time I was interviewed, the host would ask the same question: "Annie, will you ever drink again?"

This question feels like the wrong one for two reasons. First, as soon as we say "never," our brains freak out. The word alone causes us anxiety and stress. What if we find ourselves at our granddaughter's wedding when we are ninety years old and want to toast with champagne? How can we know what we'll want when we are ninety?

Second, saying we'll never drink again is a trap because it's a goal we can't reach before we die. I don't know about you, but I don't like the idea of making a goal that I won't be alive to see myself achieve.

So this is what I answer:

"I drink as much as I want, whenever I want; I just haven't wanted a drink in more than ten years."

That feels like freedom to me.

I found freedom when my desire to drink went away.

How did my *desire* go away? How did alcohol become so small and irrelevant in my life that I don't have to *try* not to drink it? I don't have to dedicate my life to meetings or give myself any sort of label, especially not the label *alcoholic*.

Understanding this is the key to your lasting freedom. To get there, we need to look a little deeper at the behaviors that we do, even though we know better, and even in the face of dire consequences.

We Know Better, But We Do Worse

My teenage son understands he's going to feel awful after an afternoon of playing video games. He even tells me—right before picking up the controller—that he's going to regret it. And then he plays for hours. He knows better. And just like me, and everyone else I know, *he does it anyway*.

The American Psychological Association (APA) studied the behaviors people turn to most often when trying to feel better. The top responses included drinking alcohol, eating, shopping, scrolling online, watching TV, and playing video games. But here's the surprising part: The same study found that while these are our go-to coping strategies, we also rate them as some of the least effective.

Scientific research confirms this strange but familiar phenomenon: We reach for the very things *we know* won't work. We do what we know is harmful, and we avoid what we know will help.

Why does this happen?

It turns out, humans have struggled with this pattern for a very long time. More than two thousand years ago, Seneca said:

We know better, but we do worse.

Ovid, an ancient Roman poet, put it this way:

I see the better way and approve it, but I follow the worse.

Paul, in the Bible, echoed the same idea:

I do not understand what I do. For what I want to do I do not do, but what I hate, I do.

Maybe you've had moments like this with drinking. You set the intention to skip the wine, but something shifts. It's like the F-it button gets pushed, and before you know it, you're waking up at three a.m. with a pit in your stomach, trying to count how many glasses you had.

What is going on here?

Something's Not Making Sense

Why does alcohol destroy lives? Why do we keep drinking, even after the costs far outweigh the benefits? Why does it feel fun at first, only to become terrifying? And why, even when we know better, do we find ourselves doing it anyway? These questions have haunted humanity since the first drop of alcohol was consumed.

In the United States we have a $5.2 billion addiction rehab industry with success rates as low as 4–12 percent. Why do so many people who try to stop drinking end up going back—often more than once? Why does living joyfully alcohol free feel so out of reach? And why do we so often associate sobriety with suffering, as if a life without alcohol must also be a life without fun?

We need to understand this problem in order to solve it, and so we don't become another statistic—one more person with the best intentions, drinking again as we watch our life fall apart.

Education is a powerful form of activism. Understanding is freedom. That's why I've spent the past ten years of my life looking even deeper into the answer to this question:

Why?

- Why do we feel smart and in control of our lives, yet alcohol is the strange exception?

- Why do we keep drinking, long after the joy is gone?

- Why, when a craving takes over, do we feel as though we no longer have a choice?

- Why, *as if on autopilot*, do we drink despite desperately wanting to be free?

- Why do we still feel tempted to drink long after alcohol has left our body and there is no longer *any physical or chemical reason to crave a drink*?

- Why are some people alcoholics and some not? And what is the difference?

- Why do some people seem to drink without problems, yet for others, drinking destroys their life and often the lives of those around them?

- Why is alcohol sold and marketed without warning labels or disclaimers, even though research clearly shows it's unsafe for human consumption?

Why?

I have answers to all of these questions—and more. Some will blow your mind. Others will make you mad. I'll warn you that the dynamics that keep us stuck in the alcohol trap are complex and multifaceted. There is a lot to learn, but I've made it interesting and even fun, and it will certainly be worth it.

The traditional approach to habit change, behavior change, and addiction isn't working—rates of addiction across many categories are at an all-time high. The strategies we've relied on for the past hundred years have, in many cases, made things worse. In this book, you'll learn why that is, through the lens of Affective Liminal Psychology, a behavior change methodology I developed by studying what truly works and what we've unknowingly been doing that makes change harder, and sometimes impossible, to achieve.

We will look at why we follow the worse not only with alcohol but in so many areas of our lives. And through this education you'll get your power back over the habits, behaviors, and addictions that keep you stuck—well beyond alcohol. Interestingly, the habit of alcohol is unique in our society; despite a 2021 study published in the *International Journal of Environmental Research and Public Health* confirming that alcohol is the most harmful drug on the planet, it remains the only drug in our culture that *you have to justify not taking*.

How did this happen? Here is the truth: We've been programmed.

———

To view the references cited in this chapter, please visit LiveNakedAF.com.

CHAPTER 2

WE'VE BEEN PROGRAMMED

Until you make the unconscious conscious, it will direct your life and you will call it fate.
—Carl Jung

What we collectively believe about alcohol is so far from the truth, it's like viewing the world through cloudy, dark-tinted lenses—lenses we don't know we are wearing. Our perspective is distorted, and we've lost sight of what's real.

It reminds me of the Allegory of the Cave.

The Cave

In this philosophical story, written by Plato in 375 BC, ancient humans live in a cave as prisoners. Their captors use fire and shadows to entertain them by projecting moving images onto the cave walls—haunting, beautiful stories that distract them from the reality of their captivity. They are mesmerized; compared to the darkness, shadow play looks like the best life has to offer.

Eventually one man escapes. He stumbles behind the wall of shadow and fire and sees something new: the light of the real world, streaming in from the mouth of the cave. It is terrifying—bright and painful to look at—but he keeps going toward it, and away from the darkness. What he finds is breathtaking: oceans and mountains, sunsets and stars, fresh food, and open skies. The world beyond shadow play is real, and rich, and wild.

Excited, he returns to help the others escape. But instead of gratitude, he's met with fear and resistance. They don't want to leave the shadows. The shadows feel safe. The real world is unfamiliar, risky.

To me, a life filled with alcohol is like being enslaved. My drinking life was just a shadow of my life today. I didn't know it at the time, but I couldn't see clearly. I was wearing—as most of us are—distorted, tinted lenses. My view of alcohol was warped by cultural beliefs. It was as if the lenses were designed to keep the truth out of focus. I now see these lenses for what they are: crafted by society and handed down through the collective unconscious in order to shape my entire perspective—without my knowledge or consent.

Living alcohol free is like stepping out of the cave. But escaping requires more than just putting down the bottle. It takes courage to leave behind what's familiar, even when the familiar is what's hurting us. As I've heard it said:

> *It's not safe because it is safe but because it is familiar, and it's not dangerous because it is dangerous but because it is unfamiliar.*

Leaving the cave means challenging everything we've been taught about alcohol. It means stepping away from the comfort of what everyone else believes and seeking truth for ourselves. It's more than a personal decision—it's an act of bravery.

Plato's allegory reminds us that human perception is limited by experience and belief, and that education and new perspectives can radically expand our understanding, influencing our actions, feelings, and behaviors. The questions we must ask include: How do we wake up from shadow play? How do we begin to see the truth that's been hidden in plain sight? How do we make our escape? How do we shift our mindset so that leaving the cave feels exciting instead of terrifying?

Our Subconscious Programming

The answers lie in the subconscious mind.

Your subconscious has been programmed. And those hidden programs—often running silently in the background—can sabotage your escape before you realize what's happening.

This programming exists, in large part, to conserve the brain's energy by creating shortcuts, or automatic habits, so you don't have to consciously think through every action. For example:

- Walk into the bathroom → brush your teeth

- Start making dinner → pour a glass of wine

- Get in your car → put on your seat belt

- Sit down at a restaurant → order a beer

These become patterns you no longer question. That's the subconscious at work. And habits extend beyond action. We have habitual mindsets and belief systems as well, programs of thought we no longer question and don't realize may not be true.

And when it comes to alcohol, the programming sounds like this:

- Alcohol helps me feel better.

- I need a drink.

- I'm not normal if I can't drink.

- Everything is more fun with alcohol.

- If I drink too much, I am broken or diseased.

- People won't accept me if I'm not drinking.

- I'm missing out if I say no to alcohol.

- I'm not strong enough to get through the day without a drink.

In today's culture, living alcohol free is still seen as a radical choice—something only people with a "problem" do. But considering alcohol is the world's most harmful drug, how does that make any sense?

Deep, persistent, unconscious programming.

Right now, thousands of these beliefs are likely running in your mind, and the easiest way to understand them is by looking at the three key categories they fall into.

Substance, Society, Self

These categories are substance, society, and self.

The first layer, *substance*, is the most surface-level, and the most conscious. It includes all the beliefs we have about the substances (and behaviors) we turn to in order to make us feel better. When we look specifically at alcohol, these beliefs are easy to hear in the reasons we give for drinking, such as "Alcohol is fun," "It helps me relax," or "It tastes good." We're usually aware of these substance-level programs, but because they are programs, rather than simply thoughts, they are automatic and tend to pass through our minds unquestioned.

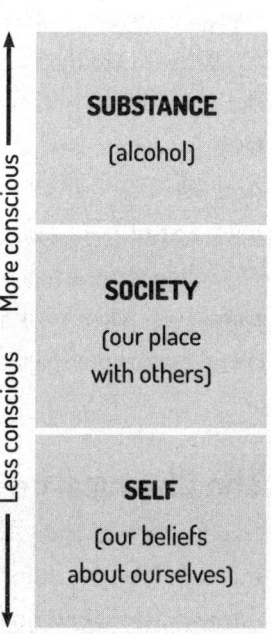

15

The second layer, *society*, goes a bit deeper—and is less conscious. These beliefs tap into a deep, primal, unconscious fear: the fear of being different, excluded, and ultimately alone. We are hardwired for connection and belonging. Throughout human history, being part of a group meant survival. Studies clearly show that children who lack emotional connection will fail to thrive, even if their needs of food and shelter are met. We are social creatures, and in our culture, alcohol is woven into almost every social gathering, celebration, and ritual, from baby showers to funerals. So choosing to live alcohol free can trigger a deep fear—one that makes us feel unsafe or isolated simply for being different. This isn't just about wanting to fit in; it's about an unconscious, survival-level wiring.

The third layer, *self*, is the deepest, least conscious, and hardest to recognize. This is when we drink to escape ourselves. We drink to numb the pain of feeling like we're not good enough, not attractive enough, not funny enough, not brave enough—or just not enough, period. These beliefs are often buried so deep that we may not even know they're there. But they drive our behavior in powerful ways.

When drinking is driven only by beliefs about the substance itself, the habit is easily broken. But when subconscious programs around both substance and society are at play, change becomes much harder. And when we drink to escape the pain we feel about ourselves, the alcohol trap can feel nearly impossible to escape.

While these layers begin to explain the mystery of why we *follow the worse* even when we know better, there's more to the story. Two additional factors complete the puzzle.

The Chemical Impact of Alcohol

Science shows clearly that alcohol is chemically addictive. This means that when we consume alcohol, it interacts with our brain cells, neurotransmitters, and hormones in a way that creates a physical need for more. Repeated exposure changes our brain chemistry, making us want to drink again, regardless of logic or intention.

For some people, alcohol is even more addictive because of variations in our brain's chemistry. If you've been diagnosed with ADHD, anxiety, depression, or a variety of other chemical differences in the brain, alcohol affects your brain differently. Your unique brain chemistry can make alcohol more physically addictive for you than for someone with different chemistry.

The same is true if you're using alcohol to cope with unresolved trauma or emotional pain. In those situations, your brain doesn't just experience alcohol as something fun or relaxing; it sees it as the relief or escape it is desperately searching for.

By contrast, if you're drinking for other reasons, like social enjoyment or out of habit, the brain is less likely to associate alcohol with emotional survival. That distinction matters. It helps explain why alcohol, and other numbing agents, can be easier to walk away from for some people than for others. When alcohol becomes chemically linked to emotional relief or survival, the path to freedom often requires more than just stopping; it requires addressing the deeper associations that have been created in the brain and body. It changes how the path to freedom looks. We will cover all points along this spectrum.

Our Internal Conflict

The final piece of the puzzle that explains why we continue to *follow the worse*, even when we desperately want to change, is the internal conflict that arises in us. The moment we try to quit, or even cut back, we unknowingly start a mental and emotional battle. Surprisingly, research shows that attempting to quit a behavior, like drinking, often leads to more of that behavior. While this seems counterintuitive, it reveals just how complex the internal struggle is.

We'll explore the nature of this conflict in the next chapter. For now, it's enough to understand that this internal battle, combined with the two other factors we've discussed—our subconscious programming and the substance's or behavior's chemical effects on the brain—are the main factors that cause us to stay stuck.

The good news is, once we understand how we've been trapped, we have the power to escape. And not just escape—we can change with clarity, confidence, and even joy. To be truly free, living alcohol free or any habitual change must become as easy and effortless as the old behavior once was. It needs to feel automatic, like second nature. A new normal.

While this book focuses on alcohol, the core principles—and many of the same chemical and emotional patterns—apply to any substance or behavior we use to escape discomfort. So even if alcohol isn't your primary struggle, you'll find insights here that can help you understand and shift any pattern that feels out of alignment. I encourage you to keep reading—you're absolutely in the right place.

The Habit of Living Alcohol Free

There was a time—often before we ever picked up a drink—when not drinking was effortless. It wasn't something we had to work at or think about. It was simply our natural state.

But over time, that changed. Through repeated exposure to alcohol and the influence of three powerful forces—our subconscious programming (substance, society, and self), our body's chemical response to alcohol, and the internal battle that rages when we try to change—drinking becomes the effortless habit. And not drinking is the struggle.

To truly break free, we need to flip that script. We must rewrite the mental code so not drinking becomes automatic, habitual, and easy—just as drinking once was. This shift is just as important for people who are already alcohol free. Why? Because unless your old programs are identified and reprogrammed, they continue to run quietly in the background of your mind. Cravings still sneak in, and the mental effort it takes to stay alcohol free wears us down. The only way to create lasting change—the kind that feels natural—is to make *not drinking* into our default mode. To make it second nature.

To show you how, I'm going to introduce the first foundational framework from Affective Liminal Psychology: Awake to Alive. This framework expands on Noel Burch's learning model, developed in the 1970s, and helps explain why certain behaviors stick despite our best efforts, and why the cycle of relapse can persist, even years after our last drink. It helps us see that the issue isn't a lack of discipline or desire; it's a gap in how we learn. And once we close that gap, lasting change becomes possible.

What if the key to transformation isn't trying harder—but learning differently?

Our journey begins in the lower-left quadrant, where we start: Asleep.

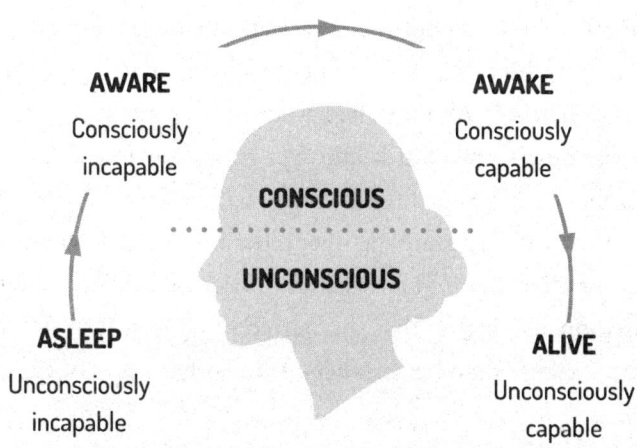

Phase 1: Asleep: Unconsciously Incapable

In the Asleep phase, we are unaware (unconscious) that change is needed and are therefore incapable of making change. We don't see a problem, so we can't solve it.

You simply can't fix a problem you don't know you have.

Before I understood alcohol was the problem, I believed it was normal to feel tired, stressed, and hungover. It seemed everyone around me felt the same. I was unaware that my misery was coming from alcohol. Instead I believed it was helping. I didn't yet see that it was actually breaking my life apart.

The first step in any change is becoming aware that something new is possible—without awareness, there's no path forward. But waking up can be painful. It forces us to question what we've accepted as normal—and that's not always easy.

Phase 2: Aware: Consciously Incapable

Suddenly—often through some type of discomfort—we wake up to the problem. We're now conscious that something is wrong, but we are still incapable of fixing it. This stage is often filled with frustration and emotional pain.

When I realized alcohol was systematically destroying everything I loved, the truth hit hard. What I once saw as an exciting romance with red wine started to look more like a toxic codependent relationship. I knew it was hurting me, but I didn't yet know how to let go.

Awareness was also painful for my daughter when she was learning to walk. She would scream when her older brothers left the room, trying to scoot after them. That frustration became her fuel. She became so focused on keeping up that she started walking at just nine months old—much earlier than her brothers. Pain, as hard as it is, can push us forward.

Phase 3: Awake: Consciously Capable

The Awake phase begins when the pain becomes a catalyst. Whether it's the frustration of being left behind or the shame of falling over drunk—again—we reach a point when we're determined to change. We enter this phase with energy and resolve.

In Awake, we not only recognize the problem but also start developing the capability to change it. For me, that meant cutting back on alcohol. I could go days without drinking. Sometimes I went long enough to convince myself I didn't have a problem. But it always required willpower. Eventually, my willpower would run out and I'd be left with broken promises, shame, and regret.

Awake requires concentration. When my daughter first started walking it took focused attention. Over time, she could walk all around the house, but she still had to be conscious of every step.

My son is in a similar place with driving. He's becoming a solid, responsible driver. But driving still takes conscious effort. He must stay alert every second he's behind the wheel. Awake is the stage of learning where we can do the new thing, but one lapse in focus, and we fall back into old patterns.

Phase 4: Alive: Unconsciously Capable

Alive is when real change sticks. The behavior becomes automatic, effortless, and deeply ingrained—no more willpower required. Alive happens once a habit is programmed into the brain. The new behavior becomes second nature—unconscious—making this phase feel magical.

Alive was the moment I no longer *wanted* to drink. My mindset shifted from *I don't get to drink* to *I never have to drink again*. Freedom came with that change in perspective.

After taking enough steps, my daughter no longer had to concentrate on every one; what once took enormous effort became easy. Today, the hard work of learning to walk is a distant memory. Walking is now an unconscious habit—as natural as breathing.

The same thing will happen for my son. Although driving is tiring now, over time and with practice, driving will become routine. Most of us know how this feels—you drive to work without thinking about every turn, not even remembering afterwards if it was raining or sunny.

Asleep to Alive is how we learn: one thing at a time. First, we master walking. Then when walking becomes automatic, we have the mental bandwidth to learn to run. Each new skill builds on what has already been mastered.

In the Alive phase, the new behavior is laid down as a neural pathway—physically embedded into the structure of the brain. When this happens, change is finally sustainable.

When you reach the Alive phase in your relationship with alcohol, everything shifts. Living AF isn't just something you *do*; it is who you *are*. So natural that it's hard to imagine ever wanting to drink. In many ways, it feels like you've become a new version of yourself—one that somehow also feels like who you were always meant to be.

Staying Stuck at Awake

But sometimes, we stay stuck in the Awake phase, like my friend Beth. A few months into my alcohol-free journey, a group of us met for a ski trip to Steamboat Springs, Colorado. One night, we were all in the kitchen of our rental, getting dinner ready. Beth and I sat at the counter while another friend—who loves whiskey—poured herself a glass, leaving it on the counter as she ran off to chase one of her kids.

Out of nowhere, Beth picked up the glass and sniffed it longingly. I was stunned—she had been sober for seven years. I asked, "Do you want that? Do you miss drinking?" Without hesitation, she said, "Yes, I miss it. Sometimes I fantasize about flying to a city where no one knows me and getting drunk in secret." I was speechless. She went on to explain that every single day, she had to put focus, effort, and energy into *not* drinking.

What if my daughter needed to think about every step she took for the rest of her life? Can you imagine how much time and energy that would steal from her? How much it would hold her back from running, jumping, or shooting baskets?

Yet this is what traditional recovery often asks us to do. In the Awake phase, staying sober requires daily effort, attending meetings, and staying hyper-focused on alcohol—which can make alcohol feel more central in our lives than when we drank. That wasn't the life I wanted—I wanted to be *Alive*. I didn't want a life that revolved around alcohol, especially after I *stopped* drinking it. And I'm guessing you don't, either. Most of us aren't looking to simply get by—we want to thrive. We reclaim enormous mental and emotional energy when not drinking becomes our brain's default setting.

But how do we get there? What bridges the gap between Awake and Alive? How does change stop being a struggle and start feeling expected?

Here's a surprising truth: The process of learning and habit formation happens naturally—unless something blocks it. And in the case of becoming effortlessly alcohol free, the main block is *emotion*.

It's simple: We do what we feel like doing and we avoid what we don't feel like doing. How we feel is what moves us from Awake to Alive. When we change our emotions about drinking, not drinking becomes easy. It becomes who we *are*.

Emotion Is the Key

Emotions program—and reprogram—our subconscious habits and routines. They shape the quality of our lives. Long before we had words, emotions were how we made sense of the world. They were how we communicated our needs and navigated our environment. Emotion is our default mode. And when willpower runs out, it's emotion that takes over.

Put simply: Everything we consistently do over the long term is driven by emotion—not logic or willpower. And science confirms this. Dr. BJ Fogg, a Stanford researcher and the author of *Tiny Habits*, said it this way in a broadcast interview:

*The positive emotion you feel as you do the new behavior is what
wires it into your brain as a habit; there is a physical restructuring
of your brain that happens because of emotion.*

If you feel deprived, abnormal, alone, or afraid, staying alcohol free
becomes harder. But if you feel strong, proud, hopeful, and maybe even
a little righteously angry about the lies you've been sold, you dramatically increase your ability to sustain change.

The latest research confirms this: Positive emotion doesn't just support habit change; it *creates* it. Emotion turns conscious decisions into
subconscious habits.

We can test this. Consider a time when you've effortlessly succeeded
in changing an unwanted behavior. How did you feel about that
change? Now think about a behavior you've struggled to change. What
emotions come up?

That difference—how you *feel*—is often the deciding factor between lasting success and ongoing struggle.

How we feel about a behavior is even more powerful in habit formation than how long we've been able to maintain the new behavior. This
challenges the long-held collective belief that time is key to habit formation. In the same interview Dr. Fogg makes an important point:
While many people believe that repeating a new behavior for a certain
number of days will lead to habit formation—the relevant number often shifting with the latest trend or challenge—this doesn't hold up
under closer examination. If we look carefully at the research, although
length of time correlates with habit formation, there is no evidence that
it causes a new habit to form. What Dr. Fogg states is *causal* for habit
formation is the emotion you feel.

I remember thinking, *If I can just string more days together, this will
get easier*. But the science is clear; that's not how it works. Time alone
doesn't guarantee long-term success. We see it over and over again—

people who've been sober for years still struggle or relapse. This is why even years of repeating a behavior aren't enough to guarantee lasting change.

Emotion-Based Change

Emotion plays a powerful role in everything we do. Nearly every decision we make is influenced by how we want to feel. We drink to change how we feel. We choose to go alcohol free for the same reason. Even tasks we don't enjoy, like going to the dentist, are often driven by emotion. We want to avoid the pain of a future cavity.

To move from the Awake phase to the Alive phase, we need to do two things:

1. Create the right emotions—the kind that support lasting change.

2. Remove the emotions that block change—like fear, shame, and guilt.

What if every time my daughter fell while learning to walk, I got angry with her? What if I scolded her, made her feel ashamed, or threatened to leave if she didn't figure it out? Would that motivate her to walk faster? Probably not. It would more likely do the opposite. She would become afraid, confused, and possibly stop trying altogether. Unfortunately, this is how our existing recovery models often treat relapse and failure—reinforcing shame instead of nurturing growth.

To successfully shift from Awake to Alive, we must understand how emotions operate within all three parts of the behavior change puzzle we've already covered:

1. Our subconscious programming

2. The physical and chemical effects of alcohol

3. The internal conflict that arises when we try to change

These three elements are deeply emotional, and they shape the feelings that either support or sabotage your progress. This dynamic is often misunderstood—and is rarely addressed directly—so we need to explore each area in more detail. I'll use myself as an example.

Subconscious Programming

When I was trying to quit, I believed I wasn't strong enough to handle life without alcohol (a self-level program). I believed that quitting meant I wasn't normal (a society-level program). And I believed alcohol helped me relax (a substance-level program). These and many other deeply ingrained subconscious beliefs kept me stuck. They made me hesitant, inconsistent, and emotionally exhausted.

Physical and Chemical Impact

Because alcohol is physically addictive, my brain was chemically primed to crave it, even after I'd decided to leave it behind. The chemical factors at play create resistance, confusion, and noise, making it nearly impossible to reach the Alive phase. Throughout this book, we'll take a closer look at both the physical and the chemical elements that can threaten our freedom.

Internal Conflict

When I was stuck in the Awake phase, I felt like I was living in two worlds. I desperately wanted to stop drinking; I saw the damage it was causing in my life. But I was also terrified to give it up. Alcohol felt like the only tool I had to cope. I was of two minds—one that wanted to change and another that couldn't imagine life without alcohol.

We'll explore each of these three blocks in detail in the coming chapters. But first, we need to take a closer look at what it really means to be Alive—and why doing the work to move from Awake to Alive is the most powerful insurance you can give yourself against falling back into the trap.

On the left of this chart is the experience of staying stuck at Awake, and on the right side is the experience of being Alive.

Awake Capability Requires Conscious Effort	Alive Effortless Capability
Fixation on alcohol even when no longer drinking	Alcohol is small and irrelevant; you can take it or leave it
Fear of missing out	Realizing alcohol was never needed for genuine enjoyment of life
Struggle with cravings and temptation	Natural state of not wanting alcohol, like a child
Feeling of being outside of society and social events	Feeling of being a trailblazer or an influencer of a new, trendy, healthy way of life
Fear of relapse and the shame and ostracism relapse involves	Living beyond fear and welcoming "failure" with grace, learning, and self-compassion
Energy spent on trying not to drink and avoiding triggers	Energy spent on learning to live joyfully and authentically
Identity centered on being "an alcoholic" or "in recovery"	Identity returned to a natural, pre-drinking state of freedom
Social life limited by avoiding cravings	Freedom to enjoy all relationships, even when others still drink
Feeling powerless over alcohol	Feeling powerful and in control
Feeling broken, of being the problem	Recognition that you are not broken and never have been

Awake Capability Requires Conscious Effort	Alive Effortless Capability
Alcohol has mental power, even in sobriety	Alcohol loses all mental power
Time spent in meetings revolving around alcohol	Time spent learning to build a life you don't want to escape
Hiding, afraid to admit struggle to friends and family	Living AF is a proud choice rather than a sad consequence

Alive feels like freedom. Freedom to choose—moment by moment—without the constant internal tug-of-war. Alive is internal emotional alignment. When that alignment happens, the desire for a drink simply fades. Not drinking becomes easy and effortless. And with that, your freedom becomes sustainable—you can live free from the fear of relapse or failure.

When it comes to living alcohol *free*, we all get to define freedom for ourselves. Some people want to be free to take it or leave it, free to drink on occasion, or free from the desire to drink so they never *have to* drink again. I want to be free to have no rules or labels, and perhaps more than anything, I want to be free to *trust myself with myself.*

To help you make the leap from Awake to Alive, the rest of this book focuses on uncovering and removing the hidden blocks that keep us stuck. We'll begin with one of the most common—and most misunderstood—barriers to lasting change: *internal conflict.* This is where so many approaches to habit change fall apart. Traditional methods rely heavily on willpower, which is a vital component for change—you cannot reach the Awake stage without willpower, but it was never designed to sustain long-term behavior change. When we depend on it as our primary tool, we often end up exhausted, discouraged, and back in the very patterns we were trying to escape.

This misunderstanding is one of the reasons success rates for overcoming addiction are so low. It's worth repeating that research by the

National Institute on Alcohol Abuse and Alcoholism found that 90 percent of people who try to stop drinking eventually relapse. To understand why this happens, let's look more deeply at why we get stuck at Awake—and why addressing internal conflict is key to moving forward.

———

To view the references cited in this chapter, please visit LiveNakedAF.com.

CHAPTER 3

THE INTERNAL BATTLE

The greatest conflicts are not between two people but between one person and themselves.
—Garth Brooks

Are you familiar with the classic image of a little angel on one shoulder and a little devil on the other? I remember it best from the cartoon *Tom and Jerry*. Occasionally, when Tom (the cat) was deciding whether to do the "right" thing or the "wrong" thing, an angel and a devil would pop up, whispering in his ears, offering conflicting advice. It's a familiar image used in movies and television to represent the tug-of-war between our inner voices.

When we're stuck following the worse, the internal battle feels a lot like having an angel on one shoulder, urging us to stop drinking, and a devil on the other, tempting us to pour another glass and sabotaging our attempts at change. This inner conflict has a name: cognitive dissonance. It's the psychological discomfort we feel when two opposing beliefs, desires, or values clash inside us.

For me, it looked like this: I both wanted to drink and wanted to stop—at the same time. Part of me loved alcohol and couldn't imagine life without it. Another part was horrified by the chaos alcohol was causing in my life.

Conflict Hurts

Recently we were picking up pizza. The kids and I stayed in the car while Brian ran inside. It was a beautiful afternoon, and our windows were open. Suddenly, loud yelling echoed from the street. Instantly we were on high alert. I felt uneasy, and my daughter looked like she was about to cry.

Have you ever witnessed a conflict between strangers? Even when you don't know the people or what's going on, just hearing angry voices can make your chest tighten. It's uncomfortable. Distressing. Watching people fight in movies, knowing it's not real, stirs up tension. And when conflict happens inside our homes, with the people we love, the pain runs even deeper.

But the worst conflict—the kind that does the most damage—is when we fight with ourselves.

For years I was at war with myself about my drinking. It may have seemed like I was holding things together from the outside, but inside, the mental battle never stopped. The pain of internal conflict built slowly, day after day, until it was my new normal.

I had a simple goal: Drink less. But I couldn't do it—not consistently. And it wasn't because I didn't know better. I did. I knew exactly how harmful alcohol was. And it wasn't because I wasn't trying—I was desperate to change.

By the time I found myself drunk in a deserted train tunnel, I had been trying to change for nearly six years. And all that time, I believed the problem was me, that I was weak, lacking willpower.

The American Psychological Association (APA) defines willpower as "the ability to carry out one's intentions." According to this definition, I just didn't have enough willpower to change. Our culture—and most traditional recovery approaches—reinforces the importance of willpower. If we could just summon more willpower, we'd be able to stop drinking or get back in control. Willpower is seen as a virtue. We associate it with strength, morality, and trustworthiness. And if you don't have it? You're labeled weak, reckless, and undeserving of respect.

But this cultural narrative is not just wrong, it's dangerous. Especially when you consider the research, which shows that willpower is not a reliable resource. In fact, it's far more fragile and limited than we've previously been led to believe.

Here's what studies show:

- A 2015 study published in the National Library of Medicine found that when individuals experience stress, their ability for self-control decreases due to reduced connectivity between the brain regions responsible for willpower. Multiple studies confirm that when you're stressed, emotional, or exhausted, your willpower is likely to falter—or disappear entirely.

- Studies show that if your brain is overloaded—maybe you've been working hard, problem-solving, or juggling too many responsibilities—your willpower can easily give out. One study published by the American Psychological Association in 2020 demonstrated that when participants were mentally taxed, they showed more impulsive decision-making or reduced self-control.

But it's not just that willpower weakens under pressure or eventually runs out. There's a more fundamental issue—and that's where we need to look next. Let's start by breaking down the word into its two component parts: *will* and *power*. *Will* is defined as "the capacity or faculty by which a human being is able to make choices and determine their own behaviors in spite of external influences," and *power* as "physical might, mental or moral efficacy, control, or influence of, relating to, or utilizing strength."

At its best, willpower represents our ability to make conscious choices in the face of external pressure. Our will is part of what makes us beautifully human. But notice something about the definition of will: It assumes the influences we are resisting are external. That they come from the *outside*.

This is where the problem begins.

In my struggle with alcohol, the battle wasn't external. It was *internal*. I wasn't using willpower to stand up to outside pressure; I was using it to fight against myself.

That's the fundamental flaw. Willpower can't work when your desires are divided. I wanted both to stop drinking and to keep drinking. My intentions were split. You become locked in an exhausting, unwinnable fight when you're trying to force one part of yourself to overpower another.

This internal war is not a failure of willpower. It's a sign that something deeper needs to shift.

On one side of the battle was my internal angel—fierce, relentless, and adamant that I stop drinking. She showed up most often at three a.m., when I woke up drenched in shame and regret, and her voice would take over:

> *"Annie, how could you? Why did you drink so much? What is wrong with you? Don't you care about anyone? What about Brian? The kids? I can't believe you did this again; at this rate you are going to end up killing yourself."*

She wasn't gentle. She was disgusted with me, convinced I was weak, selfish, and worthless. And while she raged, another part of me sat silently, absorbing the blows. I felt crushed beneath the weight of my own self-loathing—shattered by how viciously I turned on myself.

The pain was unbearable.

Instead of finding motivation to change, I just wanted relief. I would sneak into the kitchen in the middle of the night and drink more—not to celebrate or indulge, but to quiet the voice in my head. Just enough to numb my mind and let me sleep.

That voice—the one that was supposed to be helping me by telling me to stop drinking—was the most brutal. She convinced me I was a failure. She had me believing the world would be better off without me. And in those moments, it made perfect sense that the only escape I could imagine was drunken oblivion.

No matter how long or painful the nightly battle, by the next day, a completely different voice would show up. The proverbial devil would chime in just before five p.m.—soft, sweet, and strangely comforting. She sounded like a friend, full of compassion and understanding:

"It's time for wine! I know you promised to stop, but it's been a really rough day and you deserve it."

Her agenda was simple: solve my pain with a drink. I would try to push back. I'd remind myself of the night before—how awful I'd felt, how I never stopped at just one. But this voice had answers for everything:

"We can have just one. You know you will get back in control at some point; you are stronger than alcohol. You can fix this, no problem. But not today . . . today was hard. And a few drinks won't hurt—honestly, it's no big deal. You will feel so much better. And we learned from last night—no way we are drinking that much again! I promise we won't overdo it."

This voice didn't yell or accuse. She was calm and reassuring. She sounded rational, thoughtful—even kind. She soothed my doubts, and, compared to the self-loathing of the night before, this voice felt like relief.

She encouraged me. She comforted me. She genuinely seemed to care.

I found the kindness and understanding of the "devil" far more persuasive than the "angel" who demanded I quit as she told me I was worthless and broken. And so I gave in; I drank. Next thing I knew, I was waking up at three a.m. in a fog of anxiety and regret. The voice of disgust and shame would kick in—and the awful cycle repeated itself, night after night, for years. It's no wonder my mental health was a mess.

But here's the real question: Which part of me was I supposed to use willpower against? To answer that, we can't just look at their actions—we also have to look at their intentions.

I despised the voice that surfaced in the middle of the night. She terrified me. She made me feel worthless and ashamed. I hated that "angel" inside of me. But one day, I found the courage to stop and turn toward her—not with anger, but with curiosity. I asked:

"Why are you so mean? What do you want?"

Her answer came quickly:

"I see how much damage alcohol is doing. I see how much pain it's causing. I don't know how else to get your attention, so I scream and yell. I'm afraid. I'm terrified you're going to lose everything— your family, your life. I just want you to be safe. I need you to wake up. I don't know any other way to protect you."

It hit me: She was harsh, but her intention was pure. She had been trying to save me all along.

Next I turned to the so-called devil, who convinced me to reach for a drink after I had promised myself I wouldn't. I asked her the same question:

"What do you want?"

The answer surprised me. This part of me wasn't just trying to get drunk. It ran much deeper. She said:

"I'm afraid of how stressed and overwhelmed you are. I want you to feel better. I see how much you're hurting and how hard every day is. I want you to have a moment of relief, a moment of peace, a moment of joy. I want to see you smile again—even if it's only for a little while."

Suddenly it was clear: I wasn't caught between good and evil. I was caught between two parts of myself that were *both* trying to protect me. Both voices had good intentions. Neither wanted to hurt me—each was simply trying to help in the best way she knew how.

And that's what made this battle so confusing.

It was easy to assume I just needed more willpower. Easy to believe I was broken because I couldn't overpower the part of me that wanted to drink. But both voices—the one full of shame and the one full of comfort—were fighting for my well-being.

So which one was right? Which one was wrong? And maybe even more important, which one was actually driving me to drink?

When the critical voice lashed out, with vicious thoughts like *What's wrong with you?* I could feel emotion welling up inside me. I felt pressure in my chest and tears behind my eyes. That part sounded so certain, who was I to argue? Maybe she was right. Maybe I *was* awful, worthless, and disgusting.

As the pain escalated, I would hold out as long as I could, enduring the internal rage that tore me down for hours. Curled into a ball, sobbing, wishing I could disappear. Wanting, desperately, not to feel anything at all.

Eventually, something in me would snap. It felt like a survival instinct, and that's when the second voice would appear—trying to rescue me from drowning in my shame and despair. She saw how much I was suffering, how close to the edge I was, and she was desperate to help. And she knew just the thing to take away the pain—*another drink.*

The part of me that believed alcohol was the solution didn't understand that alcohol was also the problem. She had a completely different perspective from the part of me that hated my drinking. And when I gave in and drank again, the angry, disgusted voice became even more convinced that she was right; I must be bad. I must be broken. I must deserve this. And in those moments, yes, I followed the worse. I chose escape over everything else. I didn't care about the consequences. I just needed to stop the pain. And in a bizarre realization, I can now see that alcohol was a way that I cared for myself during some of my darkest moments.

But of course, drinking again only intensified my self-judgment and a shame spiral emerged, looking something like this:

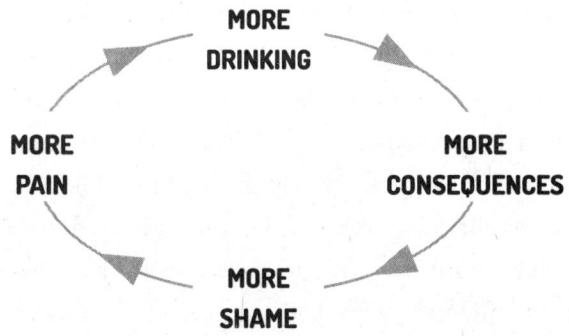

More drinking led to more consequences.
More consequences led to more shame.

More shame led to more pain.

More pain led to more drinking.

More drinking . . . and on it went.

When we rely on willpower, we're forced to take sides in the internal war. We try to pick one voice and reject the other. We have to make a part of ourselves wrong.

But it was never a battle between good and evil. There was no clear angel or devil. No one was completely right, and no one was completely wrong.

And yet, both sides kept me drinking.

Both sides were trying to help me, but both were causing harm. And because there was no unified intention within me—no emotional alignment—willpower never had a chance. It couldn't hold.

A Suppressed Part Never Dies

Some people manage to stay sober for years by using willpower to suppress the part of them that wants to drink. My friend Beth did this through her work in AA. She was able to make the part of her that drank the enemy—even naming it "the wine witch" and locking it away. But because this part still believed alcohol helped her relax, have fun, and numb pain, she avoided any situation that might trigger it. She didn't date during her first year alcohol free. She stayed away from bars, friends, and the places where she used to drink.

But here's the thing: We can't kill off a part of ourselves, no matter how much we want to. That part doesn't die; it just goes quiet, buried beneath the surface. It stays there, suppressed, waiting for the moment when it's needed again. The moment when pain resurfaces—when we experience grief, loss, stress, or tragedy—it wakes up. And because it's still carrying the subconscious belief that alcohol helps, it will push us to drink again. This is why so many people return to drinking in moments of emotional overwhelm. The side of us that relied on alcohol is still alive, buried deep inside.

This might explain a common saying in traditional recovery circles: "You need to be on guard because your addiction is out in the parking lot doing push-ups, getting stronger." That phrase is repeated because it reflects real experience. People can stay sober for five, ten, even fifteen years, and then, seemingly out of nowhere, find themselves on a dangerous multiday binge. These parts wait below the surface, ready to jump in, and when they do, it's not to sabotage us. It's because they truly believe they're helping.

Dr. Richard Schwartz, founder of Internal Family Systems therapy, has expressed skepticism about the effectiveness of willpower in achieving lasting change. He suggests that relying solely on willpower can lead to internal conflict and self-criticism. In his book *No Bad Parts: Healing Trauma and Restoring Wholeness with the Internal Family Systems Model*, he explains that parts, like people, fight back against being exiled. And the harder we try to get rid of them, the stronger they become, until eventually we are living constantly on guard against any place, person, or situation that might trigger those parts—parts we believe we've successfully repressed.

Both neuroscience and psychology confirm what many of us have experienced firsthand: Fighting with yourself in order to change is not an effective strategy. Multiple studies confirm that willpower-based strategies can lead to significantly higher rates of alcohol use when compared to acceptance-based approaches—like curiosity and compassion. In fact, a 2024 systematic review of thirty-six studies found that higher levels of self-compassion or self-forgiveness are linked to a lower likelihood of problem or hazardous drinking.

Both Sides Are Equally Matched

The internal battle can last for years—because both sides are equally matched. After all, they share the same brain and have the same level of intelligence.

Research shows that the average time it takes for someone to truly change their drinking after making the decision to do so is six to ten years. My internal war raged for six years before the train tunnel. That's a long time to stay stuck in an exhausting, painful, soul-sucking loop. Inside me, the different internal agendas would argue, manipulate, and plead. Both sides were brilliant—and ruthless.

It's time to let go of the idea that we fail to change because we lack willpower. Not only is it untrue, but it can make things worse by adding shame to the struggle. By turning us against ourselves.

In my journey, I quieted the internal war not by fighting harder, but by putting down the weapons of blame and shame. I did this when I gave myself permission to drink. As strange as that sounds, it created space. I stopped battling myself and started listening. My new goal wasn't to quit drinking overnight; it was to understand the mystery of why I kept *following the worse*.

What I discovered changed everything. I realized that the parts of me that were in conflict each had their own perspective, beliefs, emotions, and logic. Each had reasons for what they were doing. And every part had good intentions, even if their methods were painful or damaging. I wasn't weak-willed or broken. I was in a state of cognitive dissonance—conflicted, not flawed. And so are you. Here is the truth:

You've been doing the best you can with the tools you have.

The fact that willpower has become our culture's go-to solution for everything makes me angry. Our overreliance on willpower creates shame, and shame isolates us. It silences us. No one wants to admit to struggling or being "weak," so we fight these battles alone. In silence. And then we start to believe that we're the only ones who feel this way—that we're somehow broken inside while everyone else has it figured out. And we wonder why the *inside of us* is so different from the *outside of everyone else.*

Are we really meant to use willpower this way—against ourselves?

When I think about the worst things one human can do to another, it often involves overpowering someone's will. So why would we turn that kind of force inward and call it strength?

Real change starts not with more willpower, but with more compassion, more understanding, and more internal alignment.

The Paradox of Willpower

We've learned the limits of willpower, but it is important not to discount it entirely. Willpower gives us the ability to make a choice. And choice is one of the most incredible gifts of being human. Even when everything else feels out of our control, we still get to choose our response. That alone is empowering.

Willpower also plays a crucial role in moving us from the Aware phase to the Awake phase. It helps us make conscious changes. We can take a thirty-day break from drinking. We can experience the benefits—waking up without hangovers, feeling more present, and noticing how much better life feels alcohol free. And willpower is especially important when dealing with external challenges, such as social pressures.

But here's the paradox: While willpower can help us get started, it can't carry us all the way. Willpower works only when we're aligned internally. When there's conflict inside, it becomes just another form of self-punishment.

We see this occur in many behavior-change, habit-formation, and addiction-recovery models that stop at the Awake phase. The external behavior may shift, but the internal battle rages on. When we focus only on outward, behavior-based success, we overlook the deeper internal transformation required for lasting change. When we rely solely on willpower—without resolving the internal conflict behind the behavior—it eventually backfires.

So how do we move to Alive—and beyond willpower?

Alive Is Physical

The answer lies in a key neurological difference between these two phases. Science confirms that the transition from Awake to Alive isn't just mental—it's physical. It involves a literal rewiring of the brain. It's not enough to simply decide to change; the brain must build new pathways that make the new behavior automatic.

When a behavior becomes a subconscious habit (or a program), it runs without conscious thought. Again, think of how you drive to work or walk across the room. Actions that once required your full concentration now happen effortlessly. That's because your brain has created the structures to support them. These structures are physical, made of protein branches called dendrites, and they form what scientists refer to as neural pathways. When those structures don't exist, behavior change feels difficult and inconsistent. It's like trying to drive a sports car down a dirt road—slow, bumpy, and full of resistance. But once the proper pathways are built, the same car can glide down a smooth, well-maintained highway. The car is the new behavior or habit, and the highway is the neural structure that makes it possible.

To move from Awake to Alive, we need to build these highways in the brain. When the new habit is physically programmed into your neural circuitry, it becomes your default. It happens without effort, without willpower, and without constant internal negotiation.

To get there, we need to understand how the mind is conditioned in the first place. How are habits formed? How are subconscious programs written? And most important, how can we change them if they operate beneath our conscious awareness?

In the next two chapters, we'll answer those questions. You'll learn how the brain is programmed and exactly how to reprogram it. This is how we stop relying on willpower and start rewriting the code.

————

To view the references cited in this chapter, please visit LiveNakedAF.com.

CHAPTER 4

THE BRAIN'S DEFAULT MODE

We need to become more than we were programmed to be.
—The Wild Robot

There was a time when I lived out of the minibar in my hotel room. It was the first thing I checked upon arrival—was it fully stocked? And pouring a nightcap was the last thing I did before falling asleep—well, before passing out.

A few years after I stopped drinking, I was at a hotel for a magazine interview when the interviewer asked if I ever requested the minibar be emptied to avoid temptation. I was confused. I actually said, "Wait, do hotels still have minibars?" For a moment, I thought they'd phased them out—possibly for liability reasons—because I honestly hadn't noticed one in years.

Then the interviewer looked confused, responding, "Yes, of course they still have minibars."

Once I got over my embarrassment for saying something so naive, it hit me: My entire experience of staying in a hotel had changed. Despite staying in dozens of hotels over the last few years, I hadn't once noticed the alcohol in the room. My perspective had shifted so much that I no longer even registered the minibar.

That was a powerful realization. My thoughts, feelings, beliefs, and behaviors around alcohol had changed so dramatically that it transformed my experience of something as familiar as a hotel room. The room hadn't changed, but I had. And before the interviewer's question, I wasn't even aware of it—the change had happened *below my conscious awareness.*

The ancient text of the Talmud says this:

You don't see the world as it is—you see the world as you are.

Let's break down my minibar experience through the three layers of belief we've discussed: substance, society, and self. What subconscious programs were running?

From the substance perspective, I believed alcohol was essential—I thought I needed it to pregame so I could be a more confident, social version of myself at work events. I also believed alcohol was necessary to help me relax, fall asleep, and drown out the crushing mom guilt of constantly traveling, when my two young boys were at home growing up without me.

From the society perspective, I believed drinking was what everyone did. It seemed normal—even expected—to head to the minibar as soon as I walked into a hotel room. It felt like part of the script. So I didn't question it.

And from the self perspective, things went even deeper. I hated being alone. At this time in my life it was uncomfortable for me to sit with my own thoughts. My inner world was chaotic and painful. Drinking turned down the volume in my mind, and helped me numb, escape, and find relief from the noise inside my head. It reminds me of the lyrics from the song "Dear Alcohol" by Dax:

I got wasted 'cause I didn't wanna deal with myself tonight
My thoughts get drowned until I feel alright.

Years later, I found myself in the same hotel rooms, with the same minibars, but my experience was drastically different. I had a new set of subconscious programs.

From a substance perspective, I had learned the truth: Alcohol doesn't relax us; it triggers a stress response in the body. What once seemed to help me unwind was increasing both tension and anxiety.

From a society perspective, I now saw through the myth that alcohol was essential for socializing. I'd developed real confidence and communication skills. I was creating meaningful friendships. And I was doing it all without a drink in my hand.

And from a self perspective, I'd begun the lifelong work of making peace inside my own mind. I was learning how to find joy within by untangling the subconscious patterns of unworthiness, shame, and self-rejection that drove my drinking.

Because of these shifts, my experience of a hotel room—and of every situation where alcohol once played a role—had been transformed.

This kind of change isn't unique to me. It's possible for anyone, and not just with alcohol, but with any habit, behavior, or addiction.

As you read this book, you'll continue the process of rewriting your habitual patterns. But for that process to be as effective as possible, I want to give you a practical introduction to how programming and reprogramming the subconscious actually works.

As you can imagine, the human mind is incredibly complicated. In fact, scientists widely agree that the brain is the most complex—and perhaps least understood—structure in the known universe. To make this information as accessible and useful as possible, I'll continue to simplify the elements of Affective Liminal Psychology—the science-backed approach at the heart of this book—so that we can practically apply them to life. Next we are going to explore two foundational scientific concepts of the ALP approach: the instinctual brain and the pyramid of perspective.

Foundational Science Concept 1:
The Instinctual Brain

To understand why we do what we do—even when we don't want to, especially when it comes to habits like drinking—we need to start looking at how the human brain is wired for survival. From birth, our brains are naturally wired to do three main things:

1. Seek pleasure

2. Avoid pain

3. Conserve energy

These make up what's known as the Motivational Triad, introduced 2003 by Dr. Douglas Lisle and Dr. Alan Goldhamer. These three core motivators helped our ancestors survive, and they still shape our lives today.

Seek Pleasure

Our brains are hardwired to chase things that feel good. This includes obvious pleasures like food, sex, laughter, and connection, but it also includes addictive substances like alcohol. Alcohol artificially overstimulates the brain's pleasure center, chemically confusing the brain into believing alcohol is a vital part of life. This is why we go back for a second glass of wine or reach for a drink after a long day—it's not weakness; it's biology.

Avoid Pain

Just as we're wired to seek pleasure, we're also built to avoid pain, both physical and emotional. Pain tells us something is wrong and urges us away from it. The amygdala is one of the parts of the brain that detects threats and triggers our fight-or-flight response. If something causes harm, our brains remember so we can avoid it next time. This system doesn't just respond to physical danger like a hot stove or a growling dog; it also reacts to emotional threats, like conflict, shame, rejection, or fear of failure.

Because the numbing effect of alcohol helps us temporarily avoid pain—whether it's physical pain or emotional pain like anxiety, stress, or loneliness—it's not surprising that we reach for a drink when life hurts.

Conserve Energy

Our brains love efficiency. They constantly look for ways to save effort and avoid unnecessary work. This is another instinct left over from a time when food was scarce and survival meant using energy wisely.

Your brain is the most energy-demanding organ in the body. Although it makes up only about 2 percent of your body weight, it uses roughly 20 percent of your body's total energy. To manage this high demand efficiently, the brain creates mental shortcuts—automatic habitual responses.

These subconscious habits shape nearly every part of our daily lives. We develop habits of action, emotion, and belief. They run automatically in the background, helping the brain conserve energy by reducing the need for constant decision-making.

When we talk about habitual patterns in our thoughts, beliefs, and emotions, we're also talking about bias. Bias is the brain's way of conserving energy by leaning on learned patterns instead of analyzing everything from scratch.

Simply put, biases help the brain save energy by allowing certain thought patterns to run on autopilot. Bias on its own isn't always a problem. But there are two kinds: explicit and implicit.

An explicit bias is one you're fully aware of. For example, I have an explicit bias against milk—I don't like it, and I know it. It's conscious and deliberate.

Our implicit biases are the beliefs we don't know we have. You're not consciously aware of them, but they still affect your decisions, emotions, reactions, and habits. That's what makes implicit biases so powerful and so dangerous—we don't question them because we're generally not aware they exist. Since they are built into the very structure of our mind, they feel like fact. As a result, they feel *real* and influence our behaviors in ways we don't understand.

Let me give you an example.

I had an implicit—or subconscious—bias about alcohol. I believed alcohol was relaxing. Not just that it *could* be relaxing, but that it *was* relaxing, full stop. I believed it the same way I believe the sky is blue. It was *obvious*, just ask anyone. I'd never thought to question the color of the sky, and I'd never thought to question alcohol because it's not our nature to question things we already believe to be true—why would we?

But guess what? I recently learned the sky isn't blue! The gases that make up 99 percent of our atmosphere—mostly nitrogen and oxygen— are completely clear. And space, beyond our atmosphere, is black. There's nothing blue up there.

So why does the sky appear blue? It's because of a phenomenon called Rayleigh scattering. As sunlight enters our atmosphere, it interacts with gas particles. The shorter blue wavelengths of light scatter more than the others, making the sky *look* blue to the human eye, even though it's not.

If the sky isn't blue, and alcohol doesn't relax us, it's probably time to start to questioning *everything*.

Foundational Science Concept 2: The Pyramid of Perspective

My view of the minibar didn't shift overnight; it shifted over time as I changed my subconscious programs about alcohol. I now see through a new set of lenses—ones that reflect reality more accurately.

How are these programs created in the first place? The pyramid of perspective shows how our conscious perspective—how we see and experience the world—is shaped by deeper layers of subconscious programming. These layers work together to form the lenses through which we perceive reality. Here is a visual representation.

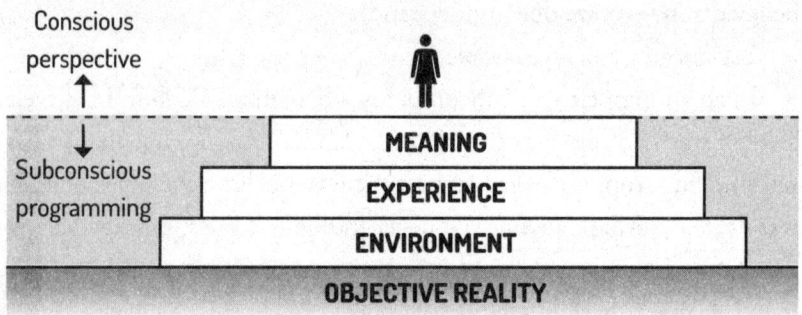

Our Reality Is Not Objective Reality

Before we get into the layers, it's important to understand that our experience of reality is not reality itself. We only ever perceive a narrow slice of what's truly happening—and even that is filtered through the limits of our human senses. Marcus Aurelius, Roman emperor and Stoic, said it this way:

> *Everything we hear is an opinion, not a fact. Everything we see is a perspective, not the truth.*

Let me show you what I mean: Imagine sitting in a courtroom. The defendant and the victim's family are both in the same room, at the same moment, hearing the same words. Yet their experiences could not be more different—one is filled with dread, while the other is full of grief or hope for justice. Same moment, entirely different realities.

Or a hospital room. A nurse monitors a screen for vitals, calmly adjusting the IV line. Meanwhile, the patient in the bed is overwhelmed by pain and fear. Same place, same time, but two radically different experiences.

Reality is further sliced based on how we direct our focus. If I'm sitting at a hotel pool, glued to my phone, I'm having one kind of moment. But if I look up and see my kids laughing and splashing, my experience shifts completely. The only difference? Where I focus my attention.

Our senses also limit how much of reality we are able to perceive. Take vision, for example. Eagles have five times more photoreceptors in their eyes than humans do. They can spot details from twenty feet away that we have to be five feet away from in order to see. Even more impressive, eagles are able to detect a wider range of colors and much finer detail than we can. Compared to an eagle's vision, human sight is like watching a black-and-white TV from the 1950s, while the eagle sees the world in full color, with ultra-high definition. And yet, even an eagle's vision is limited and still is capturing only a slice of reality.

The bottom line? Our experience of reality is unique to us. It is not reality itself. It's shaped by where we are and what we focus on. How our senses filter information is further shaped by the three layers in the pyramid of perspective—environment, experience, and meaning—through which we perceive the world. Let's take them one at a time.

Layer 1: Environment

If you were raised on the crowded streets of Mumbai, your worldview will be drastically different than that of someone raised in a one-stoplight town in the middle of the rural US. Environment shapes everything, from what kinds of monsters you believe lurk under the bed to the foods your taste buds enjoy. Our environment is not just physical and geographical; it also includes the sociocultural beliefs we are immersed in. These are the invisible backdrop of our lives, like water to a goldfish. Just as the fish doesn't know it's swimming in water, we often don't realize how deeply our environment is constantly shaping how we see the world.

My parents avoided pharmaceuticals, distrusting Western medicine. I entered my marriage with a subconscious belief that the medical system was more focused on profit than health, and when I got pregnant, I knew I wanted the care of a doula, or midwife, rather than that of a doctor. After all, I was born in a tiny farmhouse, surrounded by candlelight, music, incense, and my parents' closest friends—no doctor in sight.

This made no sense to my husband, who was raised in the suburbs, where doctors were trusted and hospitals are the obvious place to have a baby. No one was right, and no one was wrong. Our views were simply the result of our unique environments and family cultures. But once I got pregnant, we found ourselves at a crossroads, unpacking the differences in our perspectives.

Eventually we found a solution that honored both perspectives. Rather than default to my view—having all of our babies at home—or his—using an obstetrician—we chose a middle path. Our children were all born with the help of a doula and without medical interventions, but in a hospital setting—just in case.

There are countless examples in our relationship that show how people raised in the same country, even within the same race and even with similar worldviews, can carry radically different subconscious programs.

In summary, our environment—made up of our geographic location, social setting, and cultural background—shapes what Carl Jung called *the collective unconscious*. The collective unconscious is the foundation of our programming and includes the beliefs, behaviors, and expectations that seem so obvious and widely accepted that they become "common sense." We don't consciously choose these ideas—they're things we're born into and absorb unintentionally—and while most of us accept the collective unconscious narrative as true, it's often far from reality.

Layer 2: Experience

If you touch a candle flame, you automatically learn *danger, pain, don't do that again*. You don't have to think about not touching candle flames in the future—this direct experience, associated with physical pain, created a program that will stick with you for life: flame = pain.

Our experiences are influenced by our unique biology and chemistry. Research shows that physical traits—like being tall or conventionally attractive—can lead to higher pay, faster promotions, and more social or romantic attention. Your unique experience of living within the body you've been born into—including your skin color—shapes the subconscious programs that ultimately guide your behavior.

Our subconscious programs are also influenced by what we observe. Studies show that consuming certain types of media, like crime shows or murder mystery novels, can create a subconscious belief that it's unsafe to be out after dark. These aren't our direct experiences, but our brains treat them as real. The result? The night feels more dangerous, even if we've never personally experienced that danger. And because these beliefs are formed beneath conscious awareness, we never think to question them. Yet we are convinced the danger is real.

Consider what happens when alcohol enters the picture. Alcohol seems to confirm, through direct experience, that drinking removes pain. Historically, alcohol was even used as an anesthetic during surgeries before safer options were developed. Alcohol speaks directly to our most primal instincts: to avoid pain and seek pleasure. And when a substance impacts our experience by fulfilling those basic needs, our brains take notice. That's how addictive patterns begin. Not from moral failure, but from biology and experience. Not because we're weak or broken or lack willpower, but because we are human.

Layer 3: Meaning

We create meaning by interpreting our experiences. We make observations and assumptions that lead to the conclusions we make about our lives, ourselves, and other people. Let's look at an example, a story about my friend Matt.

Matt was the class clown growing up. He loved being the center of attention and making people laugh. Until third grade, when Matt stood in front of the class and mispronounced a word, making it sound dirty, and suddenly the entire class laughed at him instead of with him. Hot shame filled his belly—and a deeply rooted subconscious belief was born: *Being seen isn't safe.* The boy who loved the attention of being in front of people was locked away.

We each have countless moments like this in our lives—moments of internal disconnection where we abandon our true nature in order to become someone others will accept. Rather than showing up unapologetically as we are, we start shape-shifting, editing, and hiding.

In that moment of laughter, Matt's instinctual brain was scrambling to make sense of what just happened. You've probably heard it said that the brain is a meaning-making machine, and it's true. Our brains are constantly telling stories to explain our experiences. What most people don't realize is that the meanings our brains create are often made up. They are guesses based on our need to avoid pain, seek pleasure, and conserve energy. Mind-blowing science confirms this: Many of our deeply held beliefs are formed without much proof. We create knee-jerk meanings based on *guesses*.

Worse, these guesses are made below conscious awareness. Since the brain doesn't realize it's guessing, it treats the meanings it is creating as fact.

When the class laughed, Matt's body reacted with a jolt of adrenaline, sweaty palms, and a racing heart. His brain quickly interpreted these physical signals, creating a story to explain the discomfort in his body.

Let's consider two possible meanings Matt's brain might generate:

Meaning 1: *It's not safe to be up in front of people. They're laughing at me. I hate this.*
Meaning 2: *I can make people laugh. They're happy. I love this.*

Both meanings are plausible. Both are based on the same moment. But each leads to a completely different outcome. The brain isn't just guessing at the meaning based only on this moment or on objective reality; the guess is based on the entire pyramid of perspective. The totality of his environment and his experiences.

If Matt believes the first meaning—that being in front of people is unsafe—he may start avoiding attention. Even though performing lights him up, he might make an unconscious vow to protect himself by staying out of the spotlight. That decision becomes a subconscious program. It may keep him safe, but it also steals his dreams, protecting him from the very thing he was created for—being in the spotlight.

If his brain creates the second meaning—that it feels great to make people laugh—he may lean into that strength. Matt might seek out the stage, starting to explore stand-up comedy. That one meaning could launch him into a life of passion, laughter, and joy.

This is the power of meaning.

However, since our pyramids of perspective are not reality, the meanings we make aren't objective truth.

It reminds me of the ancient parable of the blind men and the elephant. Six blind men encounter an elephant for the first time. Each touches a different part—trunk, tusk, ear, leg, side, and tail. When asked to describe what the elephant is, each man gives a completely different answer—a guess based on their limited and unique perspective. One says it's a snake. Another says it's a wall.

None of them are wrong. But none of them have the whole picture.

Author Dave Gray makes this point brilliantly:

The point of the story is not that the blind men cannot see. The point of the story is that we are all blind.

Our perspective is limited. It's shaped by our environment, our experiences, and the meanings we assign. But perspective quickly shifts when we receive new information. Imagine if each of the blind men took a few steps to the left—they would encounter something new, gain more information, and experience the elephant differently. By going beyond their individual perspective, they would find their view of the truth expanding.

As an aside, I want to acknowledge that I naturally operate within my own pyramid of perspective. In order to minimize bias in what I write and teach, I use three filters whenever I evaluate ideas or seek truth. These filters guide me by helping me step out of my own pyramid and focus on what's useful, what's helpful, and what reflects objective reality rather than personal opinion. You can find a detailed explanation of these filters in appendix 2.

Now that we understand the layers that create our unique perspective—environment, experience, and meaning—and how they lay the foundation for how our subconscious programs are created, we need to ask ourselves: Why do certain experiences create subconscious programs while others don't?

Which Programs Stick?

At any given moment, we're taking in far more information than our brains can consciously handle. Research shows that while the brain absorbs about eleven million bits of data per second, the conscious mind can only process around four hundred of those bits. Most of what we experience passes through without leaving a trace. But some data has a lasting impact, one so powerful that it shapes how we perceive the world from that moment on. What makes the difference? What are the forces that shape the subconscious programs that ultimately become the lenses through which we perceive the world?

This is where ERA comes in: emotion, repetition, and authority.

ERA is the system our brain uses to filter the overwhelming amount of information we take in. Emotion, repetition, and authority not only create these subconscious patterns, they also hold the keys to changing them. When we use ERA intentionally, we can reshape our pyramid of perspective and create real, lasting change. Change so powerful that one day you might walk into a hotel room and genuinely believe minibars no longer exist—not because they're gone, but because they're no longer part of the world you now live in.

———

To view the references cited in this chapter, please visit LiveNakedAF.com.

CHAPTER 5

REWRITE THE CODE

All learning has an emotional base.
—Plato

My heart split open when I walked into my dad's house to pick him up for Easter dinner and found him dead in his chair. It was the worst moment of my life. My dad was *my person*, and throughout my life, whenever I've faced something difficult, one thought always brought me comfort: *I am my father's daughter*.

My dad represented love, safety, and stability. His constant presence shaped my perspective of the world. He told me that I could do anything I set my mind to. He told me that the most important wisdom for my own life would always come from within, and that, no matter what, I should trust myself first.

These were more than just words. They were deep programs written into my mind through his care, affection, and protection. Beliefs rooted so deeply that they continue to guide me, even in his absence. His influence plays a big part in why I believe I can do the things I do—like solve my own problem with alcohol and help others do the same.

The programs written in my relationship with my dad were grounded in positive emotions, but emotions have two sides, and I carry countless other programs—which were created in pain.

Pain is incredibly powerful, especially in childhood, when we're most vulnerable. The instinct to avoid pain is driven by fear, and when we are experiencing fear, the brain responds quickly and decisively. Painful experiences don't need to happen repeatedly to leave a mark. When something hurts, the brain wires it in immediately, saying, *Avoid this at all costs.* Fear writes the code, and that code keeps running in the background, unrecognized and never challenged, questioned, or rewritten.

Whether our programming came from pain or pleasure—whether it's about substance, society, or self—the formula to change it is the same: ERA, or emotion, repetition, and authority. We will start with the most powerful, emotion.

Emotion

What are the moments in your life that you remember most? Chances are, they are tied to strong emotion—either positive or negative. This isn't a coincidence. Research shows that emotionally charged events are remembered more clearly and in greater detail than neutral ones. And the memories we carry most vividly often shape our actions in the present.

Emotions also boost our brain's ability to change itself—a concept known as neuroplasticity. Studies from the University of North Carolina show that positive emotions support neurogenesis (the growth of new brain cells) and increase cognitive flexibility. In other words, positive emotions help us rewire our brains and build new, healthier patterns of thought and behavior. Equally, studies show that negative emotions like fear also lead to long-lasting changes in the brain, which influence future perceptions and perspectives.

The science is clear: Emotion plays a central role in forming new memories, reshaping neural pathways, and creating long-term behavior change. When it comes to transformation, the emotional brain is one of the most powerful tools we have.

The Paradox of Emotion

Even though emotion is the most potent force in behavior change, our emotions are often overlooked or dismissed entirely. From a young age, we're taught by parents, teachers, and other authority figures that emotions are things to be managed, hidden, or even ashamed of. The message is subtle but consistent: Emotions are messy, and they get in the way.

Let's face it: Our culture is emotionally avoidant, and these beliefs run so deep that we find ourselves apologizing for our emotion. The idea that emotions are inconvenient or weak is part of the collective unconscious, and because of this cultural conditioning, we rarely think of emotion as a valid or essential tool for change.

The Construction of Emotion

To understand the power of emotion, we need to take a closer look at what emotion really is and how to use it intentionally by turning to the latest research from Dr. Lisa Feldman Barrett.

In her groundbreaking book *How Emotions Are Made*, Dr. Barrett shares decades of research and hundreds of studies that lead to one powerful insight: Emotions are not hardwired as we once believed. For example, there is no single anger center or sadness area built into the brain. Emotions are far more complex; in fact, they are not even found in the brain—they are constructed by it. Dr. Barrett explains that emotions are created based on a combination of past experiences, context, body sensations, and learned meanings. They are constructed, not triggered. To simplify the research, we are going to focus on two key layers: *feeling* and *meaning*.

Feeling

But wait, isn't a feeling an emotion? Aren't they the same thing? Actually, no. Science shows us that our feelings are our most basic biological and chemical responses, and while they are a vital component of emotion, they are not the same as emotion.

Feelings come before language. They show up as vibrations and disturbances in the body that get our attention and drive us to act. These are primal chemical reactions, like the jolt of being startled, the ache of loneliness, or the pang of hunger. They come factory installed in the human body. This first layer of emotion is raw, automatic, and nonconscious, and it's been with us since birth.

Interestingly, feelings don't just come from our direct experiences; they also come from our observations of others' experiences. One day my friend James, who lives in Idaho, saw a mountain lion while out on his bike ride. His brain automatically reacted, triggering a fight-or-flight response and flooding his body with adrenaline and cortisol. Later, as he shared this story with our mutual friend Stacey, her body responded the same way, even though she was safe in her dining room.

If you've ever watched a suspenseful movie and noticed your heart racing or your breath growing shallow—even though you know it's just a movie—you've experienced this phenomenon. The instinctual brain reacts first, often before the conscious mind has time to step in and remind us that we are safe. And when the conscious mind does catch up, it makes sense of the distressing or surprising feelings in the body with attempts to explain it. That explanation is the second layer in the construction of emotion: meaning.

Meaning

In response to feelings, our brains create meanings. This happens automatically in order to help us avoid future pain and seek out future pleasure. We create meanings before we are even able to speak, and interestingly, even animals create meanings.

I once had a dog named Moose. He was sweet and affectionate—except around my dad. The first time they met, Moose growled and barked, completely out of character. He wouldn't let my dad near me. We later learned that Moose had been mistreated by a man with a beard before we adopted him. His brain had formed a simple meaning: *Men with beards are dangerous.* Because Moose didn't share our language, we couldn't explain that my dad—although he also had a beard—was safe.

Just like Moose, we form meanings before we have language. These early, preverbal meanings can be difficult to access and change because the part of us that created them doesn't use words.

Once we develop fluency with language, we go well beyond these basic associations. We weave complex, often subconscious stories about people, places, and events. Our meaning-making brain automatically sorts everyone and everything around us into categories like good or bad, right or wrong, safe or unsafe.

James gave his experience of seeing a mountain lion a positive meaning. For him, it was thrilling. That interpretation changed everything. His brain told his body *This is amazing* rather than *This is terrifying.* As a result, the feelings in his body changed. His brain triggered the release of dopamine and endorphins—chemicals associated with pleasure, excitement, and reward. By changing the meaning, he shifted his emotional experience.

Stacey's mind created a different meaning for the feeling in her body: *My kids aren't safe outside.* This meaning amplified her feelings of fear and stress, and as a result, her body responded by producing a stronger stress response.

The Meaning-Feeling Spiral

This is the meaning-feeling spiral. In simple terms, when the brain assigns *meaning*, the body responds with more *feeling*. Those feelings then reinforce the meaning—and the cycle continues.

Our friendly neighborhood mountain lion is a great example. It wasn't the lion itself that determined whether the experience sparked fear or excitement for James. It was the *meaning*. James interpreted the experience as exciting. Stacey, as dangerous. Those meanings shaped how their bodies reacted—and how they remembered the event. Stacey's meaning shaped her future behavior: She'd planned to visit us in Colorado until she heard we also have mountain lions. This was years ago, and she still hasn't come to visit, citing lions as the reason. The meanings we make create the emotion we feel, which in turn influences the future actions we take.

Feeling, Meaning, Emotion, and Alcohol

Let's apply this to alcohol. Imagine a socially awkward teenager who suddenly finds themselves fitting in at a party where they've been offered a drink. The brain takes note of the positive feelings, like connection and safety, and looks to understand what's changed. If the only new factor is the drink in their hand, the brain may assign the meaning: *Alcohol helps me fit in.*

Even if untrue, you can see how that meaning is based on both emotion and experience. Next, in order to conserve energy, bias kicks in—the brain will self-seal the new belief in a bubble of bias, meaning we now accept the new program as true and rarely question it.

When it comes to habits involving addictive substances like alcohol, things get even more complicated. That's because our feelings are produced by chemical signals. And here is the problem: Alcohol and all addictive substances hijack our chemical system.

To understand how, let's look briefly at one of the most well-known neurotransmitters, dopamine. Often called the "learning molecule," dopamine's job is to signal the brain to repeat behaviors that promote survival. When something triggers a dopamine release, the brain interprets that activity as important and worth repeating.

Its core message is simple: *Whatever you just did, do it again.*

That's how a false emotional message like *I need a drink* is born—it becomes more than just a thought; it becomes a physical feeling. Next, meanings are created to justify our feelings. Meanings like *Alcohol helps me relax* or *I need it to cope*. Feelings and meanings combine to create strong emotions, all of which are stored as subconscious programs. Programs that become stronger with our next element: repetition.

Repetition

You've probably heard that repetition helps form new habits, beliefs, and behaviors. This idea is so prevalent that many of us believe that if we just repeat something for long enough it will stick. And while repetition can help build new neural pathways, repetition alone rarely works—and has a significant and often overlooked flaw. Let me explain.

After hearing a well-known influencer describe how she attributes much of her success to writing mantras on her bathroom mirror and sticking Post-it notes to the dashboard of her car, I gave it a shot. I didn't feel very successful at the time, but, inspired, I wrote "I am a success" on my mirror, on notes plastered all over my closet, and even on the home screen of my phone.

Instead of helping, this practice just irritated me. Every time I saw the words, I felt worse. Eventually I learned why from neuroscientist Dr. Caroline Leaf. The problem isn't repetition—it's repeating a thought that we're not emotionally or subconsciously aligned with. When we repeat something we don't believe, it creates conflict in the brain—conflict that Dr. Leaf explains causes *neural toxicity*. I'd unknowingly made my brain a toxic place with my attempts at repetition. No wonder I was irritated. Repetition only works for things we already accept. Otherwise we just struggle against ourselves, making things worse.

This shows up when we try to quit drinking. If you're white-knuckling your way through the day and aren't yet emotionally aligned with your decision, you are creating internal conflict. The tension builds, and the more time that passes, the more discomfort you feel. This is one of the reasons people with years of sobriety can relapse dramatically—not just one drunk evening, but a full-blown multiday bender. The unresolved internal conflict becomes unbearable.

Repetition can be a powerful tool as long as we don't force a belief or action that we aren't aligned with. Neurologically, repetition works because of a principle known as Hebb's law, which states:

Neurons that fire together wire together.

In my life with my dad, this law worked for me in a useful way—my dad's steady presence allowed him countless opportunities to repeat helpful programming. But we have to be careful. Repetition shapes us in ways that go unnoticed. In order to conserve our energy, our brains tune out the familiar, our conscious attention grabbed only by what's new or different. Once we understand the power of repetition, it is up to us to become aware of both the messages subtly slipping into minds and the repeated stories that we are constantly and automatically telling ourselves.

When we use repetition—whether intentionally or not—we're building new structures in the brain. Repetition, without internal conflict, builds the very structures that move us from Awake to Alive as the neurons that repeatedly fire together wire together.

Repetition and Pro-Alcohol Programming

Consider how repetition can shape our subconscious programming around alcohol. How many pro-alcohol messages have you seen in just the last twenty-four hours? If you watched a single sporting event—most of which are sponsored by alcohol brands—you were likely exposed to hundreds of alcohol-related images, ads, and slogans. One of the most dangerous aspects of repetition is that the more something is repeated, the safer it feels. Because our brains equate familiarity with safety, even something as harmful as alcohol starts to seem safe.

But repetition alone isn't what makes alcohol such a problem.

Without the other two elements—authority and emotion—repetition isn't nearly as powerful. Let's look at authority next.

Authority

Few people have held more authority in my life than my father. At first, his authority came because he was bigger and stronger than me. Later, I intentionally turned up the microphone on his influence. I admired how he chose to live—with simplicity and contentment—so I started asking questions. I would listen carefully, internalizing his words, many of which inform this book.

Our brains assign authority automatically, without questioning why. From the moment we're born—long before we can speak—we learn that the people who feed us, comfort us, and protect us hold power. When we can't fend for ourselves, they are essential to our survival; as a result, obeying their authority and working hard to earn their affection becomes second nature.

Even if our caregivers weren't safe or nurturing, our brains still registered their authority because they were bigger, stronger, and in control of our well-being. Furthermore, we are biologically wired to appease authority. One example is the presence of mirror neurons—brain cells that have us automatically mimic the behavior of those around us. This is how a baby learns to smile in response to a caregiver. Unconscious imitation, especially of authority figures, helps us fit in and gain approval.

Another example is the authority we give to people on television or in the media. When someone is in the spotlight, we unconsciously assume they must be saying something valuable. Our brains connect visibility with credibility.

This also happens with titles. In our culture, labels like *doctor*, *lawyer*, *teacher*, *president*, or *detective* carry built-in authority. We've been conditioned to trust in hierarcy and titles, often without considering whether their expertise actually applies to the situation.

Our brain even interprets popularity as authority. That's because in our evolutionary past, social acceptance meant survival. We are wired to value the opinions of those who hold status or belong to the majority. We can see this play out when we choose to buy the products with the most five-star reviews. We figure that if many people like something, it must be good. Our brains say *Trust the crowd.*

The first time I tasted alcohol, I didn't like it at all. But everyone around me seemed to enjoy it, so I assumed I was the one missing something. My brain created the false meaning that it must be good because everyone was doing it. As a result, I made a deliberate effort to acquire a taste for alcohol.

But the strongest source of authority isn't external—it's the authority of our own direct experiences. Lived experience can carry more weight in programming the brain than anything else. We don't just *believe* what we've experienced—we *know* it.

And this is where alcohol becomes particularly tricky.

Imagine you're anxious and overwhelmed—your mind racing, thoughts spinning. You take a drink and suddenly feel calm. You experience relief. Naturally, your brain concludes that alcohol helps you relax.

But that's not what is really happening.

Alcohol doesn't relax you. It actually slows down your brain's neural activity. It dulls your thinking and reaction time, which can feel like relief if your mind has been racing all day. The contrast—between an overstimulated mind and a chemically slowed one—feels like peace. But it's not real peace or true relaxation. It's chemical sedation.

This is how alcohol tricks us. Since the experience feels real, we assign it ultimate authority. We build beliefs around it. We create unconscious programs that define alcohol as helpful, relaxing, and even necessary. That's why I believed alcohol relaxed me as surely as I believed the sky was blue. I *knew* it to be true—until I learned to question it.

We can use ERA to rewrite the code. We do this by becoming aware of where and how we've been unknowingly programmed and then using the tools of emotion, repetition, and authority to transform our beliefs. We do this by intentionally replacing the old patterns with the patterns necessary to move us from Awake to Alive.

The first step is to bring conscious awareness to our internal programs. We need to examine the layers of our perspective and uncover the emotional experiences, repeated messages, and sources of authority that shape the beliefs we hold true. We'll do this through a simple but powerful process called ACT: awareness, clarity, and transformation—a method inspired in part by Byron Katie's process of self-inquiry called The Work, Brooke Castillo's self-coaching model, and Dr. Richard Schwartz's Internal Family Systems.

Awareness

Awareness is simply paying attention to the programs running in the background of our minds. When we pay attention, we begin to see how much of what we think, believe, and feel is not necessarily ours but has been shaped by our environment, culture, and past experiences. Becoming aware can be painful. We come to realize that many of the results and limitations in our lives come from programs we never chose—that don't really belong to us. But awareness is vital because without it, we can't change.

Clarity

Clarity is the process of understanding these programs. For example, did I truly believe that great writers constantly drank red wine, or had I just absorbed that idea from books and movies? Is it genuinely classy to drink champagne, or had effective marketing trained me to think so?

When we recognize where our mental programs come from, we can begin to question them. This turns our attention inward, helping us search for the truth within ourselves. It's how we find freedom, by asking: Is this useful? Is it helpful? Is it really serving me? Once we understand the true emotional and behavioral cost of a belief, our minds naturally want to let it go—just like touching a flame once is enough to instantly create the program *Never touch that again.*

Transformation

Transformation means consciously and intentionally choosing the mental programs you want to install, using the elements of ERA. Through this process, we select beliefs that feel better, serve us, and support the way we want to live. These are beliefs we feel emotionally and internally aligned with—and that reflect reality more accurately. Transformation involves using questions and experiments to explore and try on new thoughts, beliefs, actions, and emotions.

Transformation: My Alcohol Experiment

About three months after I stopped drinking, I found myself curious about alcohol. I had gone to a St. Patrick's Day dinner where everyone seemed to be having a great time while drinking green beer. *Maybe alcohol wasn't all that bad? Maybe I'd overreacted?* But I knew that drinking again while I was already having fun, like at a St. Patrick's Day dinner, would falsely associate fun with a drink in my brain. I didn't want that. I wanted to know the truth: What was my actual experience of alcohol now that I wasn't craving it and there was no chemical withdrawal or desire for it in my body? Was drinking fun? Did it genuinely feel good? Was I was missing out?

I decided to run an experiment. I locked myself in my bedroom, turned on a camera, and drank two bottles of wine—just to observe.

It was shocking. It wasn't fun. Drinking didn't relax me. The alcohol made me grumpy, disconnected, and dim. When I watched the video, it hurt. I turned from a funny, happy girl to an angry, miserable person. I saw the light leave my eyes. Through my direct experience, I no longer *believed* that alcohol did nothing for me—I *knew* it.

My alcohol experiment was the proverbial nail in alcohol's coffin. (You can watch the video at LiveNakedAF.com.)

Transformation is powerful. It's how we reclaim our minds—breaking free from the prison of our programming and stepping outside the herd mentality surrounding alcohol.

————

ACT is the process that ties together everything we've learned so far—the three layers of belief (substance, society, and self), the subconscious motivators (emotion, repetition, and authority), and the foundational science of the instinctual brain and the pyramid of perspective.

ACT is the process that shifts us from wanting a drink to feeling indifferent about alcohol. It's how we reach a point where drinking a glass of wine starts to sound as appealing as drinking a glass of motor oil.

There are many variations of ACT. We can use awareness, clarity, and transformation to explore the mental programs we formed early in life—programs meant to protect us but that might now cause pain. With this process, we can gently rewrite those patterns. We can also practically apply it to our day-to-day thoughts, even shifting our emotional baseline. Tools from ACT can work like an emotional thermostat, helping us move from a default state of "meh" to one of contentment and joy.

I'll teach you the basics of ACT in chapter 7, but first I want to give you a direct experience of the power of the process. In the next chapter, we will transform, through the tenets of ACT, a common sociocultural program many of us carry: the belief that drinking is normal and choosing to live alcohol free is not.

————

To view the references cited in this chapter, please visit LiveNakedAF.com.

CHAPTER 6

NORMAL AF

The reasonable man adapts himself to the world: the unreasonable one persists in trying to adapt the world to himself. Therefore, all progress depends on the unreasonable man.
—George Bernard Shaw

I grew up in a one-room log cabin without running water or electricity. No indoor plumbing meant no sink, bathtub, or toilet. Our bathroom was an outhouse a short walk away from the cabin—a walk that as a little girl I absolutely loathed, especially when it was dark and snowy outside.

Here's something you might not know about outhouses: They fill up. And about every six or seven years, we'd dedicate an entire day to digging a new hole. Surprisingly, I have fond memories of the days we spent digging.

Pro tip: If you ever find yourself digging an outhouse hole, make sure it's at least eight feet deep. Otherwise, the splash-back can be a real problem!

The Tyranny of "Normal"

Growing up in a tight-knit rural community with only fifty-three students in my graduating class meant there was no such thing as privacy. Everyone knew everything about each other, including the unusual way my family lived. My classmates knew I rode a snowmobile to school because our cabin was remote and the dirt road to it was impassable for much of the year. They knew I didn't have a shower or even a thermostat. They could smell the smoke on my clothes because our heat came from a wood-burning stove.

When kids told me I smelled bad, it hurt—both because it was true and because there was nothing I could do about it. This type of teasing—for being different and abnormal—stung. And living in the jaw-dropping opulence of Aspen, Colorado—one of the wealthiest zip codes in the country—meant our lifestyle stood out in ways that were impossible to hide.

Although I now see that feeling like an outsider is part of most humans' experience as a child, at the time every difference felt enormous. It was like there was a spotlight constantly shining on everything that wasn't "normal" about me. These experiences created a constant, painful sense of otherness—a feeling of being apart, excluded, and outcast. Feelings I carried with me at all times.

How does this connect to drinking more than we want to?

The first thing we tend to do when we begin to question our drinking is look around. What is everyone else doing? How are they handling alcohol? We try to hide the problems alcohol is causing in our lives, and so does everyone else. As a result, it seems like no one is struggling quite like we are. We come to believe we're the only one having problems, the only one who can't figure it out, the only one who isn't *normal*.

Even at the height of my drinking, I looked like I had it all together. After I stopped, a few coworkers made comments along the lines of "You quit drinking? I never thought you were the one with the problem." And it made me pause: Why do we find it more surprising when someone stops drinking than when they continue, even if alcohol is hurting them?

Maybe we're asking the wrong question. Maybe instead of wondering if it's abnormal to *struggle* with alcohol, we should be asking this: Why do we think it's normal to drink a highly addictive substance in the first place?

We don't judge ourselves as abnormal for eating too much sugar or scrolling social media for longer than we mean to. We accept that it is just part of being human. Why is it different with alcohol?

Side note: You may have noticed that we've just moved through the first step of ACT—awareness. We've become aware of a belief that many of us carry. The powerful subconscious program: *It's normal to drink. It's abnormal to live alcohol free.*

Now that we're aware of this program, we can move on to the next step. Where did this belief come from? And what impact has it had on my life, my decisions, and my emotions? Let's dig in with clarity.

We can trace the idea of "not normal" all the way back to 1939. The following quotes are from *The Big Book*, the foundational text of Alcoholics Anonymous (AA):

- [The alcoholic is] . . . bodily and mentally *different* from his fellows.

- [We alcoholics are] . . . *abnormal* drinkers.

- The delusion that we [alcoholics] are like other people, or may presently be, has to be smashed.

The AA text describes people with alcohol problems as fundamentally different. Self-proclaimed alcoholics consider themselves so abnormal that they have a term for everyone else: *normies*. Normies are people who can drink "normally" and have a "normal" relationship with alcohol. *The Big Book* even goes so far as to describe people who can't drink normally as *the unfortunates*.

When we internalize beliefs like this, they shape both how we feel and how we behave. We find ourselves looking longingly at drinkers, wishing we could still be one of them. We feel alone—on the outside of regular society—carrying a sense of stigma, judgment, and shame. We even begin to feel embarrassed or ashamed about our decision to quit drinking, staying anonymous—hidden in the shadows—believing we no longer belong.

And if feeling abnormal wasn't bad enough to get help, within the traditional paradigm, we are also asked to accept the label *alcoholic*. For many, that word carries a negative stereotype—something to hide and deny rather than something to willingly embrace in order to heal.

I remember that when I first chose to live alcohol free, a colleague sent me this text message:

I'm so sorry to hear that you had to stop drinking. I can't imagine how bad it must have gotten for that to happen. I am thinking about you, hang in there.

I think the message was meant to be supportive, but I was stunned, and even insulted, because nothing outwardly terrible had happened. My situation wasn't (yet) dire. I had made a conscious decision to wake up from the cultural trance around alcohol. And yet I was the one to be pitied?

The assumption was clear: Regular people drink. People without alcohol problems drink. Choosing not to drink meant something must have gone terribly wrong.

That was more than a decade ago, and thankfully, things are starting to shift in our culture. More people are choosing to live alcohol free—not because they hit rock bottom or faced some unspeakable problem, but because they've realized that removing alcohol is one of the healthiest decisions they can make. They want more presence, more clarity, more energy, more joy—and alcohol doesn't fit into that vision.

This trend is so widespread that the alcohol industry is scrambling to respond and pushing out nonalcoholic alternatives as more and more people—many who have never had a traditional problem with alcohol—are turning away from drinking.

This is a huge step forward. But we're still grappling with a powerful subconscious belief: that if you have a problem with alcohol, not only are you not normal, but there's a label for you—*alcoholic*.

Am I an Alcoholic?

The term *alcoholic* plays a major role in the deep cultural belief that it's abnormal to stop drinking. It's time we take a closer look. We need to examine the term *alcoholic* and ask: Is it helping or is it harming? Based on my research and experience, it seems this label does far more harm than good.

I never wanted to be an alcoholic. We hope our children won't grow up to be alcoholics. I resisted the idea of admitting I was one, even when I was really struggling. Yet the only help I knew of came through AA, where the first step is to admit that you are an alcoholic and powerless over alcohol.

That label was a massive barrier for me. Just the thought of voicing the words "I am an alcoholic" made me feel sick to my stomach.

It was kind of like this: Imagine creating a room in your home where your children can go when they feel scared—somewhere they know they will be safe and can always turn for support. Now picture placing a terrifying monster right outside the door to this room. They'd have to face the monster before they could reach the safety inside. How likely are they to seek comfort? That's how the label *alcoholic* felt to me. It wasn't inviting; it was intimidating, monstrous, and lurking outside the rooms where support was found.

The weight and fear surrounding the label *alcoholic* pushed me in the opposite direction. I'm not alone in that; many people are repelled by the term. It's like building a staircase that leads to support and making the first step eleven feet tall. Most people won't even try to climb it—the first step feels impossible.

Even worse, the fear of this label stops us from opening up about our drinking, even to those we love and trust most. I certainly didn't want Brian or my parents worrying that I might be an alcoholic. Tragically, this label keeps countless people from seeking help in the early stages—when the damage is still limited and when change is more accessible.

The Label: *Alcoholic*

One of the biggest problems with the label *alcoholic* is that it ignores the majority of people who struggle with alcohol. According to the Centers for Disease Control and Prevention (CDC), about 90 percent of those experiencing alcohol-related harm don't meet the clinical criteria for addiction. When we reserve support for only those willing to take on the *alcoholic* label, we leave millions of people in the gray area—people whose drinking may not be extreme but who are still suffering.

The term also spreads the false idea that alcohol itself isn't the problem, that the real issue lies with a small group of broken people who can't handle it. But that's not true. Alcohol is addictive for everyone. Like any drug, it changes the brain, causes harm, and carries risk. No one's body is biologically built to process it without consequences.

Yet we continue to believe that some people can drink safely while "alcoholics" cannot. That belief is outdated and dangerous. It's like when doctors used to promote cigarettes in the 1950s, as if widespread use made them safe. Just because alcohol is socially accepted and culturally promoted doesn't mean it's harmless.

What makes the label even more harmful is the fear it creates. Despite evidence, many believe that being an alcoholic means you have an incurable lifelong disease. That message, which traces back to the literature from 1939, tells people that once they cross a certain line, their life will be defined by relapse, disease, and dependence. And yet there's no medical test to diagnose someone as an alcoholic. It's one of the only "diseases" you're expected to self-diagnose.

All this results in people pushing off change, waiting until things get really bad—a spouse threatens divorce, or a drunken fall—before they admit there's a problem. Denial is often blamed on the disease, but what if the label itself helps fuels denial?

Denial caused by fear keeps many people from change. Instead of seeking support early, we wait. We tell ourselves it's not that bad. And then one day something breaks—a relationship collapses or we have a health scare—and we find ourselves in an AA meeting, not because we want to be there, but because we felt forced to go. Research confirms this. According to AA's 2014 Membership Survey, most members don't start attending meetings because they choose to seek help on their own. Instead, many are forced into attendance, either referred by treatment facilities (32 percent), pressured by others (32 percent), or ordered by the court (12 percent).

And here's another problem: No other drug has a label like this. People who quit smoking aren't called "smoke-aholics." Someone who stops using cocaine isn't forever branded a "cocaine-aholic." Yet when someone quits drinking, we tell them they're an alcoholic for life.

It doesn't make sense. And worse, it puts the blame on the person, as if they are the problem. But they're not. *It's not you. It's alcohol. Alcohol is the problem.*

With that said, it is important to recognize that some people do find freedom through the label *alcoholic* and everything that comes with it. Let's take a moment to consider another perspective—when the label becomes a safe haven.

What About When the Label Works?

When I addressed the word *alcoholic* in my first book, *This Naked Mind*, I began receiving letters from people who identified as alcoholics and who were upset by what I'd written. I didn't understand, so I asked my friend Laura, who had experienced both sides. She had found sobriety through AA and credited the program with saving her life, but she no longer attended meetings. I asked her why people were angry when, from my point of view, I was simply offering science, logic, and an alternative perspective.

Her response was enlightening. She explained that for many people, once the label is accepted, it becomes a safety net. By believing that you aren't normal—that you are different, and that you have the disease called alcoholism—you accept that you can never safely drink again.

Laura told me she had internalized the belief that her next drink might kill her, and while that may not have been literally true (one drink generally won't kill someone), it gave her the resolve she needed. It kept her on the straight and narrow. It was the fear—of shame, of relapse, of danger—that helped her through some of her most difficult moments and cravings.

And I can understand that. Fear is a powerful motivator. We've learned that the instinctual brain is driven by fear—fear of pain or fear of missing out on pleasure. For some, that fear is what ensures they never return to the bottle. And that is beautiful. Painful, but beautiful.

In conversation with Laura, I gained an entirely new perspective on those who willingly take on the identity of an alcoholic: I saw courage.

I saw how brave it is to walk into a room and admit that you are broken. I saw how brave it is to leave behind your current identity and adopt a new one—one that you hope might save your life. I now see both the fear and the strength. I'll always be cheering anyone for who the label *alcoholic* has become a haven of safety rather than a barrier to change.

That being said, I'm incredibly grateful that we don't have to take on the label to make a change—and that we don't have to rely on pain and fear as our main motivators.

———

Before we go further, I want to point out that we're entering the final step of the process—transformation. We've explored the cultural programs around the idea that drinking is normal—where they came from and the harm they can cause. Next, we'll explore what's actually true—not through shame, blame, or outdated labels, but through science and evidence.

Drugs and Alcohol

As a society, we've become so confused that we no longer recognize alcohol as a drug. We separate alcohol from other substances—saying "drugs and alcohol"—even though multiple studies rank alcohol as *the most harmful drug*. Furthermore, research makes it clear: Anyone—*yes, anyone*—can become addicted to alcohol with enough exposure and the right circumstances. Studies clearly show that problematic drinking isn't limited to a small group of people labeled as alcoholics.

In fact, the term *alcoholic* is no longer used in medical or scientific settings. It's outdated, inaccurate, and hard to define. The correct term is *alcohol use disorder*, or AUD. What's even more fascinating is how AUD is diagnosed. Eleven questions outline the diagnostic criteria. If based on your experience in the last year, you answer yes to just two of the eleven questions, you meet the diagnostic threshold; you have alcohol use disorder.

Here are two of the questions:

1. Have you had to drink much more than you once did to get the effect you want? Or found that your usual number of drinks had less effect than before?

2. Have you had times when you ended up drinking more, or longer, than you intended?

Every drinker I know would answer yes to both of those questions at least once in the past twelve months. The reality is that most regular drinkers likely meet the criteria for alcohol use disorder. It appears that having AUD is much more common than not having it.

Although most people question their drinking at some point, we rarely talk about it openly. Unlike the conversations we might have around sugar or calories, we wrestle with alcohol privately. We justify, worry, and wonder in silence.

This became obvious when I started socializing alcohol free. Again and again, people would come up to me, unprompted, to talk about their drinking. They'd tell me how they only drank socially or stuck to just one glass a night. Or they'd mention the times they overdid it while insisting they were still in control. At first I didn't understand. Why were people suddenly telling me about their drinking habits? No one was coming up to me to talk about how much sugar they ate. Then I realized—they were comparing themselves to me. Deep down, they were wondering: *Do I need to stop, too?*

Just last weekend, at my son's baseball game, two different moms approached me—again, unprompted—to talk about their alcohol use. One mom told me she never drank for the buzz, only for the taste. Yet despite all the nonalcoholic options available, none of them seemed to "hit the spot." She told me that she decided to keep drinking, even though she didn't want the alcohol—because she couldn't live without taste. But science tells us something important: Alcohol is chemically addictive. Even if she wasn't consciously aware of it, her brain was craving the alcohol, not the taste. Something inside her *knew* there was more going on. Otherwise, why would she spend twenty minutes telling me about her journey with nonalcoholic drinks and her struggle to find one that truly satisfied?

Here's the bottom line—according to science:

- Alcohol is addictive to all humans. It's the circumstances, beliefs, and reasons behind our drinking that determine how quickly it becomes a problem.

- Our brains, driven by a fear of being abnormal or labeled an alcoholic, try to convince us we don't have a problem. As a result, we justify, minimize, and deceive ourselves.

Deep down, we sense something isn't right. The pull toward a drink feels stronger than it should. The hangovers hit harder. That buzz we used to get from one glass of wine now takes two or three. But instead of getting curious about our drinking, we remain afraid and alone. Perhaps the real issue with the idea of "normal" and "alcoholic" is that it teaches us that it is shameful to even *question* our drinking. We've been conditioned to believe that asking questions means we're broken or diseased. Afraid, we bury these questions as fast as we can.

What if we let go of this cultural script? What if we accept that alcohol is addictive and that everyone, no matter who they are, should be cautious? Imagine how much pain, shame, and suffering we could avoid. Imagine how much sooner each of us might change. Imagine what a better example we would set for the next generation.

I hope you can see the power of examining our perspectives with awareness, clarity, and transformation. Next, I'll share a simple formula that you can use to apply ACT in your daily life—letting it lead to real freedom. This process isn't limited to alcohol, or even to habits and behaviors. It can be used for *anything*.

———

To view the references cited in this chapter, please visit LiveNakedAF.com.

CHAPTER 7

AWARENESS, CLARITY, AND TRANSFORMATION

It is the mark of an educated mind to be able to entertain a thought without accepting it.
—Aristotle

For years, I let the clutter and mess in my house overwhelm me and ruin my mood. I'd leave everything clean in the morning, and at the end of the day, I'd walk through the door to find chaos.

I repeatedly asked my family to clean up after themselves—something that seemed reasonable. But every day, it was the same: counters covered, dishes piled up, toys scattered across the floor. The house I had worked so hard to tidy the night before was a mess.

In an instant, my good mood would disappear, and I'd go from calm to furious. Angry, I would start cleaning—*very loudly*—just to make sure everyone knew how upset I was.

As I was cleaning, I would hear the voices in my head, making meanings to explain why I felt so upset. They said things like this:

No one helps out—if they did, the house wouldn't look like this.

No one cares how hard I work—if they did, they'd clean up after themselves.

I have to do everything myself.

My kids clearly don't care about me.

My family doesn't love me—if they did, how could they treat me this way?

Wow. That got dark fast.

At the time, I didn't realize I had a choice. I just assumed the stories that appeared in my mind as I walked through the door were true. No wonder I felt irritated, negative, and angry.

I now know that our minds spiral into negativity very quickly, especially when we're not paying attention. Once I got curious about my thoughts, I was surprised. It was a big leap—from seeing a bunch of paints and crayons left out on the table to believing my family didn't love me. But that's exactly where my mind went when left unchecked. With a bit of curiosity, I had taken the first step in ACT—awareness.

Awareness is the practice of noticing discomfort in your life. I call these moments energy snags. They are times when you're moving through your day and suddenly something throws you off. I was perfectly fine until I walked through the door and saw the mess. An energy snag generally creates a wave of unease, heaviness, discomfort, or fear.

When you notice your energy has been snagged, write it down. That's first step in the ACT process. I keep a note on my phone called "ACT," and whenever I feel my energy snagged, I jot down a few notes: *What happened? What was I thinking?*

In this example, I started to notice that even if I came home from work in a great mood, I'd began to feel upset the moment I walked into a messy house. I'd throw down my bag and start grumbling—just to make sure my whole family could sense my frustration.

You don't need to act on your thoughts right away. Just write down enough about what is happening and what you are thinking so you can come back to it later. And as you write, gently ask yourself a few simple questions: *Is what I wrote actually true? If I had to prove this thought in a court of law, could I?*

These questions start to loosen the grip of old thought patterns. Even if you consider them only briefly, they can shift your perspective. Keep them in the back of your mind, and when you're ready, you can move on to the next step in the ACT process: clarity.

Clarity

Clarity is investigation; it's how to understand where your thoughts and beliefs come from, using compassionate curiosity instead of judgment. This step can include many helpful questions, and you'll find a full list at the end of the book in appendix 3.

Here are some common questions to build clarity:

- How do these thoughts make me feel?

- How do these thoughts influence my behavior—what do I tend to do when I feel this way?

- When did I first start thinking this?

- Is this belief actually mine, or did it come from someone else?

Your mind doesn't intend to cause so much pain. It's simply following the ancient programming of the instinctual brain: Avoid pain, seek pleasure, and conserve energy. These instincts keep the brain on high alert, always scanning for threats. And as you can see, even something as small as a messy house can register as a threat to the instinctual brain.

No wonder we can overreact to a bit of clutter!

But here's the problem: The brain doesn't realize that "doing its job" can actually cause you distress. For example, I didn't enjoy reacting to the mess in my house with frustration and resentment. When you start asking clarity questions—especially those that explore how a thought makes you feel and behave—you help your mind see how painful, and costly, the story you are telling yourself really is. And when that happens, the mind lets go of the thought naturally, which feels like a small miracle. With this process, we can release the negative, survival-based thoughts that don't serve us, and we begin to return to who we truly are.

We have the conscious power to change our repetitive thoughts and stories—and we can do that through transformation.

Transformation

Transformation is about creating a new meaning—a new story that serves you instead of causing you pain. Dr. Caroline Leaf taught us this isn't about forcing positive thinking. You can't fake a thought that doesn't feel true, even if you think you "should" believe it. How do you find a thought you can practice, repeat, and actually believe? That's what ladder thinking is for.

Ladder Thinking

The idea behind ladder thinking is simple: Picture a ladder you want to climb. You can't jump from the bottom rung to the top—you have to take it one step at a time. The same goes for trying on new thoughts. You need to choose thoughts that feel just a little better than what you are currently thinking. And to find the right ones, the ones you are aligned with, you can run your new thoughts back through the clarity questions: *How does this new thought make me feel? How does it influence how I behave and show up in the world?*

Remember my mantras about being a success? Let me show you what the entire ladder looked like. I knew my work was helping people, and I wanted to reach more people, so I began promoting my work more actively. But everywhere I turned, I hit a wall. Worse, since my work was controversial in traditional recovery circles, when it did get attention, that attention was often negative, which reinforced my feelings of failure. But by applying ladder thinking, I was able to successfully transform my thoughts.

The belief *I am a failure* was my starting point.

But I didn't want to stay there because of the pain that thought caused. When I believed I was a failure, I felt hopeless. I'd talk myself out of things before I even tried them, fearing rejection. I wasn't just feeling bad—I was behaving in ways that made progress impossible.

At first I tried jumping straight to the top—*I am a success*—but, as you know, that didn't work. It felt false. Once I understood ACT and the idea of ladder thinking, I searched for a thought just one step up from where I was: *I can learn to be a success.* It didn't claim I already was successful, but it was grounded in possibility. It felt empowering. It gave me energy. It made me curious. I wanted to explore what success looked like and how to learn it. That one small step changed everything.

Eventually I had some proof. I was showing up. I was learning. So I moved up another rung: *I am learning to be a success.* That one was true. I practiced it. It felt even better.

After some time, that thought evolved into *I am more successful every day.*

Now I had consistent evidence. I believed it. It wasn't toxic positivity; it was empowering reality. And finally, after more repetition and reinforcement, I could fully believe the thought I had once rejected: *I am a success!* You can see my progress up the ladder in this graphic:

You don't have to leap to the top. You just need to reach for the next believable, better-feeling thought. That's how you move through ACT and truly transform your beliefs—from the inside out.

When you're looking for the first rung of the ladder, I like what my friend Brooke Castillo suggests—she says we should try on new thoughts like we would try on a new pair of shoes. When you try on shoes, you ask: *Do they feel good? Are they comfortable? Can I walk, run, or move freely in them?* If not, you don't force it; you simply try another pair. Thoughts work the same way. If a new thought doesn't feel right or serve you well, try a different one until you find one that fits.

When I reached the transformation step with the clutter in my house, I asked myself simple questions: *What don't I see? Could the mess mean something else? What if I stopped taking the clutter personally? What if it didn't mean anything about me at all?*

I decided to try a thought experiment. I imagined walking in the door after work and seeing a perfectly clean house, with everything in its place and no clutter in sight. I teared up immediately. I could picture that house—it's the house I'll have one day when my kids are grown and gone. I'm in no rush to get there. Being a mom, even when it means a full, messy house, is one of the greatest joys in my life.

In that moment, the mess took on a new meaning: It meant my children were home. They live here. They play here. They grow up here, laugh here, and cry here. I also remembered a quote I'd heard: "Cleaning with kids in the house is like brushing your teeth while eating an Oreo." It's basically impossible.

That mess wasn't a failure, and it certainly wasn't personal—it was a sign of life. It meant my kids were safe, happy, and thriving under my roof. Just by questioning my old, painful thoughts and choosing a new perspective, I saw the clutter in a completely different way.

I started to practice these new thoughts, over and over, until they became more natural—until they felt like mine. And now, when I walk through the door after a long day and see the house in disarray, something different happens. Instead of spiraling into resentment or hurt, a new set of thoughts, and feelings, rises up automatically.

I see the mess and think: *My kids must've had a great day*. I see the chaos and feel: *They're safe here. They're happy. They are home.*

The mess hasn't changed. But my mind has.

Thoughts like these fill me with gratitude and remind me of exactly where I am in this season of life—a busy mom in a full house. And while the clutter might still be there, I have a lot less stress about it.

ACT led me to a new way of thinking—one that *changed my emotions*—which allows me to show up and parent in a different way. No more silent guilt trips and loud cleaning. I am now happy and excited to see my kids at the end of a long day. And as we now know (and science confirms), an emotional shift matters. The ripple effect of walking through the door in a good mood—rather than feeling frustrated, disconnected, or victimized—has had a profoundly positive impact on the atmosphere of my entire home, every single day.

Such small thoughts—such massive impact.

And here's what's incredible: From a clutter perspective, again, *noth-*

ing has changed. But with three kids and a large dog, lack of clutter is not realistic. What changed was my thinking, not my surroundings.

The ACT technique shows you that you have the power to transform your entire experience of life without changing anything outside you. All you need to shift is what's within.

Simple. Life-changing.

Dr. Daniel Amen, renowned psychologist and neuroscientist, puts it perfectly:

You don't have to believe every stupid lie that goes through your head. Even better, you can talk back to the lies.

ACT draws on the full psychology behind Affective Liminal Psychology. It allows us to shine conscious awareness deep into the pyramid of perspective through emotion, repetition, and authority. This is how we can uncover the unseen programs that are running our lives. By gently changing those programs—and practicing new ones—we can take back our power over both our internal experience and our outward actions.

ACT and Alcohol

Now that you know the principles and basic steps of ACT, let's apply it directly to thoughts about alcohol that threaten to keep us stuck. But first, let me show you how to gather thoughts to ACT on.

The easiest place to start is with your beliefs about the substance itself. Make a list of every reason you like to drink. What you'll see on that list are the subconscious programs that imprison you. These are the beliefs you've absorbed—that probably aren't even yours and need to be brought into the light.

Next, turn your attention to your beliefs about your role as someone who doesn't drink in your social circles and society as a whole. These beliefs can be a bit trickier to spot because they often stay quiet until you're in a social situation where you used to drink. The best way to uncover them is to step into those moments without a drink and simply listen to what your mind tells you.

You might hear thoughts like these:

"They won't invite me again."

"I don't belong here."

"These people are so boring without a drink."

Each one is part of a deeper, subconscious program. Write them down. This becomes your working list—your raw material—for the ACT process.

Okay, now that you know how to look for thoughts, let's practice ACT using a common thought that might come up as you begin your alcohol-free journey: *Tonight would be more fun if I had a drink.*

Awareness

At this step in the process, the key question is: *Are you absolutely sure this is true?*

If you're surrounded by people drinking and seeming to have a great time, your first instinct might be:

"Yes, of course this is true!"

But when we look a little deeper, asking ourselves if we are absolutely sure, the certainty begins to crack:

"Well, I guess I can't be certain about how I'd feel if I was drinking. I remember plenty of nights when drinking wasn't fun at all. In

fact, I can't even remember large parts of the boozy nights I thought were so fun. So . . . no, I can't say for sure."

Clarity

Next, we explore the cost of the thought. Ask yourself: *How does this thought make me feel?*

"It makes me miserable. I feel like I'm missing out. My mood drops. I can't focus on anything else—I just think about how I'm not drinking while everyone else is. I spiral into self-pity."

Then ask yourself: *How does this thought make me behave?*

"I stop enjoying myself. I tune out of conversations and instead focus on the drinks I'm not having. My inner dialogue gets loud: You're boring without alcohol. You'll never enjoy yourself like this. *I start believing that I'll never be fun again without a drink. I get frustrated, defeated, and sometimes I cave in, convincing myself I can handle just one."*

Transformation

Now we shift into transformation. This is, again, where we try on a new thought—a thought that feels better and, most important, one we actually believe. Ask yourself: *What is another thought I can believe that would feel more empowering?*

"Tonight might be more fun with a drink, but I don't know that for sure. I want to spend tonight seeing if I can have a good time alcohol free."

To check that this new thought is both believable and helpful, ask: *How does this new thought make me feel?*

"Tonight is suddenly an experiment. I feel curious instead of defeated. I stop obsessing about what I'm missing and start wondering what I might discover. I might even feel proud that I'm making a conscious choice."

Then ask: *How might this new thought change my behavior?*

"I'll get some food and see if anyone I know is around. I remember why I came—to connect with people—and I'll now follow through on my intention to get to know someone new. All of a sudden, alcohol feels smaller, less powerful. I remember why I stopped drinking in the first place."

During the transformation step, it can also be helpful to flip the original thought to its opposite and explore that:

Original thought: *Tonight would be more fun if I had a drink.*
Opposite: *Tonight would be less fun if I had a drink.*

Now ask yourself, is the opposite also true? Perhaps even *truer* than your original thought?

"Actually, yes. I quit drinking because I wasn't having fun anymore. I never stopped at one. If I give in, I'll drink too much, feel awful, and regret it tomorrow, which isn't my idea of fun."

This process may seem simple, but it's powerful.

I remember one of my first social events where I wasn't drinking but everyone around me was—I felt like I didn't belong. I slipped away to the bathroom, opened the notes app on my phone, and worked through the ACT process.

I wouldn't have believed it if I hadn't lived it. I walked out of that bathroom feeling completely different. I spent the rest of the night talking to new people, even meeting a woman who remains a great friend nine years later. Without these questions, I would've sat in the corner, counting the minutes until I could leave.

Don't just take my word for it—try it. The shift is real. The results are yours to experience.

Let's walk through one more example.

This one was very important for me, especially during high-pressure deadlines at work. My thought was: *I wouldn't be so stressed if I could drink.*

Awareness

Am I certain this is true? At first my brain immediately says, *"Yes! Absolutely true."* But when I paused and looked more closely, a new possibility came forward:

> *"Actually, no—I'm not sure that's true. I'm already so stressed that a drink probably wouldn't help. What would help is buckling down and finishing this presentation. If I start drinking, that won't happen."*

Clarity

How does this thought make me feel?

> *"I was only stressed about my presentation, but now I also feel stressed about drinking. I feel self-pity, frustration, and anger, both at myself and the situation. Life feels unfair. I start to beat myself up for wanting a drink. I feel grumpy, guilty, and miserable."*

How does this thought make me behave?

"I waste energy feeling sorry for myself—energy I could use to work on the presentation and actually relieve my stress. I procrastinate. I lose motivation. And the entire time I feel like I'm letting myself down."

Transformation

Now it's time to try a new thought, something I can actually believe and that feels more empowering. I searched for a new thought and found this:

"A drink might make me feel better for a few minutes, but I'd be even more stressed after it wears off."

How does this new thought make me feel?

"Better. I can see how alcohol would give temporary relief but delay the real solution. This feels empowering. I now feel like not drinking is a strong choice—something I'm doing for myself. I feel proud of that."

How does it change my behavior?

"I'm still stressed, but I'm also focused. I stop wallowing and start tackling my presentation. I'm not wasting time obsessing over alcohol. I feel energized by the decision and motivated to use my stress to fuel some productivity."

You can also reverse the original thought to see what's true in the opposite:

Original thought: *I wouldn't be so stressed if I had a drink.*
Opposite: *I would be even more stressed if I had a drink.*

The opposite felt truer:

"Yes! That feels even more true. If I drank, I wouldn't get my work done. I'd just end up more stressed—not just today but tomorrow. I know myself. One drink turns into many, resulting in avoidance, guilt, and even more stress and pressure."

I can't overstate how powerful this practice is for taming our inner voices—and for creating more peace. I use it constantly.

You can't control the weather. You can't control other people. And you can't always control your body's reactions. But you can control what you consciously think and how you interpret your thoughts. Practicing ACT—intentionally and regularly—will change your life.

As leadership expert Robin Sharma puts it:

When you control your thoughts, you control your mind. And when you control your mind, you control your life.

Repetitive Thoughts Create Pathways

One last note on the importance of starting an ACT practice in your life. Your thoughts shape your brain. Through a complex cellular process, repeated thoughts actually lay down proteins. These proteins form physical structures in the brain—structures that become the foundation for your mental habits.

Imagine living in a cabin in the woods with an outhouse a few hundred yards away. Each time you walk there, you take a slightly different route and no clear path will form. But if you walk the exact same route every day, a visible path starts to appear.

The same thing happens in your brain. Repetitive thoughts carve mental pathways. And since most of our unintentional thoughts are repetitive—and often negative—those paths become the ones we travel most often. The more we think a certain thought, the more likely we are to think it again.

These well-worn mental paths are called neural highways. They're made up of proteins, structural elements, receptors, and connections between neurons. Simply said, repeated thoughts build highways. Over time, these thought pathways become deeply ingrained, like wide, paved roads in the brain. Long-term habits even get reinforced by special cellular structures called perineuronal nets, which make the pathways stable—and resistant to change.

That's where ACT comes in. ACT helps you recognize and reshape the neural pathways that cause emotional pain.

Some of your beliefs live just below the surface, and with a little curiosity, you can begin to unravel the programs that keep you stuck. In these cases, shifting a subconscious belief can happen instantly. A single sentence in a book or something said in conversation flips a switch. You suddenly realize a belief you've carried for years was never actually yours—it came from a parent, a teacher, a friend, or society. And in that moment of clarity, the belief loses its power.

Other beliefs go deeper. They may be tied to emotional wounds, early childhood memories, or trauma. These programs take more time and care to shift. They live deep in the pyramid of perspective and can require focused attention—and possibly, professional support.

The great news is that no matter how deeply rooted a belief is, change is always possible. When we're willing to do the work to explore and rewrite our subconscious patterns, we unlock a life that feels more grounded, more joyful, and more aligned with who we truly are.

As you move into your alcohol-free life, you'll face some practical challenges, especially the first time you do something you used to do only while drinking. These "firsts" can be tough, but they also offer powerful opportunities to apply ACT, and that's where we are going next.

———

To view the references cited in this chapter, please visit LiveNakedAF.com.

CHAPTER 8

HOW TO NAVIGATE AF FIRSTS

You gain strength, courage, and confidence by every experience in which you really stop and look fear in the face.
—Eleanor Roosevelt

Living alcohol free comes with many "firsts." You'll do things for the first time that you once did while drinking. If I lived on a deserted island, I'd never think about alcohol again. But we live in a booze-saturated society—the desire to belong can lead us to give in.

The first time you face a familiar situation without alcohol may feel surprisingly uncomfortable. Even if you've been alcohol free for a while, doing something you've never done without a drink can trigger a wave of emotion, longing, and temptation.

That doesn't mean you're weak, broken, or backsliding. It's science.

Remember Hebb's law, which states that neurons that fire together wire together? Over time, your brain has connected drinking to many of your life experiences, and when you remove alcohol from the equation, your brain reacts. It's become primed to expect alcohol in certain settings while doing certain things.

My First AF Wedding

About eighteen months into living alcohol free, I attended my cousin Lucy's wedding to her wife, Tracy. The celebration was deep in the woods of New England, and all the guests stayed in cabins on the property. Because no one had to drive, the plan was clear: Drink as much as possible. People were preparing for a very boozy night, and I could feel my anxiety building.

Hoping that holding something in my hand would help ease my discomfort I ordered my first-ever alcohol-free beer. It didn't help. Even with a beer in hand, I felt awkward and out of place. I was surprised by how much internal noise came from simply *not* drinking.

The dancing started, and I love to dance. In eighth grade I was even in a hip-hop dance troupe called the Rock Jockeys. But I found myself wondering: *Could I still dance without a drink? Would it be fun?* I wanted to find out. Luckily, my three-year-old son was also excited about dancing. It was pure joy; we lost ourselves in the music.

But later, things got hard again. The kids were heading to bed, and the adults were moving to a big campfire to end the night. It was obvious I wasn't drinking. Trying to include me and wanting me to "enjoy myself," it seemed everyone there offered me a drink. The more they drank, the more they forgot I wasn't. Temptation crept in—not because I wanted the experience of alcohol, but because I wanted relief from the awkwardness.

I turned to curiosity—a powerful ally in the AF journey. I stepped back and observed my thoughts. This gave me a bit of distance from the internal voice that whispered, *Just have one.* I watched the craving rise. I imagined what would happen if I gave in. I used a tactic I call forecasting—looking intentionally into the future. Here is how it goes. I asked myself:

"If I had a drink, what would happen?"

I already knew the answer. The initial buzz might last eighteen to twenty minutes, but after that, things would spiral. I'd feel worse.

I'd want more. And I'd be more likely to give in. I knew that even one drink starts to impair the prefrontal cortex—the part of the brain that helps us make good decisions. I could see it clearly: One drink would mean a second drink, maybe a third, possibly even more. I'd stumble to bed, and when my kids woke up at sunrise, I'd be miserable.

That was all the forecasting I needed.

I made a conscious choice. I chose the discomfort of being alcohol free over the chaos a drink would bring. It was hard, but it revealed one of the most important lessons I've learned while living AF:

When I approached my craving with honest, nonjudgmental
curiosity, it became manageable—and then it faded.

I didn't need rules. I simply had to look at the truth of what drinking would bring and recognize that it wasn't what I wanted. I watched myself sit by the fire and say no to yet another drink. I watched myself make awkward small talk. I watched myself get bored as conversations looped and people got louder, slurring their words. Eventually, I quietly slipped away. No one even noticed.

I stopped about twenty yards into the woods on the path back to our cabin. Moonlight filtered through the trees. The voices by the fire were still loud, but the forest around me felt soft, quiet, and safe.

A wave of peace came over me.

I looked back at the campfire without judgment. Each person was on their own path, and I was on mine. I hadn't caved to the pressure. I hadn't given my power away by letting anyone else decide for me. I turned inward, listened to myself, and chose what I truly wanted: to live alcohol free.

I felt proud. Grounded. Aligned. The discomfort melted away. I had chosen myself.

I walked back to our little cabin, ready to snuggle up with my kids—grateful, clear, and deeply peaceful with the choices I'd made.

Vacationing Alcohol Free

Before I stopped drinking, my idea of a vacation was simple: no rules, no responsibilities—and lots of alcohol. I remember visiting the Bahamas as a newlywed on our first vacation. We kicked things off by ordering rum punches at ten a.m. From there the drinks flowed nonstop. By noon, I was dizzy. We stumbled back to our rooms for a nap, and at three p.m. I woke up with a hangover. It was brutal.

We finally dragged ourselves out of the room after dark, missing the sunset on our first day at the beach. The evening was ruined. I was dressed up, sitting at a beautiful dinner with people I loved—and all I wanted was to go back to bed. I kept drinking through dinner, hoping it would lift my mood. It didn't. No buzz. No laughter. Just a glazed-over feeling as I tried to focus enough through my stupor and keep up with conversation.

Despite how miserable day one was, I didn't drink less. Instead I tried different *strategies*: a bigger breakfast, starting later in the day, cutting back before dinner. None of it helped. The photos from that trip show a drink in my hand at all times. When we got home, the joke was: "It must've been fun; we don't remember it!" That trip stayed with me; even now, nearly twenty years later, I still feel a sense of loss.

My programming was clear: *Vacations are for drinking.* It didn't occur to me that it could be otherwise. I wouldn't seriously consider vacationing without alcohol for years.

A decade after our Bahamas debacle, I took my first alcohol-free vacation to Hawaii. It was amazing. Instead of lying in bed nursing a hangover while the kids watched cartoons, I was up, fully present, setting "missions" for my boys while we explored the beach—digging moats, chasing crabs, and building castles.

Instead of nighttime drinking, we walked on the beach as a family. I remember the breeze on my skin at sunset. We watched the stars come out. Was it all perfect? No. One of my sons got a stomach bug and spent a few days sick in the condo. But I was there for him—physically, mentally, and emotionally.

On our third day, we were lounging at the beach when a waiter came by to offer us drinks. Brian ordered our usual beach favorite: a mai tai. And I felt it—that familiar temptation. This was *the* moment. One of the most beautiful beaches in the world, and everything inside me said: *Now's the time for a mai tai.*

I reminded myself that I hadn't sworn off alcohol forever. But if I ever chose to drink again, it would be a *conscious, intentional choice*—not a default, automatic reaction.

So I consciously paused and asked myself:

- *Do I really want this drink?*

- *Will one be enough?*

- *How will I feel after the last sip?*

- *Can I even stop at one drink?*

- *Will I regret it later?*

- *How will I feel tomorrow—or for the rest of the trip?*

I realized I wanted that mai tai for two reasons: nostalgia (it's what we always did) and taste. I was convinced the nonalcoholic version couldn't possibly compare. But I can't resist an experiment. So I ordered a virgin mai tai and did a taste test: Brian's, with alcohol, and mine without. *Mine tasted better.*

In that moment, I no longer felt like I was missing out. I wasn't ashamed or deprived. I felt proud. Proud that I had made a conscious decision, choosing what I *actually* wanted. I sipped my alcohol-free drink and enjoyed the rest of the day with clarity and without regret.

Since then, I vacation very differently. I go to bed when I'm tired and wake up early—refreshed and ready to explore. We book more experiences: hiking, snorkeling, boating, biking, and fishing. My vacations are no longer about getting drunk, passing out, and recovering. They're about being present, connected, and fully alive.

You'll have lots of "firsts" on this journey—first AF happy hour, first AF wedding, and your first sober sex. (Don't worry, I have a whole chapter on that!) These moments may feel new and awkward, because for so long, we've intertwined alcohol with most of our social experiences.

Every first holds a gift, and even if it's difficult, it can become a kind of rebirth. You're learning how to do life again—this time fully awake.

The Principle of Firsts

There's a powerful ALP phenomenon called the principle of firsts. Let me explain with a story.

Recently, I talked with Sally, who had just gone on her first all-inclusive vacation. She was two years alcohol free and studying at the This Naked Mind Institute to become a coach. What happened on her vacation was surprising because she believed that at this point, she was far beyond cravings.

Warm breezes, calypso music, and a tray of tropical drinks greeted Sally at the entrance to the resort. She was overwhelmed almost instantly by the desire to drink. The craving hit so hard, she questioned everything, thinking things like: *Is something wrong with me? Should I be studying to become a coach if I want a drink this badly?*

The urge to drink lasted through dinner, and at one point it got so painful she considered flying home. *If the first night is this hard,* she thought, *how will I make it through the whole week?* But instead of running, she decided to put her tools into practice. She got curious.

She took a deep breath and leaned into her discomfort, observing her mind with compassion. What was the voice in her head saying? What was she really afraid of?

Her thoughts were loud and persistent:

- *You're missing out!*

- *This is what we always do at the beach—how can you even think about skipping the drinks?*

- *This trip isn't going to be any fun.*

- *You're wasting money—those drinks are free!*

- *Everyone else is having a good time, and you are miserable. Is that what you really want?*

Instead of pushing away the thoughts, she listened patiently. She responded by saying:

"You might be right, but I'm willing to see it through and find out."

She didn't start a battle with herself. She simply recognized that the craving came from a part of her brain that had never done a vacation without alcohol. That part didn't know what to expect.

It was a hard night. But the next morning, she woke up at peace. The mental noise was gone. Through curiosity and presence, she broke through the discomfort and gave herself a chance to see what an AF vacation could be like. That evening, when the fancy drinks appeared at dinner, she didn't have a single craving. She could even admire them—and happily order one without alcohol.

She expected that each AF night would get slightly easier, maybe going from a ten out of ten to a nine out of ten in discomfort. Instead, her discomfort was nonexistent by the second night. The cravings were gone. She said it felt like a switch flipped.

That's the principle of firsts in action.

Sally has now been alcohol free for more than five years, and even at all-inclusive resorts, where alcohol flows freely, she's never felt tempted again.

What Is the Principle of Firsts?

The first time you do something that you've always paired with alcohol—a vacation, a wedding, or a concert—you may experience discomfort at a ten out of ten. That feels discouraging, leading you to assume it's going to take a long time to get comfortable not drinking. We expect our discomfort will decrease gradually: ten out of ten, then nine out of ten, then eight out of ten. But I have great news: It doesn't work like that.

If you stay curious and alcohol free through that first experience, the discomfort doesn't just lessen—it often disappears. The second time you face the same situation, your craving may drop to a two out of ten, or maybe even zero. That's the power of breaking the old wiring—the pattern breaks down as soon as you break the association, often taking only one time.

However, it is important to know that if, during a first, you decide to drink, the opposite happens. You reinforce the neural pathway that links alcohol to that experience, making it even harder to stay alcohol free next time.

Getting through that first experience AF rewires your brain. It teaches your system: *We can do this without alcohol.* That doesn't create fear but rather motivation.

You Only Have to Do It Once

Whether it's your first happy hour, first wedding, or first all-inclusive vacation, it may be hard, but the second time is generally a breeze.

When you understand the principle of firsts, those dreaded moments become opportunities. Each one an experiment. Each one a step toward freedom.

You don't have to do it perfectly. You just have to do it once.

The Wisdom of Firsts

Your firsts hold incredible wisdom—if you're willing to stay curious and listen to yourself. They can reveal hidden beliefs about alcohol and highlight the areas where your desire to drink still lingers. You can question these beliefs with the ACT process and find lifelong freedom.

Each time you navigate a first, beyond the fact that it is an opportunity to use the tools of ACT, you build confidence and pride. You prove to yourself that you can handle life—both the big moments and the small ones—without alcohol.

When you have a successful first, you create a powerful contrast in your mind to the times you experienced the same event while drinking. Since our past drinking memories can be very unpleasant, you can feel excited about all the incredible AF experiences that are in your future.

A Final Word on Firsts

There's a Stoic saying: The obstacle is the way. When it comes to alcohol, the obstacle is the discomfort you feel as you break the associations between drinking and events. And that discomfort, when looked at directly and experienced mindfully, is the path to freedom. We've spent years associating alcohol with celebrations, connections, or relaxation, and there are deeply rooted programs that need to be rewired. Every time you are willing to experience the discomfort of an AF first, you give your mind a chance to rewire.

With every alcohol-free first, you prove to yourself that the joy was never in the drink. With each experience—whether it's dinner out, dancing, or laughing until your stomach hurts with friends—you realize the fun, the connection, the *life* is still there. It was never the alcohol that made it great.

Next, we are going to take a closer look at one of the most deeply embedded cultural beliefs—the alcohol industry's favorite and only disclaimer: *Drink responsibly.* I'll use the tenets of ACT to explore what that phrase really means and how it shapes our belief systems in powerful yet unseen ways.

———

To view the references cited in this chapter, please visit LiveNakedAF.com.

CHAPTER 9

HOW TO ESCAPE DANGEROUS CULTURAL PROGRAMMING

The idea of "drink responsibly" is a wolf in sheep's clothing. It's the alcohol industry's way of shirking responsibility while appearing concerned.
—Johann Hari

One of my podcast guests, Danielle, got drunk for the first time when she was fifteen years old. After stealing liquor from her parents' stash, filling water bottles, Danielle and her friends started drinking while walking to the high school dance. This was Danielle's first experience drinking and she downed an entire water bottle full of whiskey. The last thing she remembered was falling as she walked up the high school steps. She awoke in the hospital hooked up to an IV. Her mother was hysterical, terrified as the doctors explained how Danielle almost died from alcohol poisoning.

It would seem that nearly ending your life with your first drink would be enough to keep Danielle far away from alcohol. But the opposite happened.

Her parents were clearly upset and grounded her. But Danielle explains that she wasn't punished because of the underage drinking—they figured that's just what high schoolers do. No, what upset them most was how *irresponsible* Danielle was while drinking. The failure wasn't the drinking itself, but that they, as parents, had failed to teach her how to *drink responsibly*.

After this harrowing experience, Danielle's parents didn't have a conversation with her to encourage her not to drink. They also didn't think to reassess their own drinking. The idea that drinking alcohol might be optional didn't even cross their minds. Danielle's mom believed she needed to teach her daughter how to be *safer* with alcohol rather than encouraging Danielle to avoid it altogether.

Danielle's parents decided their house would be the "responsible" house, the place where all the kids came to drink—because at least then they could keep an eye on them. If it was going to happen, they figured it was better to happen under their roof, allowing them to protect their daughter.

Danielle spent the next fifteen years in an increasingly dangerous relationship with alcohol—blacking out, becoming violent, and carrying a deep burden of pain and regret. Research suggests that children whose parents give them alcohol, allowing the kids to drink it in their homes, are more likely to have drinking problems as adults.

When we hear a story like this, we want to assign blame. How could a mother host drinking parties after her daughter nearly died from alcohol poisoning? But let's zoom out. Danielle's mom was doing what she'd learned to do—what she believed was right. Her perspective was based on her experience, her environment, and the cultural norms of their small town. It didn't occur to her that there might be another option.

Danielle's struggles weren't her fault. They weren't even her mother's fault. They were symptoms of a deeper issue—one that affects all of us. You, me, Danielle, and her mother—all of us are caught in forces we can't see. We like to believe we're independent thinkers, immune to cultural messaging or social influence. But the truth is, none of us is immune; and fascinatingly, the more we think we're unaffected by cultural programming, the greater the impact these programs have.

Our tendency to unknowingly accept cultural programs is rooted in conformity. Conformity is a deep, instinctual human drive, and it evolved over millennia. It is anchored in seeking safety, security, and survival.

When we choose to be different from the people we love and trust, our nervous system reacts as if we're in danger. The discomfort is real. And our minds, as we've learned, create all sorts of meanings to explain those instinctive feelings. But as we discovered in chapter 4, the mind is just guessing. It doesn't realize that we're actually safe and free to make decisions that go against the grain—decisions like encouraging our kids to stay away from alcohol altogether. Until we bring conscious awareness to these cultural messages, the mind can't see that we have a choice.

This is how dangerous beliefs are unknowingly passed down. We don't recognize the unseen forces shaping our choices, so we keep repeating the patterns that are hurting us—often in the name of safety, tradition, or love.

As we look to unwind these harmful programs, with ourselves and our families, let's start with this premise: We are always doing the best we can with what we know. And when we know better—when we begin to see through the illusions—we can do better.

Drinking "Better" Makes No Sense

The main response from parents, teachers, and even hospital staff to Danielle's brush with death was that she needed to learn how to *drink responsibly*. That kind of reaction might make sense if she'd gotten into a car accident—because she still has to drive. She should certainly learn how be a safer driver—how to drive more *responsibly*. Or if a teenager is sexually active, you'd want to talk about responsibility and protection—because sex will likely remain a part of their lives.

On the other hand, if we catch our kids doing something illegal and life-threatening—like drag racing—we don't respond by saying, "You need to learn to drag race more *responsibly*."

And yet, with alcohol, we act as if there's no choice. As if everyone *must* drink. As if not drinking isn't even an option we can explore.

Let's consider the facts. Alcohol . . .

- Was declared a known carcinogen almost forty years ago.

- Is a neurotoxin.

- Contributes to more than sixty diseases.

- Causes more deaths each year than all illegal drugs combined.

And yet, the only disclaimer is *drink responsibly?*

It's mind-boggling—and frankly *irresponsible*.

We are better informed, through warning labels, about the side effects of over-the-counter medications than about the harms of alcohol. Most people could tell you more about the risks of taking too much ibuprofen than about the negative health issues related to drinking—despite the fact that, on the whole, we consume far more alcohol than ibuprofen.

Misplaced Blame

The idea of drinking responsibly is not just flawed but can be dangerous. It suggests that if something goes wrong, the problem isn't the alcohol or the industry that profits from it. The problem is *you*, the individual.

Think about what that really means: We're asking people to use a drug—one proven to be addictive—*responsibly*. It's like encouraging someone to use heroin or nicotine in a safe and controlled way. It's a contradiction.

Once you know how toxic and chemically addictive alcohol is, the phrase *drink responsibly* sounds absurd. What it really says is: "If you cannot responsibly drink a known toxic and addictive substance, then you are the problem." Let that sink in. The substance is toxic. The marketing is manipulative. The outcome is often harmful. But somehow, the blame is placed squarely on the individual for not being *responsible* enough.

Here's what I've heard from various experts about the idea of drinking responsibly:

- The phrase *drink responsibly* is a clever marketing ploy—it puts the blame on the user instead of the product.

- *Drink responsibly* is a smoke screen. It makes the alcohol industry look concerned about public health while still promoting drinking.

- The slogan is designed to look socially conscious, but it conveniently avoids any meaningful regulation or real public health solutions.

- The whole idea of responsible drinking is a myth. The industry profits off irresponsible consumption.

The last two comments are worth exploring more deeply.

First, let's talk about the avoidance of regulation. How has the alcohol industry managed to avoid regulation and transparency in marketing in ways that no other industry has? I don't pretend to have all the answers, but I'm fairly certain the reasons can be found in profits and politics. Even if we can't pinpoint the exact mechanisms, it's still a question worth asking. The phrase *drink responsibly* is a far cry from genuine responsibility in the form of proper disclaimers and education.

Second, let's look closely at the idea that the alcohol industry profits most from the most vulnerable and hurting segment of drinkers.

How to Sell Poison

I earned a master's degree in the science of marketing and spent a decade working in corporate strategy. At its core, effective marketing is rooted in psychology and human behavior. Marketers study how the subconscious mind works—and how to influence it.

The alcohol industry spends more than $6 billion each year on advertising—in the United States alone. Although we want to believe that marketing doesn't really affect us, we need to understand how promotional messages influence us, below our conscious awareness, by impacting our brain's chemistry. I'll explain that below, but the reality is that marketing works—and the alcohol industry knows it. They wouldn't invest billions if they weren't getting a significant return on their investment.

Marketing is a big reason alcohol destroys lives—and we pay for the privilege. It's a major factor in how an industry selling poison has grown into a $1.49 trillion global market. And yes, that's trillion, with a T.

To protect ourselves, we must learn how to resist and unlearn the dozens of pro-alcohol messages we're exposed to every single day—not only from traditional advertising but also from friends, family, social media, and much more. There's bad news and good news. The bad news is that we are being influenced in ways we don't even notice. The good news is that once we understand the game, we can choose to stop playing it and no longer allow our minds to be manipulated.

To fully understand the marketing of harmful, addictive substances, we have to zoom out and look at the bigger picture: why alcohol—and so many other substances sold for profit—is so addictive in the first place. The simplest way to understand this is by revisiting something we touched on earlier: our brain's chemistry and the neurotransmitter dopamine.

Dopamine, Habits, and Behavior

Dopamine is closely linked to feelings of pleasure and reward. As we've briefly learned, its main job is to motivate us to repeat behaviors. But not just any behaviors. Dopamine is released by *survival-based* behavior—like eating or having sex—things essential for staying alive both individually and as a species.

But here's the catch: Substances like alcohol—and many other addictive products—trigger *artificially high levels* of dopamine. Levels that don't occur in nature. These unnaturally high spikes trick the brain into believing that alcohol is critical.

When we drink, the brain becomes *chemically confused.* The artificial spike of dopamine that alcohol provides makes our brains mistakenly believe that *alcohol is essential for our very survival.*

That's why cravings feel so urgent. And why resisting a craving is painful.

Dr. Sara Gottfried, physician and *New York Times* bestselling author, describes dopamine as a key neurotransmitter involved in reinforcing behaviors essential for survival, such as eating and reproduction. These activities naturally trigger dopamine release, creating feelings of pleasure that condition the brain to seek them out. However, addictive substances hijack this system by flooding the brain with abnormally high levels of dopamine. This artificial stimulation trains the brain to expect heightened dopamine responses. Over time, the brain's natural ability to produce dopamine diminishes, leading to dependence on the substance—even though it can no longer fully satisfy the need it initially created.

Overwhelming cravings are not a character flaw. They actually occur because our brain is doing what it's supposed to. The problem is that these substances and behaviors hijack our brain's reward system.

Most of the things that trigger dopamine surges have massive profit margins—and massive marketing budgets. These include the following:

- Alcohol

- Tobacco

- Sugar and high-fructose corn syrup

- Processed foods

- Social media

- Gambling

- Pornography

- Recreational drugs

- Video games

Even more troubling, many of these products are deliberately engineered to be addictive. The tobacco industry is a prime example. In court, it was forced to admit it had knowingly added chemicals to cigarettes to make them even more addictive than nicotine alone. The industry deliberately engineered addiction because, sadly, addiction is incredibly profitable.

The alcohol industry is not all that different from the tobacco industry. These companies are well aware of how dopamine works, and they intentionally use this knowledge to increase profits. One way they do this is by making drinks stronger and stronger. Originally, the standard beer contained about 3.2 percent alcohol by volume (ABV). Over time, that crept up to 5 percent, and now some beers top 12 percent—the same as a glass of wine.

Wine has also become significantly stronger in recent decades—not because it's cheaper or easier to produce, but because higher alcohol content releases more dopamine. And the more dopamine released, the greater the potential for addiction.

More alcohol content = more dopamine.

More dopamine = more addiction.

More addiction = more profit.

Alcohol marketers understand how our brains respond to dopamine. And, as scary as this information is, dopamine is just one of many biological and psychological levers they pull to get us to drink more.

If you are old enough, you might remember a time when hard liquor was kept behind the counter at the liquor store. The industry discovered, through research, that if bottles are placed out on the floor, where customers can pick them up, they sell more—this is because picking up a bottle triggers a craving. This is especially true once people begin to struggle with alcohol. Bottles are now routinely stocked out on the floor where consumers can easily touch them. It's a calculated move, targeting those whom the industry has identified as their most profitable market segment, those of us for whom alcohol causes the most harm.

Should the Industry Be Held Accountable?
A Naked Mind Coach Perspective

One of our graduates from the This Naked Mind Institute spent a career in alcohol advertising. She bravely shared her experience:

I was involved at a senior level in the alcohol industry for many years, with about five thousand people working for me. We would sit in board meetings and talk about how we could get more women to drink, and how important the 20 percent [the customers struggling most with alcohol] were, how they made us 80 percent of our profit.

We used to make jokes about the alcoholics who used to come into our stores at eleven o'clock in the morning and buy booze and then come back at two o'clock in the afternoon to buy more. We knew all the science; we knew what we were doing.

This industry wants your children, and it wants your children's children, and right now it's working that out. I remember sitting in meetings talking about how we could get fifteen-year-old kids to like drinking. We invented the alcopop. We worked out that kids like sweet fizzy pop, don't they? Yeah? But they don't like the taste of alcohol. So, you know what we did, we figured it out, introducing [the alcopop] back in the nineties. And we had a whole new generation of alcoholics.

A growing body of scientific evidence supports her experiences. For example, a 2016 study reviewed materials from twenty-seven industry-linked organizations and found that most misrepresented the link between alcohol and cancer—by denying, omitting, or downplaying the risk. A 2014 study showed that alcohol companies advertise on media platforms that are hard to regulate, making it easier to reach underage audiences, despite the increased risk alcohol poses to young and developing brains. In 2017, a systematic review of twelve longitudinal studies found consistent evidence that youth exposed to alcohol marketing drink more. The researchers concluded that alcohol marketing is a significant risk factor in underage drinking. While each of these items may fit within a legal loophole, when taken together it is hard to ignore the apparent lack of responsibility coming from the industry when it comes to our children.

In 2018, an investigation revealed that alcohol companies funded the proposed $100 million Moderate Alcohol and Cardiovascular Health (MACH) trial, which aimed to show the benefits of moderate drinking. Internal emails showed that researchers pitched the trial to industry executives as a chance to show that moderate drinking is safe before any participants were even enrolled. Concerns about biased study design and ethics were serious enough for the National Institutes of Health to cancel the study.

It seems the alcohol industry is engaged in a pattern of deliberate misdirection.

Freedom of Choice

When it comes to deciding whether or not to drink, misinformation plays a critical role. Yes, we all technically have the ability to choose, but if essential information is hidden from us, is our right to choose intact? Can we honestly say we're making a conscious decision if we've only been told part of the story? It's like choosing a favorite flavor of ice cream when we haven't tried all the options. Are we really choosing freely if we don't even know what we're choosing among?

Think about it: How can we make a conscious, intentional decision about alcohol when we believe that only "alcoholics" get addicted to alcohol?

How can anyone decide to drink or not when we haven't been told that alcohol creates a chemical need for more alcohol? Or that the intense craving many people feel isn't a weakness but a biological response the brain interprets as a threat to survival?

How can someone make a health-conscious decision without knowing alcohol is a neurotoxin? Or that it's been declared a Group 1 carcinogen—in the same category as asbestos and tobacco—by the World Health Organization?

And how can we make a truly informed decision when most of what we've heard about alcohol's so-called benefits has been shaped by marketing, industry-funded studies, and trusted institutions repeating what they've been told, not what's been proven?

Exactly.

Without the truth, we can't make real, intentional choices.

And the truth is, the facts haven't just been overlooked—they've often been deliberately buried.

I know this information can be shocking. But anger, when channeled with intention, can become a powerful force for change. It can give you the energy and motivation to use the ACT process and dismantle the mental programs that imprison your mind. We may not be able to change everything at once, but we can each do our part. We can wake up, one person at a time, and take a stand, by no longer funding the industry that profits from keeping us sick and dying.

There is good news here: We are not broken, weak, or irresponsible. We've simply been caught in a powerful cultural narrative designed to protect profit rather than people. And now that you see the truth, you have the power to change the story—not just for yourself, but for future generations.

Next, let's get practical about your tools to joyfully navigate your first year AF and talk about how to say no to a drink.

————

To view the references cited in this chapter, please visit LiveNakedAF.com.

CHAPTER 10

HOW TO SAY NO TO A DRINK

I'm not drinking tonight. I've got to stay sharp in case any dragons need slaying.
—Unknown

Saying no is hard!

That's not just a feeling—it's backed by research. Studies show that we experience real psychological stress when we need to say no, even when it's clearly in our best interest.

We underestimate how difficult it will be to say no, so we say yes—even when we mean no. When we say yes but mean no, we increase our stress and reduce our sense of well-being. And beyond the chemical stress response, we worry that saying no will damage our relationships or make us seem unhelpful. These human dynamics remain true across diverse cultures; the difficulty we feel saying no is a universal human challenge, not a personal flaw. It's rooted in biology and social conditioning.

Although saying no is hard, it's also an incredibly beneficial skill to learn, a skill that can even improve mental health. The more you practice saying no with love and respect, the easier it becomes.

This is especially important in alcohol-free living. Setting healthy boundaries starts with understanding our natural resistance to saying no. Instead of judging ourselves, we can meet this resistance with compassion. By understanding the emotional patterns at play, we can start using the practical tools I'll share in this chapter to help us say no more easily.

Say No by Saying Yes

What if, instead of saying no, you could say yes? This would be great, considering how much our brains don't like saying no, especially to people we care about. Here's how that might look:

Host: *"Do you want a drink?"*

Me: *"Yes, that would be amazing. Do you have any coffee? I could use a pick-me-up."*

Host: *"Sure, give me a second."*

Let's compare this with what might happen if you were to respond with a direct no:

Host: *"Do you want a drink?"*

Me: *"No, thank you."*

Host: *"Are you sure? Why not? Are you okay? What's going on?"*

People often think they're helping us by offering a drink. The host might feel responsible for helping everyone have fun and enjoy themselves. Intentions are good, just a bit off target. Saying yes to something else, like a soda, helps preserve their intention—and your boundary—so I try to say yes to whatever is easily available. I might not even drink the soda (trust me, no one notices), but I focus on keeping the interaction light and comfortable.

Another tip: When you give a reason—any reason—for wanting a nonalcoholic drink, it can defuse the discomfort of saying no. Again, something like "Yes, I'd love a glass of water. I'm super dehydrated" can work wonders.

I love the strategy of saying yes to an alcohol alternative, but it's not the only approach. Here are a few more strategies that can help you say no with greater ease and confidence.

BYO (Bring Your Own)

One of the simplest and most effective ways to avoid the drink conversation is to bring your own. Show up with a nonalcoholic beer, a kombucha, or sparkling water in hand. When you're holding a drink, people usually don't ask what you want; they assume you're all set. And if someone does ask, remember: You don't owe anyone an explanation.

And if you do want to explain, you can always say something light, like "I love the taste of this one, even better than the real thing. Have you tried it?"

Have a Few Go-To Phrases

Sometimes we just need the right words. Here are some easy, no-drama ways to say no:

- "I'm driving."

- "Alcohol doesn't agree with me these days."

- "I've got some work to do, so none for me tonight."

- "Not right now, but maybe later." (We'll talk more about the "later" tactic in a moment.)

- "No thanks. I've got an early morning."

Pick the ones that feel natural to you and have them ready.

Use a Little Subterfuge

I call these my spy tactics. I used them often in the early days of living alcohol free. Whether they're right for you is completely up to you. Some people feel uncomfortable with this kind of light deception, but these tactics were crucial for me—especially when I was traveling internationally as one of the only women on the executive team. Everyone around me knew how much I loved my wine. So when I got pregnant and needed to abstain—but wasn't yet ready to tell anyone—I had to get creative. Here are some tactics I used:

- **Hold the gin:** This was my go-to move. I'd order a gin and tonic—perfect for this trick. As soon as I placed the order, I'd excuse myself to the restroom and quietly track down our waitress. I'd ask her to hold the gin, and for the rest of the night, any "gin and tonic" I ordered would be just tonic water. The servers were happy to help. Some nights I'd be laughing so hard, having such a good time, that colleagues would tease me for being "super drunk." And I'd smile, knowing I was completely sober. Those moments were powerful; I was proving to myself—through direct experience—that I didn't need a drink to have fun.

- **Later:** Another trick I'd use was showing interest in a drink but pushing it off for later. I'd order water or a nonalcoholic drink now, suggesting that I'd be joining in soon. Implying that you might have a drink later quiets the "just have one" crowd. If they believe you plan on drinking, they're less likely to push. Meanwhile, you stay fully in control. Most of the time, the host or bartender will forget all about my promised drink order.

Is it ridiculous that we have to resort to these kinds of tactics? Absolutely. But until we can shift the cultural narrative, this is the reality we're navigating. Let's look at some of the dynamics that explain how we got here and why we feel friction from others when we decide to go AF.

Questions Are Inevitable

In the early days of living alcohol free, I remember how quickly the questions would come the moment I said I wasn't drinking: *What's wrong? Are you pregnant? Oh, you must be taking some new medicine and you can't drink?* People rushed to fill the silence with assumptions. They wanted a reason—something that made sense to them—and I used to feel the need to offer one. I'd explain and try to justify my choice. I would try to help it make sense for them.

A powerful thing I've learned—something I didn't fully understand until recently—is this: I don't have to explain myself. I don't have to justify my boundaries, my choices, or my feelings for them to be valid. It's enough that they matter to me. You don't owe anyone a reason. "No" is a complete sentence. You can say it with kindness. You can say it with love. And you don't need to follow it with a defense, an excuse, or a backstory.

This gives you your power back.

If you find yourself in a situation where you feel the pressure to explain your choice not to drink, here are two phrases that work beautifully to shut that down—with zero defensive energy: *I just feel better this way. I'm good, thanks.* No drama. No apologies. Just truth.

Here are some other ways you can respond confidently to anyone who continues to question you:

- "You are amazing to care so much. But nothing to report—I'm just not drinking today."

- "Wow, all the questions! I love how much you care. But really, I'm just not drinking tonight."

Why Some People React Strongly

Culture is shifting. Studies show younger generations are drinking less, many describing alcohol as *their parents' drug*. These days you'll probably find at least one person who's interested in the alcohol-free lifestyle at most social gatherings. That wasn't true ten years ago when I started this journey. The landscape has changed, and people care less and less what you're drinking. Most aren't even paying attention.

However, some people do care. And a few will make a *very big deal* out of your not drinking. There will be times when someone won't take your no and may pressure you, pushing for a reason why you aren't drinking and trying to convince you that you should.

Some people even seemed to take my not drinking personally. That confused me—until I learned what was going on below the surface.

Let's look at the three main reasons some people may react strongly.

Dynamic 1: They Fear Losing You

We all run a deep, primal, subconscious program that says, *If I'm different, I won't be accepted. If I'm not accepted, I won't be loved. If I am not loved, I won't be safe.*

This is why we instinctively seek common ground, especially with the people we care about most. It's also why, when you change something big, like your drinking habits, even the people who love you most can feel threatened. The shift makes them feel different from you, and that triggers their own subconscious fear of disconnection. Even positive change can feel destabilizing in a relationship.

Here's how that fear might show up:

- They pressure you to "just have one."

- They ask how long this "thing" is going to last.

- They say hurtful things like "You're not fun anymore," or "I just miss you, and how we used to connect over drinks."

Even when those words sting, try to remember it's not really about you. It's not personal. It's fear, and fear often operates below the level of conscious awareness.

I'll never forget my most uncomfortable "saying no" moment—an evening that perfectly illustrates this dynamic. We had just moved back to Colorado from New York City and were reconnecting with Donnie and Vicki, old friends who had known me during my heaviest drinking years.

Donnie took my not drinking *very personally*. For at least fifteen minutes, he aggressively grilled me—loudly, in front of the whole table, even dragging the waiter into it and making him give me a hard time because I wasn't having wine. Donnie kept pushing for an explanation, and although his words were framed as questions, the tone underneath was clear: He was disappointed in me.

It seemed like he really felt I had let him down and ruined his night. He felt blindsided—like someone should have warned him I wasn't going to be his drunk party buddy from our NYC days. And in his blunt, East Coast way, he was making sure I knew how upset he was.

Part of me wanted to panic. But I didn't get defensive, because I understood what was really going on. It wasn't about me. His reaction was about him. I recognized the fear behind his words—because I'd felt it, too. Fear that things would be different. Fear that our friendship would change. Maybe even fear about his own drinking. Sure enough, after a few drinks, he told me how he was genuinely worried about how much he was drinking.

We ended up having a great night. He drank. I didn't. And, bonus, he left with a new perspective on what was possible. I left feeling giddy—because earlier that day I used a visualization tactic. The vision I'd held, where I had a fun night without alcohol, actually came true. Even though the night started out rough, I got back in our Jeep feeling free. Not because everyone else accepted my choice, but because I did.

This is the power of understanding why people resist your change. They're not trying to hurt you; they're just afraid of losing the version of you they've grown to love.

Dynamic 2: They're Afraid You're Judging Them

When people fear you're judging them for drinking, they stop inviting you to things. Not always because they don't want you there, but often because they assume you won't want to come.

They might hide their drinking or drink less around you. If you ask about it, they may even get defensive. This is another primal, fear-based program: *If I'm different, I won't be accepted.* Ironically, you also experience this program as a nondrinker, fearing that you may no longer be accepted now that you've chosen differently. The best way to handle this is with an offer of reassurance.

Understanding unlocks your best chance of influencing the people around you. In fact, we'll talk specifically about how to support the people in your life who are drinking more than you'd like—and how to talk with them effectively—in chapter 18.

Dynamic 3: You Become the Mirror

When you stop drinking, it can cause others to reflect on their own drinking. If they've had concerns—consciously or not—your choice might intensify those feelings. You become a mirror.

I've felt this myself. When a friend stopped before I did, I found myself wondering: *Does this mean I should stop? Am I drinking too much? Do I have a problem?*

In my drinking days, I felt shame every time I was drinking or wanted to be drinking around someone who wasn't. Looking back, I can see that my discomfort had nothing to do with them and everything to do with my own inner conflict. I even said unkind things, like "I don't trust people who don't drink." It wasn't about them. I was afraid—for myself. And that fear came out as judgment.

I now choose to be the one who is kind, because when someone is triggered by my choice to live AF, I remember, *It's not about me; it's all about them.*

Staying Off the Fence: Why Not Deciding Is Deciding

None of the strategies for saying no in this chapter will truly work if you're still *trying* not to drink instead of *deciding* not to drink.

Because our brains are wired to seek connection and avoid conflict, if we haven't firmly decided that we're not drinking, chances are we'll give in—especially in social situations. Studies show we consistently underestimate how hard it is to say no, particularly when others are still drinking.

If maybe is still an option, saying no becomes much harder. Why? Because the brain responds chemically to the presence of alcohol. Just the possibility of a drink can trigger a craving, even if you don't drink all that frequently. That little bit of pressure from your host? When you're stuck in maybe, it can easily push you over the edge into a yes.

My friend Julie has a parenting trick she calls "duck mode." When her kids start begging for something—another snack or more screen time—she switches into duck mode. It means the answer is a firm and final no. No discussion. No negotiation. Like water off a duck's back, no amount of pleading or persuading will change her mind. And once her kids realized this, something remarkable happened—they stopped asking. They might feel disappointed, but they ultimately let it go. No drama. No debate.

Our brains work the same way, especially when it comes to cravings like alcohol. Think of your brain like a small child who wants ice cream. Once the idea of a drink enters your mind, your brain won't stop asking as long as it believes there's still a chance. If there's even a sliver of possibility—if you're still debating it, still "trying to be good"—your brain keeps pushing.

That's where duck mode comes in. When you can shift your mindset to a solid, nonnegotiable no, something changes. Your brain gets the message that this isn't happening—not now, not ever—and it quiets down. Just like Julie's kids, your brain stops asking when it knows for sure the answer is final.

Duck mode is powerful. Not because it's dramatic, but because it's calm, clear, and complete. When the answer is 100 percent no, the desire begins to fade.

Or as the saying goes: 100 percent is a breeze; 99 percent is a b*tch.

Here's the bottom line:

Maybe is hard.

Maybe nearly always turns into yes.

When it comes to alcohol and how the brain works, not deciding is deciding.

How to Let Go

No matter how polished or polite your no is, some people will make it weird. They'll judge, pressure, question, or just act uncomfortable. That's on them, not you.

As author Rob Bell says, let them have their trip.

People will have reactions—*let them*. At the end of the day, Mel Robbins's *The Let Them Theory* says it best: Let people have their reactions. If someone feels uncomfortable, judgmental, or upset about your decision—that's not your problem. As Robbins explains, when you stop trying to manage other people's beliefs and emotions, you reclaim your peace and energy. Let them misunderstand you. Let them talk.

When we stop taking responsibility for how others respond, we move back into the driver's seat in our own lives and in our own decisions. You're not responsible for their discomfort—only your own clarity.

———

Saying no is one thing, but what if you still desperately want to drink? What if you still feel like you *need* it? That's a craving. It's not just an urge or a passing thought, it is much more. A craving is a physiological response to alcohol, and no amount of just-say-no skills will help unless you know how to handle a physical, biological, *chemical* craving. Let's go there next.

———

To view the references cited in this chapter, please visit LiveNakedAF.com.

CHAPTER 11

HOW TO OVERCOME A CRAVING

*Those who can make you believe absurdities can make you
commit atrocities.*
—Voltaire

Before we explore the physical, chemical, and mental aspects of cravings, we need to pause and acknowledge something important: It's
strange that we live in a culture where many people—like Danielle's
mom—don't even realize that *not* drinking is an option. Alcohol is simply assumed to be part of life. To see things clearly, we need to look
beneath the surface of this cultural trance and question what we've
accepted as normal.

Actor Tom Holland (aka Spider-Man) jokes about our cultural pre-
occupation with drinking. He asks us to imagine that alcohol was introduced today, as a brand-new product. It is expensive, doesn't taste great,
makes you dizzy, can even make you vomit, and leaves you feeling terrible the next day. Would you buy it? Would you drink it? Holland says the
proper response to being offered such a bizarre product would be:

"Nah, mate. Keep your funky juice."

I love this perspective—and it got me thinking. Why is alcohol, despite how harmful it is, such a popular and profitable product? Yes, it's
addictive, and that plays a big role. But shouldn't knowing alcohol is

addictive make us want to avoid it, not run toward it? So how do we explain our collective obsession with this toxic fermented liquid?

Even if you don't consciously feel like alcohol offers any benefits, I'm willing to bet that somewhere—deep in your subconscious—those beliefs still exist. And rewriting them with clear, unbiased information is important for any future cravings you encounter.

Let's take Holland's thought experiment one step further. We're going to imagine ourselves as aliens—outsiders observing human behavior for the first time. This will allow us to set aside bias by stepping out of our cultural trance and seeing alcohol through a more objective lens.

Alien Anthropology

We are now part of an alien research team studying humans' relationship with alcohol. After years of observation, we've gathered data on how humans drink, how alcohol affects their health, how it impacts families, and how it shapes entire cultures. (Note: Every fact in the following report is accurate and thoroughly researched. You can find the original studies and full citations at LiveNakedAF.com.)

Our report might read something like this:

To: Department of Human Research
Title: Human Consumption of Alcohol

Similar to how we use ethanol—as a fuel and a disinfectant—humans also use ethanol, commonly called alcohol, as an antiseptic and as a combustible fuel. But strangely, humans also consume this substance. This behavior puzzles us because alcohol is both toxic and nonnutritive. Despite extensive investigation, we have yet to understand why a species would regularly ingest a substance that offers no nutritional value and causes significant harm.

Here is a summary of our findings so far:

Biological Effects
Alcohol is toxic to every organ in the human body. Even small amounts of pure alcohol can be lethal. It is classified as a neurotoxin, with specific harmful effects on the brain.

Psychological Effects
Alcohol acts as a stimulant for the first twenty minutes after consumption, but then shifts to a depressant effect lasting for three or four hours. This makes its effects paradoxical; during those first twenty minutes, the stimulation phase, people often describe feeling a mild "buzz," a sense of increased energy and well-being, or a soft, fuzzy sensation.

After this short initial period, blood alcohol content (BAC) begins to drop, and alcohol becomes a depressant. People then report feeling tired, uneasy, restless, and generally discontented. These symptoms have been consistently observed after just one serving of alcohol.

The depressant effects of alcohol on the human body include the following:
• Slowed brain function and reduced neural activity
• Impaired memory, judgment, and decision-making
• Decreased coordination and slower reaction times
• Reduced breathing rate

Instead of recognizing this pattern and responding rationally, most people do the opposite. To avoid the discomfort of the depressant phase, they often reach for another drink—repeating the cycle.

Next, we explored both the costs and benefits of human alcohol use.

The Cost to Personal Well-Being

- Alcohol can trigger or worsen depression and anxiety disorders.
- It impairs cognitive function and increases the risk of dementia.
- Regular drinking causes liver damage, including fatty liver, hepatitis, cirrhosis, and even death.
- In 1987, the International Agency for Research on Cancer (IARC) declared alcohol a Group 1 carcinogen, the categorization reserved for extremely carcinogenic substances such as asbestos and ultraviolet radiation.
- Drinking contributes to high blood pressure, heart disease, and stroke.
- Alcohol reduces job performance, lowers productivity, and increases the risk of job loss.
- Drinking causes conflict in personal relationships, especially within families, in both parenting and romantic relationships.
- Over time, the body can become physically dependent on alcohol, leading to withdrawal symptoms if use stops or decreases.
- Alcohol dramatically increases the risk of suicide—up to ninety times. Approximately one-third of suicide autopsies test positive for the presence of at least some alcohol in the bloodstream.
- The harmful effects of alcohol can begin at surprisingly low levels—as little as half a beer per day.

The Cost to Society

- Children of parents who drink heavily are 200 to 300 percent more likely to suffer abuse or neglect.
- Alcohol plays a role in more than 60 percent of physical violence cases, including the majority of rapes and sexual assaults.
- Heavy drinking is strongly associated with higher rates of marital dissatisfaction and divorce.
- The risk of domestic violence is eight times higher on days when a husband drinks.

Alcohol's Financial Burden

Excessive alcohol consumption creates a massive economic burden on taxpayers—estimated at $249 billion in the United States alone. This cost comes from reduced workplace productivity, absenteeism, and premature death, as well as expenses related to health care, law enforcement, fire services, legal proceedings, incarceration, and alcohol-impaired driving accidents.

To understand why humans continue to drink alcohol—despite overwhelming evidence of its harm—we took a deep dive into the reported benefits of alcohol consumption. There was a significant amount of misinformation about the benefits of alcohol. But after rigorous filtering for accuracy here's what we found.

Benefit to Personal and Social Well-Being

While there are studies that claim to show health benefits of alcohol, a closer look reveals that many of these studies were funded by organizations or individuals with a financial interest in alcohol sales. After careful review, we were able to identify only two potentially positive effects that some humans experience when consuming alcohol:

1. THE "BUZZ"

Humans describe a buzz as a light, euphoric, slightly fuzzy feeling. When they measure how long it lasts, they report an average of eighteen to twenty-two minutes after a single drink. While drinking more alcohol can slightly extend this feeling, it follows the law of diminishing returns—each additional drink has a weaker effect. Eventually, the buzz fades away completely.

2. PHYSICAL AND EMOTIONAL NUMBING

Historically, because alcohol can numb both physical and emotional pain, humans used alcohol as an anesthetic before safer options became available. However, while alcohol may offer short-term relief, it's not a true solution. Over time, the body builds tolerance, meaning more alcohol is needed to achieve the same numbing effect. But alcohol also harms the body—so the more you drink, the more damage it causes. What begins as a coping mechanism can quickly turn into a cycle that leads to serious long-term costs to a person's health and well-being.

Final Analysis

Despite our best efforts, we still don't fully understand why humans drink alcohol. At first we assumed it was due to a lack of awareness about the harm it causes. However, we discovered numerous studies that clearly outline the serious risks alcohol poses. Recent human-conducted research has found:

- No amount of alcohol is safe for the human body, according to the World Health Organization.
- Alcohol is ranked as the most dangerous drug in the world.
- Alcohol causes cancer.
- Alcohol is responsible for approximately three million human deaths each year.
- Alcohol is the leading risk factor for premature death for adults aged fifteen to forty-nine.
- Even moderate alcohol consumption shrinks the human brain.

Strangely, despite the widespread publication of these findings, alcohol consumption among humans has not decreased.

While researching the idea of alien anthropology, I used AI to help keep my sources organized and fact-checked. Partway through, I realized AI is a lot like an alien—it knows only the data, with little cultural bias. And it's never had a drink, meaning no personal bias either. The AI offered this insight:

> *It's crucial to note that these potential benefits of alcohol must be weighed against the significant negative impacts of alcohol on public health, safety, and social welfare. The overall societal cost of alcohol consumption generally outweighs its benefits.*
> —Notion AI

I agree with Notion AI. And if we are honest, and when we remove both the cultural and the personal biases inherent in this conversation, we can see that our society views alcohol through a lens that defies logic. It's expensive, harmful, and incredibly destructive—and yet we treat it like it's normal, harmless, and even *important.* Everyone I know has a loved one whose life has been deeply damaged by alcohol.

I'm with Tom: *Nah, mate. Keep your funky juice.*

You might be wondering what a detour through alien anthropology has to do with overcoming a craving. The answer: a lot. Because cravings have two parts: the mental aspect and the physical aspect. The mental aspect is what keeps us stuck long after alcohol has left the body and physical withdrawal symptoms have passed. It's why people return to drinking even after they've sworn it off.

Cravings are complex, layered responses driven by both the body and the mind. And once your brilliant brain consciously understands the pieces of the puzzle, you can learn how to navigate cravings effectively—no matter how intense they might be.

When we face the cold, hard facts, we see the truth: Alcohol is not a sexy, exciting companion, but a thief that is quietly stealing from us. And with that mindset shift, the physical cravings become easier to manage.

So what exactly is a craving?

I remember how intense cravings felt. Sometimes I wanted to crawl out of my skin. It was as if I were on fire, the battle raging inside me. The emotions were so overwhelming that I'd often give in—not necessarily because I wanted the drink, but to escape the awful experience of the craving itself.

Cravings, especially in the early stages, can feel like real physical pain: headaches, nausea, stomachaches, and even nerve pain. But the most intense part of a craving is often the hardest to describe. It doesn't always show up as something specific, but it can feel as overwhelming as anything I've ever experienced.

How awful a craving feels is in part due to a network of neurons that automatically fires in response to certain triggers—places, routines, emotions, anything your brain has linked to drinking. Maybe it's walking into your favorite bar. For me, it was opening the cabinet where my glass and wine box lived. That simple act would activate my brain's wiring, telling it to increase the release of dopamine in anticipation of a drink.

If I chose not to pour a glass, my brain would rebel, completely cutting off dopamine production, and the experience of going from dopamine acceleration to a complete shutdown *feels awful*. This triggers a crash that can feel, both physically and emotionally, like a painful emergency. Chemically, we feel as though we are suffocating, as though we'll fall apart if we don't get the drink and restart our dopamine production. Our brains aren't just addicted to the substance; they're addicted to the internal, survival-based, chemical response triggered by it.

The Neurochemistry of Alcohol Cravings

Understanding the brain's chemistry helps explain why alcohol cravings feel so overwhelming. Here are the key aspects of the neurobiology of cravings (detailed sources for this information are available at Live NakedAF.com):

- **Dopamine surge:** As we now know, drinking causes a surge of dopamine, the brain's reward chemical. Dopamine then sends this message: "That thing you just did? Do it again. It helps us survive." The intensity of this response can make our brains believe—at an instinctual level—that alcohol cravings are a literal life-or-death situation.

- **Neurotransmitter imbalance:** Regular drinking disrupts the balance between excitatory (glutamate) and inhibitory (gamma-aminobutyric acid, or GABA) neurotransmitters. This imbalance creates anxiety, triggers cravings, and leads to withdrawal symptoms.

- **Increased sensitivity to stress:** Over time, alcohol reduces your brain's ability to handle stress. This makes you more sensitive to difficult situations, leading to a marked increase in physiological and chemical stress and cravings that feel out of proportion to the reality of what they are.

- **Hijacking of the brain's pleasure center:** Alcohol alters the function of the brain's pleasure center—especially the nucleus accumbens—causing natural rewards (like food, love, or achievement) to feel less satisfying in comparison to alcohol. This rewiring makes alcohol feel essential while other pleasures lose their appeal.

- **Disrupted prefrontal cortex function:** Alcohol impairs the prefrontal cortex, the part of the brain responsible for judgment, decision-making, and impulse control. This damage weakens your ability to resist cravings, even when you consciously want to quit.

- **Craving triggers encoded in memory:** Environmental cues get strongly associated with alcohol in memory. These cue-induced cravings are stored in the amygdala and hippocampus and can persist long after detox—leading to relapse even after prolonged abstinence.

- **Relapse as a learned habit:** The brain forms habit loops that involve the basal ganglia. These loops can drive automatic drinking behavior in response to emotional triggers—often before conscious awareness catches up.

Chemical reactions aren't logical or deliberate; they happen automatically. Cravings bypass your conscious thinking and feel intense, urgent, and real. And you don't decide to feel them; they just show up.

This feels both confusing and frightening. People describe the experience by saying things like "I don't even know how it happened. One minute I was fine, and the next I was checking out at the liquor store."

It can feel like something foreign takes over your actions—and there's nothing you can do to stop it.

But that's not true. Once you understand what's happening in your brain, you can learn how to interrupt the cycle and reclaim your power over cravings. Before we dive into specific tools, it's important to understand a few big-picture principles.

First, cravings are temporary. Once you work through them, they don't often return in similar situations. As we discussed in chapter 5, cravings are usually tied to neural associations (Hebb's law) and tend to fade after the first or second time you face a trigger (principle of firsts).

Second, we can intentionally choose which problem we want to face: the discomfort of a craving or the consequences of drinking again. When we understand that cravings are temporary—and that we have tools to manage them—we can reframe the discomfort of both withdrawal and cravings. We can start to see our distress as something we are intentionally choosing. After all, growth lives outside our comfort zones, and knowing the pain is temporary and that we can find a much happier and more joyful life on the other side gives us the motivation we need to get through our cravings.

Third, the light of understanding reduces shame. By understanding the reality of how your brain works in reaction to alcohol, you've already reduced shame. Without this knowledge, cravings can feel like a personal failure—as if we put ourselves in a bad situation or didn't try hard enough. Shame, guilt, and fear increase stress, which further intensifies cravings. Just by learning this information, you've taken a huge step in decreasing the power of future cravings.

What Doesn't Work

Let's look at what doesn't work. One of the most common—and least effective—ways we try to overcome our cravings is through direct opposition. We try to fight the craving head-on. We might repeat mantras, like "I will not drink. I will not drink." Or pace around clenching our fists as we tell ourselves "Alcohol is poison. Alcohol is poison."

Science shows that this kind of opposition is one of the least effective strategies. It puts your prefrontal cortex—the part of your brain responsible for logic and self-control—into a battle with your limbic system, the part of your brain that craves. Experts agree that trying to overpower a craving through sheer willpower can be a recipe for giving in. This is because when we repress a thought or craving—whether by ignoring it, distracting ourselves from it, or trying not to think about it—we actually make it stronger.

The good news is that although cravings feel intense, they aren't permanent. You can interrupt the automatic craving-response cycle through intentional, proven techniques. The rest of this chapter focuses on the principles behind the most effective method that studies have found to overcome a craving—*urge surfing*.

A Pathway to Freedom: Surfing the Urge

Urge surfing is a powerful technique developed at the Addictive Behaviors Research Center at the University of Washington. Originally designed to help with smoking addiction, this method is effective for all kinds of cravings, including alcohol.

The concept is simple: Instead of resisting or reacting to a craving, you learn to mindfully observe it. You sit with it, notice it, and let it rise and fall like a wave—without getting pulled under. Let's start by looking at evidence that supports the effectiveness of this technique.

In one study, researchers observed people who smoked but had no intention of quitting. Participants were split into two groups. Both groups were asked to abstain from smoking for twelve hours and then track how much they smoked afterward. Before lighting up, one of the groups completed an urge surfing exercise.

After twelve hours without smoking, all participants were experiencing strong physiological cravings—understandable, given that nicotine is one of the most chemically addictive substances. With cravings fully present, participants sat down at the table with an unopened pack of their favorite cigarettes. They were instructed to observe their cravings mindfully as they held the pack, unwrapped the cellophane, smelled the cigarettes, and even placed one in their mouth—without lighting it.

They were told to simply notice their physical and emotional responses and watch what happened. Once the exercise was over, they were released—and every single participant went outside and lit a cigarette. This result wasn't surprising. Again, they weren't trying to quit, and they had been deprived for half a day, so naturally they reached for a cigarette.

But something remarkable happened with the group that practiced urge surfing. Over time, researchers tracked their behavior, and by week seventeen, an impressive 37 percent of participants had quit smoking completely. Even those who didn't quit reduced their smoking by 44 percent compared to the control group. Again, this held true even for participants with no intention to quit.

Further research in neuroscience supports these surprising results. Studies show that mindfully observing a craving—even if we eventually give in—leads to real, measurable changes in the brain. This practice reduces cravings and strengthens self-control by weakening the brain's automatic response loop.

Before we get into the specific how-to, here are the key elements of why mindful observation is so successful:

Awareness: Notice the craving as it arises, without judgment. Accept the feelings, allowing the urges to exist without trying to fight or suppress them.

Clarity: Observe the physical sensations and emotions that come with the urge. Notice how they make you feel, and what actions they make you want to take.

Transformation: Recognize that you can shift the urge through nonattachment and see the experience as a temporary experience, not a command you must obey. Let the urge rise, peak, and pass naturally—without consciously acting on it.

How to Surf the Urge

What does it really mean to surf the urge of a craving? It means staying with it—watching it, feeling it, and getting curious about it. *What exactly is this feeling? Where do you feel it in your body? What thoughts arise alongside it?*

As you sit with and put your conscious attention directly on the uncomfortable sensation, notice something important: Even though the craving feels intense, you are still okay. You are still breathing; your heart is still beating. The feeling itself isn't actually dangerous—even though it can feel that way. You can witness it without reacting. It's important to remember that our resistance makes the craving more intense. You might hear thoughts like these:

I shouldn't feel this way.

I've been alcohol free for so long—why is this happening?

What's wrong with me?

These thoughts build on one another and amplify the discomfort. But if you approach yourself with curiosity instead of judgment, your experience shifts dramatically. Studies confirm that most cravings last less than fifteen minutes. I bet you can do almost anything for fifteen minutes.

Cravings can feel overwhelming, like a storm moving through your body. You want to run, escape, or give in. But those feelings can't hurt you; they are just chemistry in the body. You know the feeling of the spins after getting really drunk? It's absolutely *miserable*, but you also know you are okay—and that they won't last forever. Cravings are the same, and even if the feelings are out of control in the moment, they won't last forever. When you acknowledge a craving, sit with it, and let yourself fully feel it without acting, you begin to break the automatic loop in your brain. Every time you do this, you weaken the neural connections that create and reinforce the chemical desire for alcohol.

The more you practice, the more you'll notice that cravings become less intense and less frequent. Brain imaging studies show that practices like this change the regions of the brain involved in craving and self-control. Over time, your relationship with cravings transforms—and eventually fades away.

Remember: Cravings are just neurological patterns. And patterns are both temporary and can be changed. Freedom doesn't come from resisting or avoiding your feelings. The way out is through. Don't fight cravings. Don't ignore them. Move through them. Lean in. Feel it all. Even the discomfort.

We are not powerless. We are powerful, conscious human beings. We have the ability to choose—even in the midst of the most intense, painful chemical cravings. Think about it this way: If someone held a gun to your head and told you they'd pull the trigger if you drank, no matter how strong the craving was, you wouldn't give in.

An Important Note on Chemical Addiction

That said, science shows there comes a chilling point in addiction when our ability to choose completely shuts down. With alcohol—and any addictive drug—the brain becomes so hijacked that a person *would* drink even if a gun were pointed at their head.

A few of you reading this may meet the criteria for true chemical addiction—and there is no shame in that. It's a biological reality.

We can look at some quick math based on US research to understand how many drinkers this applies to. According to the Centers for Disease Control and Prevention (CDC), only about 10 percent of excessive drinkers become chemically addicted in a way that leads to severe, sometimes life-threatening withdrawal. Another CDC study shows that approximately 25 percent of adults drink excessively, and the

2023 National Survey on Drug Use and Health (NSDUH) reported that 67 percent of US adults drink. Based on these numbers, around 3.7 percent of adults who drink meet the criteria for chemical addiction that leads to severe withdrawal.

For the remaining 96 percent, the power to choose remains intact—but that doesn't mean it's easy. And importantly, *anyone* who drinks can still face the intense, sometimes terrifying discomfort of chemical craving and withdrawal. The withdrawal effects of alcohol on the brain are so intense that they can begin as quickly as twenty minutes after consuming alcohol—*even if it's the first drink you've ever had.*

And again, tragically, for some of us the chemical disruption in the brain becomes so severe that cravings can't be overcome without medical help. Let's take a closer look at why that is.

With a true chemical addiction, the instinctual brain—sometimes referred to as the "lizard brain"—takes over and prioritizes survival over all else. However, because alcohol has confused the brain, those survival circuits misfire, and the confused brain believes alcohol is key to survival. The individual then becomes powerless against the drive to drink—even to the point of death. True chemical addiction is not a failure of willpower. It's a neurological shutdown.

One of my dad's best friends, now decades sober through AA, told me his experience of chemical addiction:

> *I would be fine for days, sometimes even years. And then—boom. I'd wake up throwing up in my bedroom or a parking lot. And as soon as I finished puking—if I didn't pass out—I'd reach for the bottle. I was drinking the thing that was making me sick, while it was making me sick. It was like watching someone else. I had no control over my body or my choices, and deep inside, a part of me was screaming: "No! No! Please stop. We're going to die. Can't you see what you are doing? You're killing yourself."*

This story is confirmed with research. In studies, scientists will force-feed their subjects, most often mice, the addictive substance until the mice become chemically dependent. This is possible with highly addictive substances, like alcohol, because the act of repeated ingestion can lead to a chemical addiction in anyone.

Once addicted, the mice are observed walking over hot, electrified metal sheets, burning their paws just to reach the drug. Subjects choose the drug over food or water, even to the point of starvation. They will choose the drug over caring for their young, even to the point that their offspring are dying of neglect. I know these studies are awful to think about, and tragic, but we need to face the reality of chemical addiction—when this is no longer a habit or behavior but deserves to be called a disease.

At this point, medical detox and professional supervision become essential. Chemical addiction doesn't just impair decision-making; it shuts it down completely.

We must try to stay aware of our limits when it comes to resisting cravings. A clear sign that you may need additional support is if, even after learning everything in this chapter and throughout this book, you still can't resist a craving. This could mean that you need to be physically separated from accessing the substance in order to move through the physical withdrawal process.

Please consult your doctor. This is not something to take lightly or attempt to manage alone.

On a lighter note, for most of us, the power of choice remains. Again, for about 96 percent of drinkers, once we see that cravings are just chemistry—not truth—we can step back. Even if it feels like you might not survive without that drink, you will. The feeling is a chemical trick. And you now know how to spot it. We are powerful. We can escape the trap. We are smarter than mice—and even mice can avoid a trap once they understand how it works.

I love how Viktor E. Frankl put it:

Between stimulus and response there is a space. In that space is our power to choose.

In the previous two chapters, you learned essential skills for living joyfully alcohol free. We explored more comfortable and effective ways to say no to a drink—and uncovered why saying no feels so difficult in the first place. We also learned about the three common dynamics that create tension with friends after you stop drinking and how to navigate those situations with confidence and clarity.

Then, with a brief but educational detour into an alien's perspective, we uncovered the most research-backed, science-supported technique for handling cravings.

In the next chapter, we'll explore how to build deeper, more connected relationships—so your relationships become more joyful, more supportive, and more fulfilling than ever before.

———

To view the references cited in this chapter, please visit LiveNakedAF.com.

CHAPTER 12

HOW TO BUILD STRONG AF RELATIONSHIPS

To be yourself in a world that is constantly trying to make you something else is the greatest accomplishment.
—Ralph Waldo Emerson

We talk about social skills as if they're something we're born with. If you've ever taken a personality test and been labeled an introvert or an extrovert, you might assume your social ability is fixed. But social skills are just that—skills. And skills can be learned, improved, and strengthened.

Many people believe alcohol makes socializing easier. That seems true—you feel more relaxed and a little less tense when you first start drinking. Your brain slows down, the sharp edges dull, and your inhibitions lower. With that combination, it's no wonder being outgoing can feel easier with a drink.

Although it's deceptively inviting, alcohol eroded my social skills. I remember embarrassing myself by talking too loudly and making jokes that no one laughed at—unless they were also drunk. I remember thinking I was hilarious—until my boss pulled me aside to tell me I needed to get it together and sober up. And the next morning was always the worst part. I'd wake up in a hotel room, sometimes not even sure what country I was in, as dread coated my insides. Little by little, the memories would come back. Bits and pieces of the night before—conversations, laughter, confusion. Sometimes I'd recall something fun, but more often it was flashes of getting scolded by a bartender, peeing behind a dumpster, or crying in the hotel lobby as if the world was ending. I'd remember slurring my words, embarrassing my colleagues—and myself.

Looking back, alcohol didn't give me social skills. I wasn't building confidence or relationships. I was leaving behind an alcohol-fueled wake of awkwardness and regret.

Alcohol Stunts Our Social Skills

Strider bikes were just hitting the market when my oldest son, Turner, was learning to ride. A strider is a bike without pedals that helps kids learn to balance by using their feet and weight, rather than relying on training wheels. The key difference? Striders teach the most important skill of riding a bike—balance—from the very beginning. Training wheels, on the other hand, remove the need to balance altogether.

Drinking alcohol in social settings is a lot like using training wheels. The most important part of meaningful social connection—being present, listening, staying attuned, and actively engaging with others—gets bypassed when alcohol is involved. Just like training wheels, alcohol can delay the development of these essential skills. And just like a child who struggles when the training wheels come off, adults who remove alcohol often feel unsteady in social situations because they never learned how to connect without it.

If you've used alcohol in social situations for a long time, you probably haven't had the chance to build the foundational skills necessary to feel comfortable socializing without booze. You might not feel confident reading social cues or participating in conversation without something to take the edge off. Alcohol steals the learning process, robbing you of the chance to develop and strengthen authentic social abilities.

Yes, alcohol can make us feel more social in the short term—just like training wheels make riding a bike easier at first. But neither one provides us with the skills we need for lasting success. And here's another powerful twist: Building real social connections—the kind that come from honesty, presence, and trust—isn't just what allows us to socialize without alcohol. True connection also helps us break free from alcohol altogether.

Connection Can Prevent and Heal Addiction

Research shows that meaningful connection can both prevent and heal addiction. One well-known example is the Rat Park experiments. In these studies, rats placed in isolation were given a choice between plain water and morphine-laced water. Time and again, they chose the drugged water, developing addiction and dependence. But when those same rats were moved into "Rat Park"—a stimulating environment with social interaction—they avoided the drug-laced water. Even rats already addicted *stopped using the morphine water* once placed in a healthy, connected, *social* environment.

This phenomenon isn't limited to rats. After the Vietnam War, many American soldiers returned home with heroin addiction, a habit they formed while coping with the trauma of war. The government braced for an addiction crisis. But something unexpected happened: Despite being regular heroin users in Vietnam, roughly 95 percent of returning soldiers stopped using the drug. They reconnected with their families, communities, and everyday routines, and the addiction simply faded. These results challenged prevailing addiction theories.

A similar pattern emerged in Portugal. In the early 2000s, Portugal decriminalized the personal possession of drugs and redirected its resources away from punishment and toward connection-based rehabilitation. It opened community-centered facilities instead of jails. The outcome? Problematic drug use dropped significantly despite drugs being both legal and accessible. Once again, the data pointed to connection as a powerful antidote to addiction.

When someone experiences long-term success in AA, the connection they find plays a key role. My friend Beth, now sober for more than sixteen years, credits a large part of her continued success to the community she found within AA.

These examples challenge the traditional narrative that addiction is a matter of genetics, biology, or willpower. Instead, we see that social connection is not just helpful, but essential. Connection protects us from addiction and supports lasting change. Learning the skills of both socializing and forming deep, connected relationships doesn't just feel good; it is vital.

The Magic of Authentic Connection

Over the past year I've led a small group with six This Naked Mind coaches. We ended our year together with a two-day retreat. During our time together, a very unlikely group of people—and complete strangers—came together and formed some of the closest relationships I've seen. Friendships built entirely on mutual acceptance and support.

On the final day of the retreat, I led a closing exercise. It was simple. Each person took a turn sitting in the center of the room while the rest of us shared something we had learned from them. I thought it would take about forty-five minutes. It turned out to be so profound, touching, and magical, that instead of forty-five minutes, it lasted more than *three hours!*

What happened in that space—connection, appreciation, joy, and deep laughter—was more nourishing than any substance could ever be. It was real. It was human. We had spent a year being vulnerable, curious, and radically accepting of one another despite the extensive differences in each of our pyramids of perspective, as defined in chapter 4. And that level of authentic connection changed each of us. We challenged one another, cracked one another open, and helped one another heal—and in doing so, we each found out how to listen more deeply to ourselves.

I laughed harder during those two days than I had in years—sometimes until I couldn't breathe. That's the thing about authentic, accepting connection: Joy, true joy, arises naturally within it.

Connection thrives when we're accepted as we are. In relationships, this is when we have learned how to show our weaknesses, our strengths, and our fears—and realize we are still loved. We don't have to perform or hide. We feel seen. We feel known. Not for who we think we should be, but for who we truly are.

And that's the real gift—being known. But to experience that kind of connection, we have to be brave and vulnerable. We have to show up fully. We have to be exactly who we are.

So how do we build deep, meaningful, life-giving connections—especially when we're no longer using alcohol as a social crutch? Here are some of the most powerful social skills and relationship dynamics that I've learned during my alcohol-free journey. These have helped me not only form strong relationships but also nurture and grow them over time.

Curiosity Is a Social Superpower

Curiosity is one of the most powerful and underrated social skills. When you become curious about others, a few important things happen. First, you become genuinely interested in the people around you. And here's the secret: Being interested in others makes you magnetic. *When you're interested, you become interesting.*

Dale Carnegie said it best:

You can make more friends in two months by becoming interested in other people than you can in two years by trying to get other people interested in you.

Second, curiosity helps you become a better listener. When you're truly curious about someone, you actually listen to their answers. But most of us haven't been taught to listen—we've been taught to wait for our turn to speak. Real listening is a gift, one we're all starving for in today's fast-paced, one-way-communication culture.

I asked a few friends to name the top people they go to for wisdom, advice, or perspective. An overwhelming number named their therapist. Why? Because we're listened to when we see a therapist. A therapist is a paid listener—and that is part of what makes them so valuable.

Now, I'm not suggesting that you need to turn into a therapist at a dinner party. What I am saying is that listening is a generous act. I've tried both listening while drinking and listening while alcohol free, and I'm absolutely a better listener without a drink in my hand.

Psychiatrist and author Karl Menninger put it beautifully:

Listening is a magnetic and strange thing, a creative force. The friends who listen to us are the ones we move toward. When we are listened to, it creates us, makes us unfold and expand.

At social events, I like to challenge myself to learn ten new things. It might be ten things about one person, one thing about ten people, or any combination—it doesn't matter. The goal is to get curious. Every time I've used this approach, I've been amazed by how much fun I have and how easy it is to form real, lasting connections.

Curiosity is a skill you can practice. And once you do, it opens the door to meaningful relationships—authentic, connected, and completely alcohol free.

Connection, like many things we've explored, isn't sabotaged on purpose—it erodes when we're unaware of the subconscious programs running in the background. These hidden patterns create conflict between us and others, leaving us clueless as to the real reason why. We just feel the frustration or the disconnection from the people we care about most. Let's take a closer look at some of the roadblocks to connection—the unseen programs that create distance between ourselves and others.

Roadblocks to Connection

We all have subconscious programs governing our relationships in ways that sabotage our connection with others.

We blame others or ourselves when we have conflict or disappointment in our relationships and we don't understand what's really going on. In these knee-jerk patterns of blame and shame, we are blinded from underlying issues.

We have the power to break free once we shine a light on them. Here are some of the most common ways we unintentionally sabotage connection in our relationships.

The Need to Be Right

Sarah, one of our This Naked Mind coaches, shared a phrase that she claimed transformed her life—just four simple words:

"You might be right."

Sarah says these words saved her marriage.

Like many of us, she had a deeply ingrained belief, held over from childhood, that being right was how she earned worth, stayed in control, and even kept herself safe. She didn't realize that this need to be right was actually sabotaging the things she valued most—love and connection. It wasn't until she looked honestly at her behavior and prioritized her deeper values—connection, care, and love—that she could see the impact of her need to be right. When she focused on showing her loved ones how much she cared instead of proving she knew everything, her relationships shifted. She let go of the need to be right and prioritized making her family feel loved, which did in fact change her life.

It sounds simple, but there's deep wisdom here. Putting down the need to be right doesn't mean you're wrong. It just means you're choosing peace over power. When Sarah chose connection over control, everything shifted. Her marriage got stronger, her conversations got easier, and her family felt more supported.

These four words—*You might be right*—are some of the most powerful I've heard in the context of relationships. They invite openness. They de-escalate tension. And most important, they send a clear message: *I care more about this relationship than about winning this argument.*

Byron Katie puts it this way:

You get to be right, and I get to be free.

And in that freedom—freedom to be ourselves and allow others to do the same—relationships thrive.

Invalid Expectations

Another common—and often invisible—way we sabotage relationships is through invalid expectations. We all have expectations we don't realize we're holding but that shape how we feel, how we treat those we care about, and how we judge the people around us. When reality doesn't match these unconscious expectations, we feel more than disappointed—we often feel hurt.

Tal Ben-Shahar, a psychology professor, explains it simply through what he calls the "Happiness Equation":

Reality – Expectations = Happiness

Happiness equals reality minus our expectations. If our expectations are too high—or worse, completely unrealistic—we're setting ourselves up for pain.

Let's say you decide to stop drinking. You expect your partner to celebrate you. You imagine that they'll be proud, supportive, and maybe even inspired to join you. But instead, they seem cold or distant. Maybe they tease you. You feel hurt—even betrayed. Underneath that pain are probably a few unspoken expectations. Things like: *If I make a healthy change, the people I love should cheer me on,* or *If they really cared, they would support me by joining me.*

Or maybe you host Thanksgiving for your extended family. You go all out—clean the house, prep the food, and set the table just right. You imagine your mother-in-law will notice and compliment your efforts. Instead, she comments on how dry the turkey is. You don't just feel annoyed—you feel unseen, unappreciated, and unwanted. Because somewhere inside lurks the expectation that she should say something kind. These expectations aren't wrong; they're human. But when they go unspoken or unnoticed, they create conditions for suffering.

This is why awareness is so powerful. When we take a moment to name our expectations, we reclaim the ability to adjust them. And when we can adjust or let go of expectations, we open the door to happiness. Letting go of the belief that others must behave a certain way for us to feel okay allows us to build relationships based on acceptance and understanding instead of control and disappointment.

Letting go of invalid expectations doesn't mean we stop hoping for kindness, support, or recognition. It just means we stop tying our happiness to whether or not those things show up.

One of the most helpful frameworks I've come across to understand expectations was developed by Pete and Geri Scazzero. They outline four criteria an expectation must meet in order for it to be valid:

1. **Conscious:** You are aware of the expectation.

2. **Realistic:** The expectation is achievable and reasonable.

3. **Spoken:** The expectation is clearly communicated.

4. **Confirmed:** The expectation is agreed upon.

Let's look at each point more closely.

1. Conscious: You Are Aware of the Expectation

When we first got married, I had an unconscious expectation that we wouldn't have a television in our bedroom. I grew up without television, and having a TV in the bedroom felt intrusive. Brian grew up differently, and from his perspective, a bedroom TV was essential. I didn't realize I was carrying this expectation—and I certainly didn't communicate it. When we moved to Brooklyn and into our first apartment, I was furious when he put a TV in the bedroom.

2. Realistic: The Expectation Is Achievable and Reasonable

It was unrealistic to expect my husband to share the same point of view I did. I've had many other unrealistic expectations, too—like expecting guests to stop bringing wine to dinner without being asked. But by far, the most painful unrealistic expectations are the ones I place on myself.

I've held myself to impossible standards in nearly every area of my life, from always being calm and holding it all together to being the best mom, wife, author, and friend. I've even had the unconscious (and, frankly, hilarious) expectation of never aging.

Taking an honest look at the unrealistic expectations we put on ourselves can make us laugh because they are so extreme. And in that laughter—the moment of recognizing how impossible these standards really are—we gain the power to finally let them go.

3. Spoken: The Expectation Is Clearly Communicated

In the early years of my marriage I assumed that if Brian loved me, he'd just *know* what I needed. He should know not to come home after nine p.m. without calling first. He should know when I needed a hug.

Brooke Castillo uses a powerful metaphor to explain this relationship dynamic—*an owner's manual*. She explains how we all walk around with an invisible manual for how we want to be treated. And our manuals are incredibly detailed—they can even include things like how the dishwasher should be loaded or what it means if someone doesn't text back right away.

We carry around a long list of expectations—many of them unmet—and here's the kicker: Brooke explains that not only do we have detailed manuals for how others should treat us, but *we don't share them with the people we love.*

I know I certainly didn't share mine with Brian. I never clearly told Brian what was in my manual. I couldn't express myself without frustration, anger, or tears because of the subconscious program I had running: *If he doesn't [insert action], that means he doesn't love me.* As a result, my attempts at communication came out as criticism or judgment, almost guaranteed to start a fight. I was upset because he wasn't following a manual he had never been given—*unspoken expectations.* And because we come from different backgrounds, carry different beliefs, and have different programming, how could he possibly—*just know?*

4. Confirmed: The Expectation Is Agreed Upon

If we manage to communicate our expectations to those we expect them from, the next critical step is gaining agreement. Not forced agreement—real agreement. As relationship-development expert Stacey Martino explains, when someone is pressured to say yes, that's not agreement; that's compliance. It probably won't hold.

When I look back, most of my expectations—both for myself and others—didn't meet the validity criteria for this framework. No wonder I felt hurt and disappointed.

Uncovering Expectations

Here are some journaling prompts that will help you become aware of and uncover the hidden expectations that might be quietly sabotaging your connection with others and with yourself.

What expectations do you have of others that are . . .
- Unconscious?
- Unrealistic?
- Unspoken?
- Unagreed upon?

What expectations do you have of yourself that are . . .
- Unconscious?
- Unrealistic?
- Unspoken?
- Unagreed upon?

Appreciation Heals What Expectations Break

If you are anything like me, you'll probably find that you're holding on to quite a few invalid expectations. For me this realization was painful, but again, we can't fix a problem we aren't aware we have.

Here is a specific practice called "Funeral for Your Partner" (see the following box) that helped me move beyond invalid expectations in my marriage and into a place of genuine appreciation and healing. This practice was taught to Brian and me by Jay Pathak, a coach, mentor, pastor, and one of the wisest people I've met. When Jay first started meeting with us, he could see my unmet expectations before I could. He could also see how they were making me, and Brian, miserable.

The "Funeral for Your Partner" Exercise

This practice uses all the key components of awareness, clarity, and transformation as a way to work through invalid expectations. It's simple, and you can use it with anyone in your life—your mom, dad, sibling, boss, friend, or even your former drinking buddies. If you have a relationship with them and carry expectations they haven't met, this exercise helps bring clarity and healing.

Step 1: Make "The List"
Write down everything you wish your partner—or anyone you are in a relationship with—would do differently. Be honest and detailed. I wanted Brian to compliment me more, prioritize me in ways that I didn't think he was currently , and show up differently in our business. You may want your partner to do more around the house or to be more patient with your children. Everything you wish they'd do that they aren't currently doing is fair game.

161

Step 2: Mourn "The List"

Read the list, letting yourself grieve. Why? Because the person you wrote about doesn't exist. They are a figment of your imagination. More accurate, they are a reflection of your programming. When I laid my imaginary husband to rest, I stopped measuring Brian against someone who never even existed.

Step 3: Express Gratitude for What Is Real

After this exercise, the next time you sit across the table, the screen, or the telephone from this person, really experience them. See the person you married. Hear the sister you've known your whole life. Notice the living, breathing human. Recognize how they, like you, were once just a child. Next, look for things to appreciate. Each day, add something new to your gratitude list for the *real* person in your life, and let go of the version of them you made up.

After this exercise, I saw how I'd invented a false version of Brian. A phantom husband. One who had never existed and would never exist. Even worse, I measured his love for me against how much he resembled my imaginary version of him.

But once I let go of the illusion, and my manual, and saw Brian for who he truly was, things shifted. I realized how much I loved him, not my false idea of him. I buried the pretend Brian, and our marriage has become better than it's been in a long time. And I know Brian's life has improved, too.

In this chapter, we discovered how some of the biggest blocks to connection live in the subconscious. And we've learned how these dynamics sabotage relationships. As you work to unwind these dynamics in your life, you will notice energy snags, moments when something stirs discomfort. That's not a problem; it's an opportunity. Use these moments to apply the ACT process and unlock the freedom that lives on the other side of your programming.

Since we're already talking about relationships, let's explore one of the key reasons many people keep drinking—intimacy, and the belief that alcohol makes sex better.

———

To view the references cited in this chapter, please visit LiveNakedAF.com.

CHAPTER 13

HOW TO ENJOY SEX ALCOHOL FREE

Drunk sex might get your body there, but sober sex? That's when your soul shows up too.
—Anonymous

When I was drinking, I had a little routine before sex. I'd tell Brian I needed something from the kitchen or that I had to make sure the stove was turned off. Then I'd sneak into the kitchen, find my box of wine, and chug just enough to take the edge off. I would stop in the hallway bathroom to rinse with mouthwash before heading back to the bedroom. He never suspected a thing. But for me, that quick drink felt like the only way I could relax enough to get in the mood.

It wasn't aways like this. From the beginning, Brian and I had a very strong connection—physically and emotionally. While our sex life started off strong, and I am happy to say that post-alcohol it is better than ever, it wasn't always like this. For many years, alcohol quietly stole this simple joy from our lives.

As a disclaimer, writing about something as vulnerable and potentially sensitive as sex requires acknowledging that I come from my own body, gender, orientation, and experience. I also speak from my unique pyramid of perspective. And when it comes to sex—as with everything else—you are your own wisest resource. Listen to yourself. Be gentle. Honor what's true for you.

Sex and Drinking

Over time, I forgot how to feel relaxed, open, or sexy without alcohol. I stopped enjoying sex and didn't know why. I now know that one reason sex felt so different when I was drinking was because alcohol was changing my body's ability to experience pleasure. Alcohol dulls our physical senses—especially touch. Studies show that alcohol can impair men's performance, and it can make climax nearly impossible for women.

What the Science Says

Alcohol consumption has a significant and well-documented negative impact on sexual health for both men and women. While alcohol may temporarily reduce inhibitions, its physiological effects often weaken both performance and satisfaction.

Chronic and heavy alcohol use is strongly associated with various forms of sexual dysfunction in men. A clinical study conducted in 2012 found that alcohol caused up to 76 percent of male subjects to experience at least one form of sexual dysfunction, including erectile dysfunction, premature ejaculation, and reduced sexual desire.

Physiologically, alcohol acts as a central nervous system depressant, which can interfere with the nerve signals responsible for sexual arousal and performance. It can also lead to hormonal imbalances, such as reduced testosterone levels, further contributing to decreased libido and sexual function.

Women are also adversely affected by alcohol consumption in terms of sexual health. A meta-analysis of seven studies involving more than fifty thousand women found that alcohol consumption increased the likelihood of sexual dysfunction by 74 percent, with common issues including decreased vaginal lubrication, reduced sexual arousal, and difficulties with orgasm.

Because I didn't realize alcohol was a key reason that I no longer enjoyed sex, I internalized the issue. Losing interest in intimacy triggered a wave of self-doubt. How could I not want to be close to the man I loved? Alcohol also chipped away at my self-image. Two bottles of wine a night took a toll on my appearance: I hated my body—not just because of how I felt physically, but because I was in conflict with myself emotionally.

———

Sex is one of the most vulnerable areas of our lives, and many of us carry things into the bedroom that sabotage intimacy without even knowing it. Here are a few of the most common patterns:

Internalized Sexual Shame

Many of us hold a deep, subconscious belief that sex is somehow wrong, dirty, or shameful. This comes from cultural, historical, and religious conditioning. Even when we're talking about joyful, healthy sex within a loving relationship, sometimes a part of us may feel uncomfortable. That discomfort? It's probably not actually yours, but leftover baggage that was handed down to you. And the great news? You now know that these programs can be rewritten.

Past Trauma

It is important to gently acknowledge that for some of us, alcohol hasn't just been a social habit—it has felt like a means of survival. For those who carry the weight of sexual trauma, drinking may have been a way to quiet the alarm bells in the mind or dull the pain held in the body. It may have been used to numb what felt too overwhelming to face, or to navigate intimacy when consent, desire, and safety felt tangled with confusion, pressure, shame, or unresolved pain—whether conscious or not. If this is part of your story, know that your experience matters. You are not alone, and you are not invisible in this conversation. While this book doesn't dive deeply into trauma healing, support is available. Safety, healing, and wholeness are possible—and you deserve all three.

When we carry unresolved emotional wounds, the bedroom no longer feels safe. As a result, we naturally—and subconsciously—protect ourselves against vulnerability, openness, and intimacy: key factors in a satisfying sexual relationship. This is normal, this is human, and unfortunately, alcohol—because it numbs us—can feel like safety when it is really sabotaging your ability to heal and move beyond your past. If you don't feel safe in the bedroom, get the help you need. The work of going deep inside your mind to heal is warrior work—it's courageous and on the other side is freedom.

Insecure Body Image

When we don't feel good about our bodies—whether we're aware of it or not—it can be hard to relax and enjoy intimacy. Some insecurities are obvious, with thoughts we can hear, like *I hate my thighs* or *I have too much cellulite*. But others are buried deeper. Maybe early on you were teased about your body, and now, without even realizing it, you feel uncomfortable undressing in front of your partner. Again, alcohol seems like the solution, but true healing comes from making peace with your body—not because it is perfect, but because it is the incredible vessel that allows you life.

Performance Anxiety

A lot of us carry unconscious pressure to perform during sex. I used to think intimacy had to look like it does in the movies—that there was a right way to do it, and I had to get it right. But pressure pulls you out of the experience. Instead of being present and feeling pleasure, you're busy trying to meet some imagined standard. And that disconnection can steal the joy right out of the moment. Alcohol seems to make it easier to perform, but what if performance was never the goal?

Fear of Abandonment

It might seem extreme to bring the fear of abandonment into this conversation, but this is one of the most common subconscious programs operating within us when we feel uncomfortable with intimacy. Without realizing it, we wonder if we're enough—attractive enough, sexy enough, lovable enough. And fears, which are both primal and instinctual, can keep us from fully opening up during intimate moments. We unconsciously protect ourselves from intimacy by holding ourselves at a distance, even from those closest to us, out of fear of loss. This can hold us back from surrendering to connection, despite wanting it.

No wonder sex can feel complicated. And because so many of these patterns are unconscious, we might not have any idea what is really happening. All we know is that we are resistant to sex, and with all of this going on, it might not even feel good.

We understandably turn to alcohol, which feels like it works, at least on the surface. By impairing the prefrontal cortex, alcohol quiets the thinking mind and allows us to act from a more primal, instinctive place. By slowing down the brain's communication pathways, alcohol can feel like relief from the mental chatter about body image, performance anxiety, or rejection. Because of this, it seems to help us get "in the mood" and into the bedroom.

But getting into the bedroom is very different from enjoying what happens there. I remember nights drinking with Brian when things would heat up fast . . . but the sex itself? I barely remembered it. I'd be drunk, sometimes in a blackout. And let's be honest—alcohol doesn't just impair memory; it also clouds judgment. Many of us have ended up in bedrooms we never would have chosen if we weren't drinking.

Here's the truth: Alcohol may take the edge off our fears and insecurities just enough to get us to have sex, but at the same time, the physical pleasure of sex itself might be ruined because alcohol numbs our sense of touch. And let's face it, touching that feels good is kind of the *whole point*. In trying to fix the problem, alcohol steals the very thing we've come to get.

We think we "need a drink" to loosen up, when what we really need is healing, compassion, and one of the best things to bring to the bedroom, a little playfulness.

The First Time

We can't discount the fact that alcohol-free sex is a first. When I stopped drinking, sex felt nerve-racking because I didn't have my usual crutch. But I also knew alcohol had taken so much from me that even my marriage was at risk. I decided figuring this out was worth the effort. I reminded myself that just because something feels unsafe or uncomfortable doesn't mean it is—it usually just means it's unfamiliar.

And at first, alcohol-free sex was unfamiliar. But interestingly, that unfamiliarity sparked something new: a fresh energy. After all, sex wasn't familiar on our wedding night, either, and part of the excitement came from unfamiliarity. We found that again with AF sex, and these days, we both agree things have never been better.

I want to share more than my perspective, so I asked the This Naked Mind community this question: What have your experiences with alcohol-free sex been like?

Here are some of the responses:

- My sex life has been amazing. The sense of touch, the intensity, and the orgasms—better than anything I've experienced. I feel fully in control of my body and the moment.

- Alcohol-free sex is incredible. Being present from the start, enjoying foreplay, and experiencing full-body freedom during orgasm—then remembering it the next day or even days later. It feels like natural ecstasy.

- Drunk sex doesn't compare. It honestly felt like more effort than it was worth. Sober sex is so much more enjoyable.

- I used to believe I needed alcohol to have sex. But I realized I couldn't even orgasm with my husband when I was drinking—my senses were too dulled. It was frustrating and embarrassing.

- At first, alcohol-free sex felt awkward. But we figured it out. Now it's deeply satisfying—physically and emotionally. We both smile afterward and say, "That was the best sex ever." Every time.

- Speaking as a man . . . it's way better. I just wish I could get her to try it!

- I used to drink before sex, thinking it enhanced the experience. Now I know that removing alcohol is like taking off a condom from your pleasure center—everything becomes more intense and connected.

- It feels healthier. More mindful. The choice to have sex always comes from a clear, conscious place.

- I can fully enjoy the intimacy. It's easier to climax. I highly recommend sober sex. Honestly, there's no downside. It's beautiful. For the first time, the phrase "making love" actually makes sense.

- Since I stopped drinking, I'm not ashamed to admit—I want sex more than ever. It's deeply satisfying. I've even been complimented on both my stamina and technique.

How to Have AF Sex

If you've used alcohol to lubricate your sex life (pun intended), the first time without it can feel as uncomfortable as losing your virginity all over again. Instead of approaching it with fear, try to see alcohol-free sex as an experiment. It's okay to take your time and figure out what feels good for you. It might not start with kitchen counters and instant orgasms, and that's okay. Like anything new, there's an adjustment period—and that can feel intimidating at first.

When you're brave enough to learn the skill of alcohol-free sex, you discover more about yourself, your body, and your partner. Over time, AF sex gets better and better. Not only does the physical experience improve, but so does the emotional connection—sex without hiding, numbing, or disconnecting is on another level.

Here are some practical things to bring to the bedroom instead of a glass of wine:

- **Open communication:** Research shows that honest communication improves sexual satisfaction. Talk with your partner about your desires, boundaries, and expectations.

- **Mindfulness:** Mindfulness can increase arousal and satisfaction. Stay present, and focus on how things feel in your body.

- **Foreplay:** Longer foreplay builds anticipation and helps with natural lubrication. Take your time. It might feel awkward at first, but just breathe and allow yourself to ease into it.

- **Sensate focus:** Sensate focus is a therapeutic technique that uses mindful nonsexual touch to build intimacy and reduce performance pressure. It's easy to research online and practice at home.

- **Lubrication:** Don't be shy about lubrication! It can enhance comfort and pleasure, making the whole experience more enjoyable.

Most important, make sure you feel safe and be kind to yourself. This is new—and new things might feel awkward because they are unfamiliar, but even that can be part of the fun. Think of it like teenagers in the back of a car after prom—all nerves, fumbling, and apologies—but that's okay! Give yourself time. You will find your rhythm. And in my experience—and in the experience of thousands of others—alcohol-free sex is absolutely worth the effort.

Some fears about living alcohol-free life go deeper than missing out on parties or facing awkward moments in the bedroom—they strike at the heart of something essential to a good life: our happiness. Many of us carry a powerful, deeply ingrained subconscious belief that alcohol is a big part of what makes life good. We associate alcohol with fun, connection, laughter, celebration, and joy. But what is true? In the next chapter, we'll explore the cultural programming that links alcohol to happiness and see if those beliefs hold up.

———

To view the references cited in this chapter, please visit LiveNakedAF.com.

CHAPTER 14

HOW TO FIND HAPPINESS WITHOUT ALCOHOL

The belief that unhappiness is abnormal or a sign of failure causes more suffering than the unhappiness itself.
—Dr. Russ Harris

One of the most profitable lies in human history is that *you should be happy all the time.*

You can test this idea with a simple experiment. Just look around and notice how many things have been marketed or sold to you with the promise of happiness:

You'll be happy if you . . .

. . . drive this.

. . . watch this.

. . . play this.

. . . eat this.

. . . wear this.

. . . look like this.

Most promotional messaging leads with the belief that happiness is just one product, experience, or purchase away. This idea is misleading and deeply harmful. Not only does it encourage us to suppress natural, yet uncomfortable emotions—the ones that allow us to learn and grow—but it also has us forever chasing an unrealistic, impossible ideal. As writer and Buddhist monk Matthieu Ricard says:

The pursuit of happiness has become a billion-dollar industry, but true contentment cannot be bought or sold.

This subconscious program—that we should feel happy all the time—is a key aspect of addiction, and feeds dissatisfaction. Research shows that the more we chase perpetual happiness, the more we increase our risk of stress, anxiety, and depression.

Emotional well-being isn't about always feeling good—it's about learning to feel everything. And knowing that feeling everything, no matter how difficult, is not just okay, but a big part of being human.

I cry often and easily. That might sound strange in a chapter about happiness. But after a lifetime of making peace with the storms inside me, I've come to love a good cry. I pushed down and buried so many emotions with alcohol for so long that I became terrified of all emotion. I feared that if I let the floodgates open, I'd be swept away and the tears would never stop.

Even the smallest emotional twinge sent me running to my favorite numbing agent—alcohol. Because hard emotions don't wait until after five p.m. to surface, alcohol began to seem like a good idea any time of day. I was desperate to hold back the pain that constantly threatened to spill out. On a work trip to London I walked into the wine aisle at ten a.m. just to find something to numb my internal pain before heading back to the office.

Now when emotions show up, even intense ones like sadness, I make space for them. I welcome them. As hard as it can be, I've learned how to hold, and even love, myself through the darkest emotional waves.

We've been conditioned to believe that tears are weak, wrong, or shameful. I can't count how many times I've told my kids, "Don't cry." Crying has become such a social faux pas that we often feel the need to apologize for a single tear in public—even at something as tragic as a funeral.

Suppress the Pain and Numb the Joy

Why are kids so joyful? What changes between childhood and adulthood? I've researched this question and discovered how our unwillingness to feel the hard stuff—the pain, sadness, fear, and despair—is a big part of why we lose our joyful, childlike approach to life. As children, we move in and out of intense emotions with ease. I watch my daughter soar to emotional heights, proclaiming, "This is the best day ever!" only to sink into despair and declare, "This is the worst day ever!" less than thirty minutes later.

What if the reason we lose our capacity for joy is because we start suppressing, distracting ourselves from, and numbing what hurts? What if, in doing so, we also numb ourselves to the feelings that bring us to life? After all, you can't numb selectively. Numbing pain simultaneously numbs pleasure.

When we allow ourselves to feel what's been buried—even if it's painful—we make space for joy to rise again. I like how author Mark Manson says it:

Happiness is not about feeling good all the time, but about learning to accept and manage the full range of emotions that we experience.

We aren't allowing ourselves to *be* fully human when we suppress our emotions. The pursuit of happiness becomes toxic when we chase it and, in the process, demonize our natural, human emotions. The cumulative result of chasing happiness? Ironically, greater unhappiness.

Few things have improved my well-being more than letting go of the idea that I should be happy all the time. Once I stopped chasing this impossible goal, I also stopped turning to the harmful substances and behaviors I thought would make me feel better. Let's stop trying to be happy and simply learn how to be human.

Alcohol = The Thief of Joy

There is a substance-specific subconscious program running in your mind that needs to be rewritten—it's the belief that alcohol makes us happy. This belief is powerful because our direct experience seems to confirm it. Let's run this program through the ACT process. First, we recognize that it's just a program—awareness. Next, we explore where it came from and what it's costing us—clarity. Finally, we examine what's actually true—transformation.

If this program isn't true and alcohol doesn't make us happy, why do we believe it does? Let's start with our direct experience—alcohol appears to bring laughter, connection, and fun.

Alcohol does make us feel good—at first. It overstimulates the brain's pleasure circuits, including the nucleus accumbens, the ventral tegmental area (VTA), and the amygdala. This surge in pleasure may sound like the whole point, right? But there's a problem—and it's a big one.

Just like any powerful piece of technology, your brain requires the right conditions to operate. A computer needs to stay cool; your brain needs balance and stability.

When your body gets hot, you start to sweat. When the brain's pleasure center is overstimulated by alcohol, it works to restore balance. It does this by dialing down the pleasure you feel from drinking. This is part of the reason why you have to drink more over time to get the same buzz. This is tolerance. I remember getting back to my hotel room after a night of heavy drinking and realizing I hardly felt buzzed at all.

But it doesn't stop there.

The brain also creates a chemical called dynorphin, a peptide that diminishes pleasure. Dynorphin's job is to restore balance by suppressing the overstimulation to the brain's pleasure circuits caused by alcohol.

You might be wondering why, if alcohol makes you feel good, your brain would fight back by creating a chemical that makes you feel bad. The answer is simple: Your brain sees this level of stimulation as unsafe or disruptive. Dynorphin doesn't get released during ordinary pleasures but only when the brain is reacting to an artificial chemical stimulation and needs to restore balance.

And while we might be able to trick our taste buds into thinking alcohol is enjoyable, the body knows better. Alcohol is still ethanol—the same substance used to fuel cars. Once it enters your system, the body goes on high alert, even stopping normal functions like digestion and blood sugar regulation in order to focus all its energy on removing the alcohol, which your body experiences as a toxic threat to your system.

So the alcohol gets flushed out. But what about the dynorphin?

Since dynorphin is produced by the body, it's not toxic. That means it sticks around. And here's the kicker: Dynorphin doesn't just block the pleasure from alcohol; it turns down all enjoyment. Everyday pleasures—like laughing with friends, reading a book, or watching a movie—become muted. Things that used to be fun before your drinking days no longer feel fun. This leads you to believe that alcohol is what makes life fun. But in reality, the opposite is true. It's alcohol—and your brain's reaction to it—that's been stealing your joy.

You've probably heard someone say they can't seem to have fun without a drink—or maybe you've felt that way yourself. Sadly, because of the neurochemical process I just explained, that becomes true. With regular drinking and elevated levels of dynorphin, life begins to feel dull. Flat. Even miserable. But when we stop drinking, our joy returns—often with surprising intensity. People report experiencing lasting euphoric feelings when they first go alcohol free.

Here is the bottom line: Alcohol is the thief of joy. It steals your happiness.

Happiness You Can Count

Let's explore the truth about alcohol and happiness by taking a closer look at just how happy—or not—alcohol actually made you from a measurable, numbers-based perspective.

Social psychologist and researcher Barbara Fredrickson, well known for her work on positive emotions, identified ten emotions that create our experience of happiness: love, joy, gratitude, serenity, interest, hope, pride, amusement, inspiration, and awe.

Use the chart below to reflect on how alcohol has influenced each of these emotions in your life. For each one, ask yourself:

- How did alcohol contribute to this emotion in my life?

- How did alcohol diminish or steal this emotion from me?

For clarity and easy reflection, number each of the points you make so you can tally them later. Be honest with yourself. This is your opportunity for clarity, to see your experience clearly and begin to shift it.

Emotion	How Did Alcohol Enhance This Emotion in Your Life?	How Did Alcohol Diminish This Emotion in Your Life?
Love		
Joy		
Gratitude		
Serenity		
Interest		
Hope		
Pride		
Amusement		
Inspiration		
Awe		

When you are done, simply count the number of items you listed in each column.

For example:

Emotion	How Did Alcohol Enhance This Emotion in Your Life?	How Did Alcohol Diminish This Emotion in Your Life?
Love	1. Alcohol made it easier to loosen up in the bedroom.	1. Even when we had sex, it was hard to remember, and I never really felt connected. 2. My kids didn't want to be near me when I was drinking. 3. Alcohol-fueled fighting has taken a toll on my marriage. 4. I've yelled at my kids more times than I can count when drinking. 5. I drink heavily on work trips, leaving Brian feeling afraid of what I might do.

I could go through another, but I want you to do this part for yourself.

Here's what a quantitative analysis might look like:

Alcohol enhanced my happiness in one way
Alcohol diminished my happiness in five ways
Alcohol = 1
Living AF = 5
Winner = Living AF!

It's eye-opening to see just how much happiness alcohol actually takes from us—and spoiler alert: Living AF always wins. Alcohol promises happiness, but it never truly delivers.

Finding Joy

Happiness is deeply human. It's beautiful, needed, and absolutely worth pursuing. I've spent years chasing it. But in the seasons when my mental health struggles made happiness feel impossible, I began to look beyond happiness. And that's when I found something even more powerful—*joy*.

Happiness is an experience that shows up when many, if not most, of the positive emotions on Fredrickson's list are present. Happiness feels good—but it's also more dependent. It needs things to line up. It needs conditions to be just right.

Joy is different; it doesn't wait for everything in your life to be perfect. It doesn't depend on checking off goals or finally becoming who you think you're supposed to be. It's not about your career, your appearance, your relationship status, or any future version of you.

Joy doesn't need everything to be okay. Joy can exist all on its own. And it's always here, present in each moment. It lives in the beat of your heart. The rise and fall of your breath. The wind outside your window. The quiet support of the chair beneath you or the ground under your feet. Joy lives in the present moment, always available when we pause long enough to notice that joy is as simple as a life being lived—this life. Your life.

I wonder if joy isn't so much an emotion as a kind of awareness—a way of paying attention. A shift in consciousness. When we wake up to the reality of being alive; when we touch this improbable, mysterious experience we call existence; when we brush up against something eternal. Something real.

Joy can be found in the moment you stop and really see what's in front of you—not what needs fixing, but what simply *is*. Joy arrives when we slow down and stop striving, numbing, or rushing. Joy arises when we find gratitude—not because everything is perfect, but because we're awake to the miracle that we're even here on a wild ride of life unfolding, moment by moment.

Joy doesn't need a grand stage. Often it shows up quietly in the background of the ordinary—waiting to be noticed. I can find joy washing my hands in the warmth of the water. In tending to myself, there is joy. Even the buzzing of a fly once made me smile. And that moment, like most moments, was ordinary—until I paid attention.

Surprisingly, and perhaps counterintuitively, when I let myself feel grief, sadness, or heartache—fully, without resistance—I'm also opening the door to joy. There's something deeply human and strangely joyful about honoring your full emotional experience. The more I accept my emotions, the more peace I feel. With peace comes joy. And the more compassion I offer myself, the more joy grows.

Joy doesn't mean we skip over the hard parts. It's in the tears, in the ache, in the quiet moments when we stop trying to outrun what hurts and sit with it that joy can arise.

I've spent my life believing that joy will come once I finally fixed myself. What I now see is that joy has been here the whole time. The road to joy winds through the very emotions I desperately tried to avoid.

There is always somewhere else to go. More to achieve, more to discover, more happiness to find, more connections to make, more presence to embody.

And at the same time, this moment—just as it is—holds all we've ever searched for. In a very real sense, although it can be hard to understand, we've *already arrived*. No matter where we are on the path or how far we think we have to go, when we take a minute to connect with the depth of this moment, we realize that here, now, in this, is the only place we need to be. The only place we can be.

Neither the past nor the future actually exist. We can only experience the past within the thoughts we have about it, thoughts we are thinking right here, right now. We can only experience the future in our imagination, and that imagined experience is happening right here, right now. We can't touch the past; we can't change it or relive it. We can't touch the future, either. We can only touch, change, and live *this*. This moment isn't just part of life—it *is* life. And it's the only place where joy can be found.

This quote is written in large script on my office wall:

I have arrived. I am home. My destination is in each step.
—Thích Nhất Hạnh

What we're searching for is already here. In your body, your breath, your being. It is the quiet realization that you are enough—simply because you exist. You get to be *here*, experiencing your unique slice of reality. And that is everything.

Because with joy, we don't need to go search for it—we just need to remember *it already is*.

———

To view the references cited in this chapter, please visit LiveNakedAF.com.

CHAPTER 15

HOW TO HANDLE "RELAPSE"

The curious paradox is that when I accept myself just as I am,
then I can change.
—Carl Rogers

A few years ago, I was invited to Will and Jada Pinkett Smith's house to appear on the show *Red Table Talk*. I wasn't allowed to know the address, so a driver picked me up. As we wound through the hills outside Los Angeles, I'm not sure I've ever been more nervous. I kept reminding myself: *Annie, you'll never have this experience again. Yes, your body is freaking out, but that's okay—it's just part of it. Breathe. Just breathe.*

Security was so tight that I'm surprised I wasn't blindfolded. I was dropped off at a movie trailer with my name on it—which was very cool. But then I noticed Kelly Osbourne's name was on the trailer next door. Even cooler.

I tried on outfits while hair and makeup artists came in and out. I even video-chatted with some friends, showing them the dressing room, and then . . . I waited, nerves building. I kept peeking out to see if anyone else was around, but it was clear we weren't supposed to wander around the Smiths' property without an escort. Finally, when my nerves were at an all-time high, a team wearing Secret Service–style earpieces arrived to pick me up in a black golf cart.

They drove me to the main house and set me up in the green room, which was the Smiths' personal theater converted into a television production studio. Cameras were rolling, and Kelly was at the famous red table with Jada and her cohosts, Gammy and Willow. I could see them live to my left, and in front of me was a full media wall, screens showing every camera angle.

Although each episode runs for about twenty minutes, they film for two or three hours to capture the best possible material. I had plenty of time to watch Kelly's conversation before it was my turn at the red table. I even had a chance to use the bathroom and couldn't resist snapping a selfie on the toilet and sending it to my girlfriends with the caption (just in case it wasn't obvious): "Peeing in Will Smith's house!"

But mostly, I was riveted by the conversation. Kelly was telling her story of drinking again during the pandemic after years of living alcohol free.

We'll return to Kelly's story, but first, I want to introduce the ALP concept of a data point so you can understand why what Kelly said next made me cry.

Data Points

A data point is when you drink—whether it's one or several—after you set an intention not to. It can also mean drinking more than you mean to after setting a limit. A data point isn't exclusive to alcohol; it can apply to any habit or behavior. But let's focus on drinking.

The premise of a data point is that mistakes are information—simply data that helps us learn and grow. That was the lens I was looking through, and as I listened to Kelly, I realized she had an entirely different lens. For Kelly, drinking again wasn't just a data point; it was a shameful experience of failure.

This anonymous quote exactly captures how I was feeling at the time:

Why does one drink mean "game over" instead of "reread the instructions"?

185

Why was Kelly so upset about drinking again—especially since she quickly got back on track and we know that almost everyone who tries to stop drinking will drink again? What was the big deal?

Then she said something that brought tears to my eyes. Gammy, Jada's mother and cohost, asked Kelly if she was still attending her support group. Kelly shook her head and explained that more than 90 percent of the women in her group also relapsed, and the group had *dissolved.*

This is when a pit opened in my stomach.

How could this be? It was a global pandemic. People were scared, isolated, restless, and uncertain. Lives had been turned upside down. It made sense that drinking, society's favorite coping mechanism, had spiked. At This Naked Mind, we saw this, too: Our members had an increase in data points. But no one was *leaving*; our groups weren't *dissolving.* If anything, people were leaning on one another more than ever.

My mind was racing. I tried to calm myself with the fact that Kelly was doing so well—she was positive and hopeful. But my thoughts kept spinning. What about the other women in her support group? Did they give up? Were they able to get back on track?

The Rat Park experiments show us how connection, community, and acceptance are vital to successful change. Based on this, if the women in Kelly's group were drinking again *and* no longer together in community, would they really be okay?

What was so different between my experience and Kelly's? Why did the group fall apart when they needed one another the most? Why did they leave one another instead of coming closer together?

I believe this dynamic is driven by shame; the women walked away, too ashamed to return because of failure. But what exactly had they failed *at?* If we look carefully, we see they had failed at never drinking again. This is what relapse culture teaches: The goal is 100 percent, and if you fall even a fraction short, game over.

100 percent = success

99.9 percent = failure

Where else in life do we measure success this way? We don't apply this thinking to exercise, healthy eating, parenting, or relationships. Even surgeons account for mistakes, realizing a 100 percent success rate, although ideal, is impossible. And the best baseball players? They fail to hit the ball *most of the time.*

When a computer learns something new, like how to play chess, it's programmed with the rules and then it starts making moves. It learns by trying. It makes mistakes, stores the data, and plays again. The faster it makes mistakes, the faster the learning process.

Now imagine if that computer had an inner critic:

Stupid machine! I can't believe it's taking you so long to figure this out!

What's wrong with you? You're not even worth the parts you're built from.

It sounds ridiculous, right? A computer doesn't shame itself. It doesn't carry guilt. It just learns. And interestingly, that's how humans naturally learn as well.

How Babies Walk

When babies learn to walk, they fall—a lot. But it's the process of falling that helps them succeed. Each time they get back up after a fall, they strengthen the muscles in their legs. It is the failing and trying again that builds the physical strength necessary for the baby to succeed at walking.

Failure is not the opposite of success—it's the *path* to it. Without failure, there would be no success. Mistakes aren't detours; they're the way forward. Science is crystal clear on this point. Studies show that when we approach our mistakes with curiosity and compassion, they catalyze growth and change. Change isn't linear. Progress isn't linear. Success isn't linear. None of these things go simply straight up and to the right. They wind, twist, and double back, and even though progress can look like chaos, it is slowly marching forward.

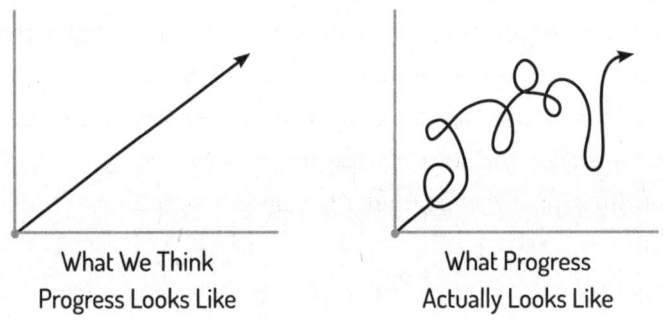

What We Think
Progress Looks Like

What Progress
Actually Looks Like

Let's stop measuring success against the impossible standard of perfection. Let's start to measure progress instead. Let's focus on how quickly we get up, not whether or not we fall down. When mistakes are treated as data, not failure, we don't quit—we grow.

The truth is that people have free will. They're going to do what they are going to do, and if they feel shame, they will just hide from us when they do it.

The idea of a data point instead of a relapse removes shame. And removing shame supports how the brain learns best: through trial and error.

Here's a simple logic question: Who is more likely to succeed in living alcohol free, the person who slips up and then quits their support group, or the person whose slipup is met with empathy, encouragement, and a supportive discussion about what they might do differently next time?

The research backs this up. Compassion, both from others and from yourself, strongly predicts long-term behavior change. These two forces go hand in hand.

Now, I know what you might be thinking: *But, Annie, if everything is a data point, then I'll just be tempted to gather more data. I'll end up on the couch, drunk, with a pint of ice cream, a remote in one hand and a bottle of wine in the other!*

I get it. I had the same fear. But I can say from science, experience, and observing thousands of our coaching clients who have successfully navigated the journey of data points, the opposite is true. When people live by a data point philosophy, their drinking drastically decreases over time.

Now, I won't sugarcoat it. You might end up on that couch—TV on, ice cream in hand, two bottles deep—*in the short term*. But you won't stay there.

What the Science Says

A 2023 systematic review of multiple studies found that higher levels of self-compassion led to reduced problem drinking. Self-compassion and self-forgiveness were identified as protective factors against harmful alcohol outcomes. A longitudinal study conducted in 2017 showed that individuals with higher self-compassion scores exhibited decreased alcohol consumption.

I love how Louise Hay put it:

You've been criticizing yourself for years and it hasn't worked. Try approving of yourself and see what happens.

A Compassion Experiment with ACT

This is a simple, practical experiment to help you respond to yourself with compassion instead of shame. Commit to twenty-eight days—four weeks—of treating yourself with kindness. Every time you make a mistake or fall into an old pattern, choose compassion and understanding over criticism.

You can simply practice being kind for the full twenty-eight days, and it will be an amazing experiment that can change your life. But if you want to go even deeper and follow the ACT compassion process, here it is:

Week 1 = Awareness
Your only task this week is to notice the voice in your head that gives you a hard time. Don't try to change anything—not the voice, not your behavior. Just listen.

Each time a harsh, critical, or unkind thought pops up, write it down. After writing it down, gently ask yourself: *Is this true?* And let your brain consider the answer. That's it.

Weeks 2 and 3 = Clarity
Each day, pick one of the thoughts you wrote down in week 1 and use the ACT process from chapter 7 to walk through it fully until you reach a "transformation thought," a more compassionate belief to practice.

Keep a running list of these new thoughts. You'll continue with them in week 4.

Week 4 = Transformation
This week is again all about paying attention to the voice in your head. When a critical thought arises, consciously replace it

with one of your new transformation thoughts from weeks 2 and 3.

And all this week (and hopefully for the rest of your life) when you slip up or do something you regret, practice talking to yourself the way you would speak to a friend: *It's okay. That wasn't ideal, but you're learning. I see you. You're doing your best.*

This is about practicing internal kindness—on purpose.

Final Reflection

At the end, reflect on your results by asking these questions:

- Did the behaviors you usually beat yourself up over begin to shift? A little or a lot?
- Did your inner peace or sense of well-being improve?
- Did your urge to escape decrease—or increase?
- What else did you notice?

The Infinite Game

In his book *The Infinite Game*, author Simon Sinek explains the importance of knowing which kind of game you're playing—a finite game or an infinite game. The danger comes when we play an infinite game as if it is a finite game.

A finite game has a clear beginning and end, fixed rules, a path to win, and a path to lose. An infinite game has no set endpoint. It changes and evolves as we do. There is no winning or losing—and the primary goal of an infinite game is: *Keep playing*.

Why does this matter? It's not just because it feels better than shaming ourselves and creating goals we can't achieve, although that's true. The real reason is because science shows us that this approach is what actually works. Research consistently proves that lasting behavior change doesn't come from guilt, shame, or punishment. It comes from grace, curiosity, compassion, and persistence.

There's no finish line. It's a process. The rules evolve as we do—as we learn more, we do better. We honor every version of ourselves that existed before today—recognizing that each one brought us to this moment. And we extend that same grace to our future selves, no matter how imperfect they turn out to be.

In an infinite game, where you measure progress rather than perfection, there is always something to celebrate. Let's say you try a thirty-day break, but you only have two alcohol-free days. That's progress! In fact, it's a 7 percent improvement. We'd never dismiss a 7 percent growth in business as meaningless. Most entrepreneurs would be thrilled. Seven percent is significant! And what if you only have two slipups in the thirty days? That's a 93 percent success rate—*amazing*.

When we play the infinite game, we approach the learning process the same way babies approach walking: try, fail, learn, build strength and resilience, and try again. No shame. No judgment. Just forward movement. And like a baby, we need encouragement, support from a community that sees our effort, not our setbacks.

On the other hand, when we treat behavior change like a finite game, we invite unnecessary pressure. That mindset has us believing that every attempt is our last chance. Even worse, learned helplessness is possible. Learned helplessness is a psychological occurrence that manifests when we no longer believe we have a chance, so we stop trying. It is one of the most dangerous results of framing our alcohol journey as a finite game—if we don't believe we can win, we are in danger of giving up altogether.

Let's stop calling it failure. Let's call it what it really is: feedback.

Remember that as long as you're still *in the game*—no matter how winding the road—there's *always* a path forward.

Data Points Versus Moderation

We can't have a conversation about data points and relapse without discussing moderation. In fact, when people hear the term *data point*, they often ask me, "Isn't that just the same as moderation?" or "Aren't you just giving people permission to drink?" Fair questions—and ones that deserve a clear answer.

A data point is when your intention and your outcome don't match. Maybe you meant to have just one glass of wine, but you ended up drinking four. Or maybe you promised yourself a night off but still poured a drink. The gap between what you planned and what actually happened is data—information you can learn from.

Moderation is different. Moderation is when you intentionally try to control your alcohol so you can keep it in your life but reduce its harm.

At some point along our journey, most of us ask ourselves: *Can I moderate?* Research supports this. Most people don't start this journey planning to quit completely. I certainly didn't. We want to drink *less* or drink *better*. The subtitle of my first book was *Control Alcohol*. It was intentional, honoring the reality that most of us begin this conversation through the "control alcohol" door, not the "stop drinking" door.

The Third Tradition

Traditional recovery models conflict with this reality. Take Alcoholics Anonymous (AA), for example. AA follows two sets of guidelines: the Twelve Steps and the Twelve Traditions. Tradition three states: The only requirement for AA membership is a desire to stop drinking.

You gain membership by attending a meeting, receiving your day-one chip, admitting that you are an alcoholic, and declaring your intention to leave alcohol behind forever. On the surface, this tradition seems reasonable and even motivational.

And I can understand why having a space where everyone is committed to quitting for good might even feel more secure than a meeting where people are still unsure if the "stop drinking" door is the one they want to walk through. But the research tells us it takes six to ten years from the time someone starts questioning their drinking to when they're ready to quit. And it's hard to fully address the problem until we face this reality.

Because AA is seen as the default solution—so much so that many don't realize alternatives exist—we leave countless people outside the door. They're left to struggle alone, feeling unwelcome until they are finally desperate enough to walk through the "stop drinking" door, often only when their lives are falling apart and they are out of options.

Tradition three immediately excludes anyone who isn't ready to quit. It sends the message: Unless today is day one of never again, you don't qualify for membership.

Moderation: The Real First Step

In the journey to take our power back from alcohol, moderation is almost always the real first step, whether we want to admit it or not. A friend who attends AA told me that when people decide to see if they can drink "normally" again, they may disappear from meetings for months or even years. When they return, *if* they return, they'll say they were doing more "research" to find out if they really have to stop drinking. This "research" is actually exploring moderation, an attempt to keep drinking but reduce the harm.

When done consciously, moderation is a way of applying the scientific method. We form a hypothesis—*If I just stick to one drink, I'll be okay*—and then we test it.

We're trying to answer questions like these:

- Can I enjoy the buzz without the hangover?

- Can I drink on date night without getting into a fight?

- Can I sip cocktails on vacation without ruining the trip?

It's human nature to want to figure things out for ourselves. We want to hold on to the benefits of drinking while reducing the pain. We test, fail, and get up again as part of the change process.

Many of us have been down the painful path of moderation. And it's also human nature to want to prevent undue pain for someone else, warning them about how painful the trial and error of moderation can be. We know the pain that moderation caused us, so we try to encourage those we care about to enter through the "stop drinking" door sooner and leave the "control alcohol" door behind.

And although the theory sounds great—wouldn't it be nice if we could simply explain the dangers of moderation and save others from years of struggle?—humans just don't work that way.

We're not ready to let go of alcohol—not because we're stubborn and need to learn the hard way, but because alcohol still feels important in a real, chemical, unconscious, survival-based way. In a way we don't understand.

Even if a thousand people say moderation is impossible, most of us still need to find that out for ourselves. That's not being stubborn—it's being human. After all, *direct, lived experience* is the most powerful way to rewrite subconscious programming.

We need to stop pretending that the path to change is linear, neat, or immediate, and that moderation is the enemy. Attempts to moderate are often part of the process, just like a baby falling while learning to walk. The stumbles needed to build the strength to move forward. Not detours, but the *path*. And if we're more honest about where people start instead of leaving them out in the cold to do more "research," we can't meet them there.

Moderation According to Science

But we can educate ourselves and be better prepared by looking at moderation from an objective, scientific perspective. We'll examine what the research says—what actually happens in our brains and bodies when we try to control alcohol. We will learn if moderation is really working for us or if we're just tricking ourselves. We'll look at this question through lived experience, science, and evidence, rather than opinion.

Before we start, I want to offer an important disclaimer: Because alcohol alters the brain, the results of your moderation experiments can be hard to interpret from your own perspective. You might think you're learning, but your brain—affected by even the very first drink—can become chemically confused, making the data unreliable.

Let's explore what science says about moderation and the key questions you should be asking yourself along a moderation journey. These insights will help you get honest about your experience and determine whether moderation is truly working or just making things worse. Here are seven important scientific truths about moderating alcohol:

1. Alcohol Creates a Need for Itself

When you reduce your drinking, your brain goes through withdrawal. This doesn't just include the physical symptoms; it also involves a mental itch. Your brain has learned to expect alcohol, and when it doesn't get it, it sends urgent signals that something is missing. This creates a powerful belief system—that alcohol is necessary for relief. That belief doesn't go away just because your body rebalances. It can persist long after the physical cravings are gone.

2. Moderation Creates Decision Fatigue

Decisions, no matter if they are big or small, take energy and can be exhausting. In psychological circles, this is known as decision fatigue. Every time you think about whether to drink, when to drink, or how much to drink, your brain uses significant energy. The more decisions you have to make, the more worn out your brain becomes. Eventually you hit a tipping point—your willpower collapses, and you override your own rules. Moderation often fails not because of lack of effort, but because your brain simply gets tired.

3. Alcohol Damages the Brain's Decision-Making Center

Alcohol directly affects the prefrontal cortex (PFC), damaging your brain's ability to make thoughtful, goal-oriented, and future-based decisions. Even one drink impairs the function of the PFC, and over time, repeated drinking causes long-term damage, making it harder to moderate. The part of your brain that promises to stick to "just one" is the very part being dulled by the substance you're trying to control.

4. Willpower Is Limited

Moderation depends heavily on willpower. But as we've learned, willpower is a limited resource, and just like a muscle, it gets fatigued. Eventually it fails. Willpower also creates internal conflict, as you are pitting the part of you that wants to drink less against the part that thinks moderation is stupid and just wants to get drunk. Moderation is a constant internal negotiation that intensifies your internal battle and drains you.

5. We Want What We Can't Have

Human psychology works against moderation. The more you tell yourself "just one," the more your brain rebels. As soon as I tell myself I am not ordering fries, *the only thing I want is fries*. Because of this, moderation feels like deprivation, like being on a constant alcohol diet. You're not satisfied, you're anxious, and part of you is plotting when and how you'll bend the rules.

6. Alcohol Makes You Thirsty

It's a small but important factor: Alcohol dehydrates you. When you're thirsty, you want to drink more. Combine that with impaired decision-making and social pressure, and it's no wonder one drink often leads to many.

7. Moderation Creates Denial

When you attempt to moderate, you're still holding on to a subconscious belief that alcohol is beneficial—otherwise, you wouldn't want to keep it in your life. That underlying desire means that when moderation begins to fail, your brain, especially the parts chemically altered by alcohol, goes into panic mode. It starts to suppress the evidence that moderation isn't working because as long as moderation seems like a viable option, your brain feels safe. It won't have to give up alcohol, something it believes is beneficial, for good. So rather than accept that moderation isn't working, your brain denies it, doing everything it can to keep you from facing the truth.

———

If you decide to explore moderation, it's important to go in with a clear plan. Know your reasons, your boundaries, and your goals. Ask yourself:

- Why do I want to moderate?

- What am I hoping moderation will give me?

- What will success look like for me?

- How will I know if it's not working?

It's also important to ask yourself who you can involve—perhaps a coach or a trusted friend—to help you clearly see the results of moderation. This helps remove the lens of personal bias that results from the chemical confusion alcohol creates in the brain.

Once you've clarified your reasons, made a plan, and involved a coach or friend, the next step is to stay mindful and connected to your experience. It's important to check in with yourself regularly—not with judgment, but with compassion and curiosity.

The following questions, adapted from *The Diagnostic and Statistical Manual of Mental Disorders*'s criteria for addiction, are designed to support honest reflection. They can help you assess whether moderation is truly working for you and give you a clearer picture of your relationship with alcohol—or any substance.

- Are you drinking more than you mean to? Or are you consistently able to stick to your limits?

- Have you tried to set rules for yourself—like "only on weekends" or "not before dinner"—only to find yourself breaking them?

- Have you devoted significant time and energy to moderating? Not just drinking, but thinking about drinking, recovering from drinking, and planning for it?

- Have you skipped out on social events, hobbies, or even your responsibilities because of how you felt after drinking?

- Has drinking in moderation kept you from showing up as the parent, partner, or professional you want to be?

- Have you kept drinking even when you know it's making things in your life worse?

- Do you notice withdrawal symptoms—headaches, anxiety, irritability, or trouble sleeping—when you cut back or go without alcohol?

- Have there been consequences during your attempts to drink in moderation? Have you missed work or taken risks that you wouldn't otherwise?

- Have there been consequences in your relationships? Are there ongoing tensions or arguments about your drinking?

- Have you avoided people, changed social groups, or withdrawn emotionally to protect your attempts to moderate?

- Are there internal cravings, urges, or mental negotiations that feel louder and more all-consuming than you want them to be?

- Once you have considered all these questions, is moderation worth it?

This is about deciding whether moderation supports or sabotages the life you want. These questions can be painful, because awareness often is. But they're also essential. Moderation without awareness isn't moderation—it's wishful thinking.

These questions aren't a diagnosis; they're a flashlight. They can reveal the real reasons—both conscious and subconscious—you're still drinking. They help you uncover the beliefs, thoughts, emotions, triggers, and patterns that are perfect to bring to the ACT process. As you do the ongoing work, unwinding your subconscious programming, you'll eventually reach a point where the question isn't "Can I moderate?" but "Why would I want to?"

———

To view the references cited in this chapter, please visit LiveNakedAF.com.

CHAPTER 16

BUILDING A JOYFUL AF LIFE, PART 1: SWITCHES

You yourself, as much as anybody in the entire universe, deserve your love and affection.
—Buddha

Life hurts—and sometimes the pain is more than we can handle.

I still remember the first time I learned that people die. I was hysterical for days. Growing up without television (we had no electricity in our cabin), I may have understood this truth a bit later than most children—around age ten—and when I did, it shattered my world.

For weeks, I lived in acute panic about my parents dying. And if I'm honest, that fear never fully left. When I lost my father, my fears were realized. One day, out of the blue, he was gone. In the early weeks after his death, I felt like couldn't even breathe.

How can I possibly live in a world without him? In the lyrics of Dean Lewis:

How do I say goodbye to someone who's been with me for my whole damn life?

Life hurts. People die. And perhaps the only certainty life offers is that everyone we know, have known, love, have loved will die. And yet we are expected to get up, go to work, function, and remember to pick up groceries on the way home. It feels like a miracle that any of us are even upright and vertical.

The need to escape being human—even for a moment—is primal. It's deeply rooted in our biology. We all reach for *something* to take the edge off. Even if that something might be as innocent as a warm cup of tea or a Netflix binge. The impulse to self-soothe is universal, inevitable, instinctual, and as old as the first people who existed.

I have three kids, and chances are, they'll try alcohol at some point. Of course I hope they don't, but I have to be realistic. I already see them reaching for things—screens, sugar, or video games—and it's this basic need to feel better, to self-soothe, that can get us in trouble if we aren't paying attention.

Some substances clearly cause more harm than others. So how can we become mindful about the things we use to navigate life? How can we set aside our biases and take an honest look at what truly works for us—especially when our culture is full of opinions, stigmas, and misinformation? Author Rob Bell illuminates this with a concept he calls *switch versus seed*.

Switch Versus Seed

Switch versus seed is a way to categorize the things we do—or take—to help us feel better. Switches work just like they sound: They're instant. When you use a switch, you get immediate relief. But that relief often comes with a downside. It is usually short-lived, and many switches cause harm, especially the ones we reach for most. Some switches cause clear, immediate harm—think a cigarette—while others carry a lower risk. Many become more harmful over time, and although not all switches are bad, most come with a cost.

As you may recall from the APA study I mentioned earlier, we often default to switches that don't truly help—like drinking, scrolling, or binge-watching TV—while ignoring the things that actually support our well-being.

Seeds, on the other hand, take more effort up front. You have to plant them, water them, and tend to them. A seed doesn't sprout the moment it hits the soil. It might take days, weeks, or even a full season to grow. Seeds require patience, intention, and consistency. Their benefits aren't immediate, but they're deep, lasting, and life-changing. Seeds create cumulative long-term relief. These are practices like exercise, meditation, and creating meaningful connection—things that take more energy but offer restoration, peace, and personal growth.

One small seed can grow into a massive tree. A tree that becomes your anchor, helping you find peace no matter what storms are happening around or inside of you.

Switches are short-term tools. Seeds are long-term strategies.

Before we dive into the most effective seeds, we need to take an honest look at switches. The idea of eliminating them entirely sounds good in theory, but it's not realistic. We need switches. That might be surprising—after all, if switches like alcohol have done so much damage, shouldn't we try to eliminate them? It's a fair question. But just like the path to abstinence often begins through moderation, behavior change rarely starts with perfection. That's simply not human nature.

Exploring Switches

Switches can help us get through the acute phases of discomfort while we work on planting seeds. They offer a brief pause, a breath of relief, a moment to rest. And sometimes that's exactly what we need. In the beginning, when you remove your main switch—like alcohol—you'll feel raw and emotionally exposed. If you don't have something else that soothes you, even temporarily, it's easy to spiral. Your brain will start shouting, *Go back to what worked!* That doesn't mean you're weak. It means your brain is searching for safety. When I stopped drinking alcohol, I consumed massive amounts of gummy bears and potentially harmful levels of caffeine. It worked for me in the short term. I'm not advising anyone to binge on sugar or espresso, but I am asking you to be gentle with yourself and consciously reach for switches that help more than they harm.

In order to have a mindful, conscious conversation about switches, we need to understand them a bit better.

The Chemistry of a Switch

The first thing to understand about switches is that they can be both things we do—like watching television, gambling, or even looking at porn—and things we take—like a Xanax, a cup of coffee, or a drink.

Interestingly, both switches we take and those we do can cause chemical addiction. For example, gambling is highly addictive, even though it doesn't involve ingesting a substance. That's because it triggers a strong dopamine response and overstimulates certain areas of the brain, similar to how alcohol works. The same is true for video games, social media, and doom scrolling. Anything that creates an instant chemical shift in the brain has the potential to become a problem, even if you're not putting anything physical into your body.

Many mind-altering substances act as switches, too, including pharmaceuticals like stimulants and prescription painkillers such as opiates and fentanyl. These substances work by chemically targeting the instinctual brain, either turning on pleasure or turning off pain. Recreational drugs like cigarettes and alcohol, as well as more dangerous substances like heroin, function the same way.

Different switches have different costs. Using heroin to take the edge off carries a very different level of risk than binge-watching your favorite show. Some switches can even be healthy—if used intentionally. One of my personal favorites is sex. Sex creates an instant chemical shift in your brain chemistry—just like any switch—and although it can be incredibly destructive if used mindlessly to escape your life, when shared with a loving partner, science shows that sex can instantly calm your mind, release endorphins, and shift your entire mood.

Switches and the Collective Unconscious

Unfortunately, our perception of both the costs and benefits of certain switches is wildly inaccurate, shaped by layers of inherited perspective rather than either science or our direct experience. Culturally, we tend to view some substances—like a glass of wine after a hard day—as completely acceptable, while others—like the idea of microdosing mushrooms—trigger fear and resistance. That reaction isn't based on research; it's rooted in the subconscious beliefs we've absorbed from the media, government, and our families.

Recently, I watched a *Saturday Night Live* skit that illustrated how deep our cultural programming is.

In the skit, a college student named Zachary casually mentions that he's microdosing mushrooms to manage stress. Two of his friends panic, treating his admission as a dangerous confession. Their over-the-top reactions—complete with frantic calls to authorities and dramatic warnings—mirror the exaggerated fear tactics of 1990s antidrug campaigns. Meanwhile, the absurdity lies in their obliviousness to their own behaviors, such as stress-eating, over-caffeinating, and of course, heavy drinking—all of which are socially accepted yet carry significant harm.

This skit underscores the irrationality of our attitudes toward different coping mechanisms and how, out of fear, we dismiss things that may be helpful—perhaps even more helpful than the solutions that come in a prescription bottle.

We need to question societal norms and consider evidence-based approaches to foster well-being, rather than relying solely on culturally ingrained beliefs.

Many substances have been criminalized as Schedule I drugs, not based on evidence but due to political agendas and governmental control. The fear and stigma around these substances has hindered medical and scientific research into their potential healing applications. As a result of this classification, pharmaceuticals have become the default for treatment of addition, some with serious and sometimes dangerous side effects.

Luckily, we are waking up to the collective unconscious, and recent studies are challenging long-held beliefs. For instance, psilocybin, the active compound in "magic mushrooms," has shown promise in treating addiction. In a randomized clinical trial, published in 2022, participants receiving psilocybin reduced heavy drinking by 83 percent.

The bottom line is that we need to stay consciously aware and take personal responsibility for what we put in our bodies—and what we do to feel better.

Switches and Brain Chemistry

To better understand switches, it helps to know that the type of switch you're drawn to—and how harmful it may be for you—can depend on your unique neurochemistry. Some switches are more harmful for certain people than others, and one key factor in this equation is your brain's balance of neurotransmitters. For example, if your brain is low in gamma-aminobutyric acid (GABA), a calming neurotransmitter, you may be more likely to use alcohol as your go-to switch. If you're low in dopamine or endorphins, you might be drawn to something else—like stimulants or prescription painkillers.

Understanding your unique chemistry matters. It's a vital part of making informed, adult decisions—decisions that reduce pain for yourself and the people you love. After looking carefully at myself, I've come to realize that some switches, like alcohol, are simply too costly to ever justify.

One of the most important things to understand about any switch—especially those with addictive potential—is that the level of harm can depend on both how and why we're using it. The moment we begin using any switch to self-soothe or escape discomfort, the risk increases. Chemical confusion in the brain intensifies, leading to increased use and, for many, a path toward dependence or addiction.

We typically reach for switches for two main reasons: to enhance our experience (fun, celebration, enjoyment) or to numb or escape our experience (stress relief or avoidance). And chemically addictive switches like alcohol carry more risk when they are used to escape. That's why planting seeds—and building a life you don't want to escape—is such an essential part of healing.

There are switches we can reach for that help us relax, unwind, or enjoy life, without the risks and consequences of alcohol. But how do we navigate the growing rise of alcohol alternatives marketed as "healthier" switches? All sorts of alternatives, such as mood-lifting nootropics and adaptogens, and calming herbs like kava and cannabis, are being marketed as alternatives to alcohol. The research is still emerging, especially around some of the more recently decriminalized options, but early findings are promising. Many of these alternatives appear to deliver similar effects with far fewer physical or emotional downsides. They seem to offer the same benefits, with significantly less harm.

As these products, such as functional beverages, calming drops, botanical blends, and herbal gummies, become more widely available, how do we make informed choices?

There are a few main ways to think about alcohol alternatives.

Short-Term Switches

Again, in my early days, I found myself reaching for gummy bears— lots of them. I kept them in my pockets and purse. This gave me a bit of the dopamine it was no longer getting from alcohol. While it wasn't a long-term solution, this temporary switch made the transition easier. It's the same reason coffee and cigarettes are often staples at support meetings—and that's not necessarily a bad thing. But I didn't want to live off sugar forever. Over time, my brain and body began to rebalance and I began to add seeds—as a result, my sugar cravings faded naturally. But giving myself permission to be extra gentle with myself during those early days was a game changer.

There are also pharmaceuticals you can talk to your doctor about that can support you through the transition. Naltrexone is one option; it reduces cravings and helps promote abstinence by blocking the brain's reward response to alcohol. Acamprosate works differently, helping restore chemical balance in the brain after drinking, especially in people who experience mood swings or sleep disruptions in early sobriety. There are even medications that make drinking physically unpleasant, helping break the brain's association with alcohol and reward.

There are also non-pharmaceutical alternative remedies that can ease the transition. Herbal remedies like kava or valerian root have been shown to help relieve stress. Cannabidiol (commonly known as CBD), a nonpsychoactive compound found in cannabis, has antioxidant properties that may protect brain cells and support the body during alcohol detoxification. In fact, studies have shown that CBD can reduce anxiety and alleviate stress, and some animal studies suggest that it may even mitigate alcohol-induced liver damage.

If, like me, alcohol was your go-to form of self-medication for decades, you may have a serious adjustment period after stopping, and that's when short-term switches can provide relief. Everyone's journey is unique. While some may find solace in nonalcoholic beverages (I love kombucha and Guinness 0), others might explore different avenues. The key is to be gentle with yourself, recognize your needs, and find switches that support your health and happiness.

But wait. What about the idea of a gateway drug? Isn't it a slippery slope? It might be. And that's why this is *your* journey. You have to be both brave enough and conscious enough to find out what is right for you. And if staying away from all switches—especially in the early days—feels best to you, then that's what you need to do.

I know people who tried nonalcoholic beers and felt so triggered and tempted that they ended up drinking again. For them, the nonalcoholic beer *was* a gateway. And there is a neurological reason to be cautious.

The taste of beer—even if it's nonalcoholic—can trigger psychological cravings.

But the opposite is also true. There is also a neurological case to be made that drinking nonalcoholic beer, without the addictive substance of alcohol, can help *weaken* the association between alcohol and enjoying friendships, sporting events, or a social barbecue. Nonalcoholic alternatives make it much easier for some people to continue socializing with their drinking friends.

That was Mike's story. After finding freedom with This Naked Mind, he explored all kinds of alcohol alternatives. He even sought out bars and nightclubs that didn't serve alcohol. At first, he found that he always needed a nonalcoholic drink in his hand while socializing with drinking friends. But over time, that association faded. Now he won't waste the calories on a nonalcoholic beer; he prefers sparkling water with lime.

For some of us, it's not just about the transition—it's about finding something that works long term. Something we can turn to when we want to celebrate, unwind, or just feel like we're really living. While the ideal of being "clean and sober" forever is an interesting idea, for most of us, it's just not realistic.

Long-Term Switches

We didn't just drink to self-medicate—we drank to socialize and celebrate. And while learning real social skills and building a life you love is the goal, it would be naive to think that we, as humans, don't also crave switches that make life a bit more enjoyable. Again, human nature. We can't just ignore reality or pretend it won't happen, as traditional models often do.

One of my closest friends, Yardley, read *This Naked Mind* in secret after her friend's therapist recommended it. Yardley had been a casual social drinker, but once she understood the true cost of alcohol, she easily gave it up. After a few years alcohol free, she started missing that social "something" and began to explore alcohol alternatives.

Yardley lives in California, where cannabis is legal and widely used, and the term "Cali sober"—using cannabis but not alcohol—is popular. She began researching and experimenting with CBD and eventually found THC gummies. Now she takes a gummy a few nights a week to relax. She'll also have one before social events where she knows others will be drinking.

It works for her. Compared to alcohol, the benefits are greater, and the costs—so far—have been minimal. Will it stay that way? Only time will tell. But right now, Yardley is consciously and intentionally choosing a long-term switch that works better for her—with more benefits and less harm than alcohol.

When it comes to switches, we can experiment and decide if there are things that carry less harm than alcohol that we want to incorporate—*intentionally*—into our lives. The key is to be aware of the habits you're forming. Ask yourself: Are these new switches truly serving you? Or do they carry the same risks and consequences alcohol once did? As you move through this journey, it's important to stay conscious of your patterns and your reasons. Support yourself with compassion but also with clarity. The goal isn't to swap one harmful habit for another—it's to heal.

When Switches Cause Problems

Because nearly all switches can cause chemical addiction, we need to be careful and mindful of the potential harm. I saw this most recently with my daughter's video games. She loves playing *Roblox* with her cousin, who lives far away, and when they first started playing together, it was a joyful shared time. I even marveled at how these two little girls could "hang out" in a virtual world as if they were getting together for a playdate. But eventually, after long gaming sessions, my daughter would become restless, irritable, and bored with everything else. If she wasn't playing, she was thinking about playing. She stopped enjoying activities she'd once loved, and suddenly everything was *boring*. When "I'm bored" became her favorite phrase, it was clear her brain was becoming chemically confused and even dependent.

Rather than banning the games altogether, Brian and I gathered data. We talked about what was happening, limited screen time to break the dependency, and gave ourselves full permission to take away the game entirely. The last thing we wanted was for her to experience the hallmark of a switch causing dependency—when playing the game became the only fun moments in her day while stealing her happiness from all her non-gaming moments.

Not all switches are created equal. Some help us relax, connect, or recharge in ways that align beautifully with the life we want to live. Others quietly pull us away from it—chipping at our energy, joy, and relationships, often without our even noticing.

ACT Questions for Switches

Awareness, clarity, and transformation are essential ingredients for navigating switches. We can't know if something is helping or hurting unless we pause to really look. That's why I developed a few simple but powerful questions that lean into the principles of ACT. These are questions I use as I navigate my own switches as well as when parenting my children. They allow us to look within and find our own guidance, asking ourselves if the switch is doing us more good than harm.

Start with the Benefits
- What are the benefits of this switch to me personally?
- What are the benefits of this switch to the people around me?

Consider the Costs
- What are the potential costs or harms of this switch to me personally?

- What are the costs or harms of this switch to those around me?

Since many switches alter your brain chemistry—whether it's sugar, cannabis, video games, shopping, or prescription drugs—we need to make sure our switch of choice isn't hijacking our ability to choose. In addition to the science-based questions from the previous chapter on moderation, here are a few additional questions to spot the subtler signs of emotional or chemical dependence:

- Do I think about this switch when I'm not using it?
- Are those thoughts distracting me or stealing joy from the present moment?
- Do I feel frustrated, sad, or irritable when I can't use this switch?
- Have things I used to enjoy become less fun without this switch?
- Does this switch create internal conflict or cognitive dissonance?

These questions aren't here to judge. They're here to guide. To help you make conscious, compassionate choices about how you care for yourself. To remind you that the goal isn't perfection. The goal is a life that feels good and true—on your terms.

My Personal Switches

You may have noticed that—aside from gummy bears and coffee—I haven't told you what switches I use or which ones I recommend. That's intentional, for three important reasons.

First, because you're reading this book, your brain will subconsciously give my words authority. As we've learned, influence from perceived authority figures can bypass conscious thought, directly influencing the subconscious. Your brain may, at a subconscious level, interpret what I do as what you should be doing. I take the responsibility of authority very seriously. And since my experience is a case study of one, it's not enough data for you to be influenced by. But it is important that you also take care to make your own choices, rather than allowing me—or anyone—that level of authority in your life.

Second, I have my own unique brain chemistry, health history, diagnoses, and medications. What works for me might not work for you. Sharing my switches would invite bias and comparison and perhaps unintentionally steer you away from what your body and mind truly need.

Third, I believe you already have within you the most significant wisdom for your life. That wisdom lives in your experience, your self-awareness, and your willingness to get curious and explore what works for you. You can feel your body; you know its signals. You don't need to follow me or anyone. You can follow you.

After my dad passed away, and I was going through his things, I came across a letter he had written to twelve-year-old Annie Grace. He'd given it to me for my first wilderness solo, camping alone in the wild for twenty-four hours. The guides hiked us into the woods, leaving each of us at a different site, one mile apart, without food or a tent but with a sleeping bag and a tarp in case it rained.

We were also given a bottle of water and a single Snickers bar. The challenge was simple: If your Snickers was untouched in the morning, you passed. If it was eaten, you failed. Along with the tarp, water, and Snickers bar, we each received letters from our parents.

All these years later, I found that letter. In it he said:

The importance of being yourself to the fullest and highest possible degree always becomes clearer in situations where you have to rely <u>only</u> on yourself.

You can be trusted with you. When you slow down and pay attention, you start to understand what truly serves you and what doesn't. Whether your path is traditional, alternative, or somewhere in between, the key is learning to trust yourself. Only you can hear the quiet signals of your own biology—what helps, what harms, and what heals. This is an inside job.

You are the adult in this story. You get to decide what's right for you—whether that's moderation, switching to something else, or walking away entirely. As you begin to choose yourself first and make choices that fit your life, your inner wisdom will grow clearer.

If something genuinely feels good to you—when you consider the full picture, including the costs and benefits—and you stay awake to the impact, then using a switch isn't failure. It's part of your unique journey toward healing and wholeness.

Now that we've explored switches, let's turn to my favorite part of an alcohol-free toolbox: seeds. Unlike switches, which can carry the risk of harm or dependency, seeds are inherently beneficial. They don't deliver immediate gratification; they take time, attention, and care. But their impact is deep and lasting. In my experience, seeds build something far more powerful and life-giving than anything quick or convenient ever could.

———

To view the references cited in this chapter, please visit LiveNakedAF.com.

CHAPTER 17

BUILDING A JOYFUL AF LIFE, PART 2: SEEDS

I believe depression is legitimate. But I also believe that if you don't exercise, eat nutritious food, get sunlight, get enough sleep, consume positive material, surround yourself with support, then you aren't giving yourself a fighting chance.
—Jim Carrey

When I first stopped drinking, I clung to my switches—sugar, coffee, and social media. Anything to take the edge off. And honestly, they helped. They softened the edges and gave me something to hold on to when everything felt uncertain.

Over time, I began to see that while switches can soothe us, they can't sustain us. They're like matches—they spark, they flare, and then they're gone. You can't build a life you love on borrowed comfort. For that, you need seeds.

Seeds take time. They need patience and consistency. They don't offer the instant hit of relief, but they do offer something far more powerful—roots. One of my parents' hippie traditions was to bury our placentas under a sapling when we were born. Both my brother and I have trees growing at my dad's cabin—trees that have slowly matured over decades. I remember being so excited when, at three years old, my mom and I planted my brother's tree. But after we planted it, for years, it looked like nothing was happening.

While visiting the cabin for my dad's seventy-seventh birthday, I stood under my brother's tree, one we planted more than forty-five years earlier. It is very tall now and beautiful, and its shade on that hot September day was life-giving.

When life gets heavy, the shelters you've grown—those small daily choices, the morning walks, choosing nourishing food over junk, practicing stillness, the effort to build lasting relationships—become your trees. The forest that holds you, shields you from the wind, and cools you with its shade.

When I live in the shade of the seeds I've planted, my life feels rich and joyful. There are days that feel so amazing that I can't believe one person can hold this much joy. That's what seeds do. They grow slowly but steadily—and they change everything.

The best part? Once your seeds start growing, it becomes easy to move beyond the switches that carry a cost. And you won't need to white-knuckle your way through change because you'll have something better—something more meaningful—to nourish you.

I want to share some of my favorite seeds, which are also the ones science proves most effective. But I know that if I mention things like exercise or meditation, the eye-rolling will begin. And I get it. These things can be hard, uncomfortable, and discouraging.

And if we're honest, most of us have tried them before without success. That makes them feel even harder—the feeling of failure, paired with the belief that we've already "been there, done that," becomes resistance. We hear suggestions like these and immediately, often subconsciously, we tune out, thinking, *Yeah, yeah. I've heard it all before.*

So how do we break through the personal bias and unconscious resistance that keep us from doing the things we know will help? I've written this chapter in a way that will lower that resistance. I'm not saying you'll read this chapter and suddenly wake up tomorrow a vegan–

yogi–weight lifter who meditates. But I am saying that this chapter is designed to disarm resistance so that you, on your own terms, feel safe and powerful.

You can treat these tools like a smorgasbord, choosing and experimenting with what works best for you. Approach seeds as part of the infinite game, one of the most joyful games of all, a game of building a life that brings you happiness both now and in the long term. Let's start with the seed I had the most subconscious resistance to: *meditation*.

Meditation

New research shows that regular meditation practice helps people quit smoking, lose weight, kick a drug habit, and stay sober. Just five minutes of daily meditation is a powerful brain training exercise.
—Dr. Kelly McGonigal

Did I guess it? Are you groaning, *No, not meditation?*
Maybe you've said:

- *I've tried it. I'm terrible at it.*

- *It's so boring.*

- *I don't have time.*

- *It's just not my thing.*

I get it. I felt the same way. The idea of being still and quiet with my own thoughts? Terrifying. For those of us with busy, anxious minds, meditation feels like a setup for failure.

My parents always meditated. They described it as "no mind," "no thoughts." For me, meditation was impossible. As an anxious teen, I couldn't quiet my mind for two seconds, let alone twenty minutes. Because I felt like I was doing it wrong, I gave up. As I got older, I kept hearing how effective meditation could be, but I still resisted it. It seemed like a waste of time—especially for someone like me, who uses busyness to manage anxiety. Meditation didn't feel peaceful; it felt torturous. I couldn't even sit still, let alone clear my thoughts.

But about a year after I stopped drinking, I started searching for ways to further improve my mental health and continue to manage my depression and anxiety. That's when I discovered *The Power of Now* by Eckhart Tolle. He introduced a practice so simple it surprised me: Pause for a few seconds, several times a day, and just notice what's happening around you.

That's it.

So I did. I'd pause while making breakfast or rushing out the door. I'd notice sunlight, the dog, a bird near the window. At first I had to set alarms to remember. But within a couple weeks, I started craving those pauses—and no longer needed reminders.

It was the first time I found myself witnessing my thoughts instead of being ruled by them. Those tiny moments of presence were making a big difference. And if just a few seconds of stillness felt that powerful, I wondered what a few minutes would feel like, and my exploration of both mindfulness and meditation began.

What the Science Says

Again, alcohol damages your prefrontal cortex—the CEO of your brain. This is the part responsible for decision-making, impulse control, and planning for the future. Even one drink affects your PFC, and over time, the damage adds up, making it harder to stay alcohol free. Meditation is one of the few tools proven to strengthen this vital part of the brain. It increases blood flow to the prefrontal cortex and, like lifting weights, builds cognitive strength over time.

Today's research confirms what's been said for thousands of years: Meditation works. It reduces anxiety and depression, sharpens your focus, and improves your ability to regulate emotions. It builds mental resilience and helps you step out of old unhealthy patterns—making it a potent practice for lasting emotional and behavioral change. For me, meditation has made me calmer. I don't snap at my kids as easily. I handle stress better. I feel more present and more like myself.

You don't need to meditate for a long time. Regular, short bursts of meditation can improve attention, self-control, and impulse regulation. MRI studies confirm physical changes in the brain after meditation. And you don't need to be "good" at meditation for it to work. New meditators experience these changes, too.

Candles and cross-legged poses aren't necessary. Just find a quiet, comfortable place. Sit. Close your eyes. Bring your attention to your body, your breath. That's it. You might get distracted—totally normal. When it happens, just notice. Label the thought if it helps (*planning, worrying, remembering*), and return to your breath. Another trick: Repeat a phrase silently. I use "Be still": Inhale "be" and exhale "still." This helps anchor my thoughts when my mind feels busy.

Tips and Tricks

Here are a few more helpful tips to try as you consider meditation as one of the seeds to plant in your alcohol-free life.

Failing Isn't Failing

At first I thought I was failing because I couldn't stop thinking. But I've since learned that getting distracted is the point. Meditation isn't about stopping your thoughts; it's about noticing when you've drifted and gently bringing your focus back. The fact that you noticed *is* the point—that's the rep that builds the muscle of meditation, the action that builds the new neural pathways and strengthens your brain. Every time you bring your attention back to your breath, you're literally rewiring your mind.

Start Small

Set yourself up to win. Don't start with ten minutes; start with two. Even one counts. When I started to meditate, I began with three minutes a day. That small, easy-to-meet commitment changed everything. Eventually, I attended a meditation retreat where I meditated for five hours straight. I'm still amazed I didn't need a bathroom break. Importantly, for the start-small strategy to work, your goals must feel easy and almost effortless. Otherwise, you'll be forcing something that doesn't feel aligned. Habit expert James Clear popularized the idea of micro-commitments in his bestselling book *Atomic Habits* by sharing his habit of doing just one push-up a day.

Frequency Over Length

The research is clear: Shorter, frequent meditation sessions work better than long, occasional ones. Two or three minutes a day is enough to start. It's consistency that rewires your brain, not duration.

Make It a Treat

This is your moment. You don't have to fix or solve anything. You don't have to prove anything. Just breathe. Just be. That's the gift. This is your opportunity to put the most valuable and powerful resource you have—your ability to direct your conscious attention—toward what is happening within. For me, this can feel like the ultimate act of self-care.

Be Flexible

Meditation can happen anywhere. I often meditate in my car while waiting to pick up my kids. A few quiet minutes with the windows down, eyes closed, breath slow. It's powerful, and I miss it when I skip it.

———

The bottom line is that alcohol damages your brain. Meditation heals it. Meditation strengthens your focus, restores emotional balance, and reconnects you to yourself. You'll feel it, little by little, from the inside out. Start small. Stay curious. And remember: The goal of meditation isn't to clear your mind; it's to witness it. That moment of awareness is where the shift begins.

And sometimes—if you're lucky—it even gets quiet.

Movement and Exercise

Exercise turns out to be the closest thing to a wonder drug . . . it not only relieves ordinary, everyday stress, but it's as powerful an antidepressant as Prozac.
—Dr. Kelly McGonigal

Moving is essential to a joyful and peaceful life, yet for many of us, exercise feels like a chore. We associate movement with obligation, something we "should" do. But what if it could become something you genuinely want to do? What if it felt like a gift instead of a task? Think back to when you were a kid between ages seven and eleven. How did you love to move your body? That joy is still inside you, waiting to be rediscovered.

What the Science Says

Exercise isn't just good for your body; it's also transformational for your mind. It reduces anxiety and depression, improves cognitive function, boosts self-esteem, and even helps your brain grow new cells, especially in the prefrontal cortex—which is great news because the prefrontal cortex is the part of the brain alcohol damages.

Years ago, I injured my knee and couldn't run, bike, or do tae kwon do. My mood tanked. I eventually turned to meditation, which helped immensely, but the truth was clear: Movement isn't optional. It is crucial to my well-being.

Why do we struggle with exercise? It can be because we don't extend the same care to ourselves that we do to others. We'll walk our dogs, rain or shine, but we ignore our own body's need for movement. Our cultural perspective is also a factor; it seems we've made the word *exercise* synonymous with something physically boring and unpleasant.

To change our perspective toward our body, we need to start with love—not the conditional kind based on how our bodies look, but the deep, nurturing love we would offer a child. Your body shows up for you every day. It's literally the reason you are here. No body, no life. I think it's fair to say the body deserves to be treated with respect and compassion rather than judgment and criticism.

Try this simple but powerful practice: Take fifteen to twenty minutes, put on some music, and write a letter to your body. Thank it. Think, deeply, about it. Apologize if you need to. Acknowledge how it has never stopped supporting you. This act alone can reframe your relationship with exercise—it can become an act of devotion rather than a form of punishment. We can care for our own bodies the same way we might care for a young child. When we shift into appreciation, even small movements, like a big stretch first thing in the morning, feel like a gift.

Our bodies don't like being still. While lounging around all day might sound appealing, research shows that passive rest doesn't feel good for very long. In fact, studies reveal that active hobbies make us significantly happier than passive ones. Other research shows you are *three hundred times* more likely to feel joy playing a sport than watching one on TV. Some studies even show we're often happier at work than doing nothing at all.

Tips and Tricks

Here are a few more helpful tips to try as you consider exercise as one of your seeds.

Create Momentum and Milestones

Studies show that we thrive in an atmosphere of growth. When our brains are focused on reaching the next milestone, the discomfort of exercise fades. That's why competitive sports are so popular—there's always something to work toward, something to win.

You can create this for yourself. At This Naked Mind, we host step challenges a few times a year. Coaches and team members compete to hit their step goals—and it's the only time of year I consistently get my steps. For those few weeks, getting outside for a walk feels easy, as the community carries us along. Momentum is another reason I love martial arts; with belt levels and milestones, growth and progress are built in.

Micro Commitments

Just like meditation, this is also true for exercise: A five-minute walk is more effective than a sixty-minute session you'll never repeat. A 2010 study found major benefits from just five minutes of regular exercise. My best habits started small: one minute of meditation, two sentences of journaling, a quick walk. Over time, these grew into lifelong practices.

Make It Playful

I don't enjoy traditional workouts. But kicking, punching, yelling, and breaking boards? That's fun. It's physically intense and emotionally freeing—my brain turns off during the practice; it has to. After I quit drinking, my family joined a martial arts studio. It gave us connection, joy, and purpose—all without alcohol.

Temptation Bundling

Temptation bundling is a strategy that involves pairing what your brain sees as a chore with a treat. Watch your favorite show while walking on the treadmill, or listen to a great podcast while doing the dishes. I love bundling social time with movement—for me, exercising with friends makes it effortless. Exercise doesn't have to be solitary. Join a walking group, cycling club, or gym class. Movement can be social, even celebratory, especially when drinking isn't the focus.

Keep a Record

Recording your direct experience is a powerful tool for future motivation. On days when you're too tired or when you're tempted to skip a workout, it can be the reminder that gets you back in the game.

One evening, I'd had an awful day and was miserable, crying in the parking lot of our tae kwon do studio, feeling certain exercise wasn't the answer. I just wanted to sit in my Jeep and feel sorry for myself.

I couldn't imagine feeling better, and I certainly didn't think a tae kwon do lesson would help. But I always love a good experiment, so I decided to find out. I recorded a tearful voice memo to myself about how I felt and why going in was stupid—but then I went. Ninety minutes later, I recorded a second voice memo, and I was laughing and elated about how good I felt. And since exercise creates a physical afterglow—the good feelings last well beyond the workout itself—I felt better into the next day. I now listen to that second voice memo whenever I need motivation.

Breathwork

Because the "higher power" language in traditional recovery can be a barrier, I've intentionally stayed away from spirituality, but it's hard for me to tell you about breathwork without telling you about my direct experience of its spiritual aspects. Before we talk about anything spiritual, I want to give us a definition of the term. When I think of *spiritual*, I think about the science that is now proving what the ancients knew, that we each exist within a vast, mysterious system. A system of life, death, and ultimately, energy. I think of how all around me, when I am curious, I find the mystery, the unexplainable, and even the magical. I think about the universe—the entire known system that we exist within—and I can't help but notice the intelligent design of it all. And breathwork is the perfect time to introduce the spiritual dimension to this book because recognizing the mystery is essential to building a life you don't want to escape.

Breathwork is intentional, focused breathing—sometimes guided— and it can be profoundly healing. I was first introduced to it by my friend and biohacker, Anthony DiClemente.

Through breathwork I felt fully connected—to everyone and everything. Moments like these move my faith in this wonderful, intelligent, mystery past *belief* and into *knowledge*. Moments when I felt gratitude for the things I haven't been able to explain and joy in things I can't yet name.

What the Science Says

Breathwork's emotional and physical benefits are well documented, and it is a powerful tool for calming the body and mind. When you practice intentional deep breathing, it activates your autonomic nervous system, which helps reduce anxiety and improve mood. Over time, breathwork also boosts brain function by enhancing focus, processing speed, and decision-making.

What's happening is this: Slow, steady breathing sends signals from your lungs to your heart and brain, creating a calming feedback loop. This helps your entire system work in better balance. Certain breathing techniques have even been shown to help people recover from burnout. In short, how you breathe can change how you feel—mentally, emotionally, and physically.

One simple and powerful method is the four-seven-eight breath:

1. Sit comfortably and close your eyes.

2. Inhale quietly through your nose for four seconds.

3. Hold your breath for seven seconds.

4. Exhale through your mouth with a whooshing sound for eight seconds.

5. Repeat four times, and notice the shift in your body and mind.

For more intensity, try inhaling for another seven seconds before your exhale. You can gradually lengthen the inhale—go from seven seconds to fourteen if it still feels good. Customize it. Anthony would tell you to challenge yourself because the magic is found on the other side of discomfort—which seems to be true for most of life's most magical things.

Sunshine, Nature, and Dirt

We overlook the simplest tools because they seem too obvious. Getting outside, touching the earth, and soaking in some sunlight can drastically improve how you feel.

What the Science Says

Spending time outside is one of the simplest and most effective ways to improve your mental health—and the science proves it. Sunlight acts as a natural antidepressant, helping lift your mood and regulate your sleep-wake cycle. Activities like gardening boost serotonin levels in the brain, which can ease anxiety and create a sense of calm. Even a ninety-minute walk in nature has been shown to reduce anxious thinking. Being outdoors also helps your body recover from stress more quickly and thoroughly. This results in increased happiness, greater self-confidence, and a deeper sense of well-being—all by simply reconnecting with the natural world. Don't underestimate the power of the outdoors. You don't need anything fancy—just fresh air and a patch of earth can help restore balance.

You can enhance this connection through primal grounding. Walk barefoot on natural surfaces like grass, rocks, soil, or sand. Studies show that this practice allows your body to absorb the earth's electrons, which may help reduce inflammation, improve sleep, and boost overall well-being. Some studies suggest that grounding can positively influence mood and decrease stress levels by stabilizing the body's electrical environment.

Scientists believe this is because the earth's natural frequency, known as the Schumann resonance, resonates at approximately 7.83 hertz. And a frequency of 7.83 hertz aligns with the alpha brain wave state, which is associated with relaxation and mental clarity. Alpha brain waves are measured when we are calm, relaxing, focused, or meditating.

The next time you feel overwhelmed or disconnected, step outside and feel the ground beneath your feet. This simple act serves as a powerful reminder of your connection to the world and everything in it. Even the beautiful and mysterious aspects of some of my most peaceful moments are in the vast wilderness, where I feel small—and so do my problems.

Music and Dancing

I was crying while driving and Turner, my son, wanted to make me feel better. He took my phone to queue up a playlist of songs he'd heard me listening to lately. Within twenty minutes, I was laughing through my tears. I felt lighter. I could breathe again.

What the Science Says

Music is more than entertainment; it's medicine. A meta-analysis of more than three thousand studies shows that music can significantly reduce anxiety, ease symptoms of depression, and even help relieve physical pain. Tibetan singing bowl meditations can calm the nervous system and reduce fatigue and tension, all while boosting mood. Whether you're moving your body or simply listening, music has the power to shift your emotional state and support your well-being. Dancing offers additional benefits. It improves body image, supports mental health, and enhances overall quality of life.

Dancing—oh, groan! Double groan. I get it. I've felt that way, too. Somewhere along the way, many of us developed a subconscious resistance to dancing. We made it wrong. Just the thought of dancing brings up discomfort—feelings in the body and critical thoughts in the mind. We tell ourselves dancing is silly, only for children, dark nightclubs, and free-spirited hippies.

But if we step outside our bias, it's easy to see the truth: Dancing is a powerful feel-good activity. Moving to music is one of the first things babies do, even before they can crawl. It's universal, across every culture and generation. And when we allow ourselves to give in to it, to the silliness of it and the joy of it, and really dance, it can be life-giving. Science says so.

But we are resistant because somewhere along the line we internalized a resistance to dancing. We may have been teased—or teased others—for how our bodies moved. And in that moment, perhaps a program was written, one that said that dancing was no longer about how it feels but how it looks.

It's time to rewrite that.

How? By dancing. Maybe it's alone at first, in an empty house. Or maybe you are brave enough to look up local alcohol-free dance events, such as ecstatic dance, where everyone goes nuts, dancing like their childlike selves and learning how to dance for the *feel of it*.

To plant this seed, you have to face your dancing demons. Look them straight in the eye. Move toward the fear, not away from it. Let go of the noise, the subconscious voices insisting you just aren't someone who dances.

———

These practices—breathwork, meditation, exercise, sunshine, dirt, music, and dancing—are just a few of the incredible science-backed seeds we can begin to plant to support our emotional well-being and restore balance to our nervous system.

My friend Mike started planting seeds seven years ago when he stopped drinking. A few years into his journey, he sent me a selfie video. Smiling at the camera, he said:

> *"Annie! Who am I? I've lost sixty pounds. I'm out biking in the sunshine and prioritizing my health. I even do yoga now. I hardly recognize myself—and I love my life! I couldn't have done it without you—thank you so much!"*

I love the Jim Carrey quote that I shared at the beginning of this chapter. I've struggled with depression and anxiety my entire life, and I've explored it all, from traditional antidepressants, to self-medicating with alcohol, to some of the most radical alternative treatments. And I've come to see that Jim is right: It's the seeds—like enough sleep, nutrition, exercise, friendship, and sunlight—that have made the biggest difference in my mental health.

That doesn't mean switches don't have their place. They do. Just like I need prescription lenses to correct my vision, I'll probably always need some sort of chemical support to rebalance my brain. There's nothing wrong with that. But when it comes to living well, even living with true joy, we are not powerless—not even close.

One of the core principles of ALP is also one of the most obvious yet overlooked truths about being human: We are *biological* beings. I've tended to ignore this, especially in my youth. I deprived my body of sleep, nutritious food, sunlight, and movement. I flooded it with alcohol and demanded more from it than I would ever ask of another person.

And still, it showed up for me.

These days, when I'm doing the right things (and I'm not always doing the right things), my life is truly joyful—*joyful AF*. And in my experience, when you've tended enough seeds to awaken joy, your need for switches disappears.

———

To view the references cited in this chapter, please visit LiveNakedAF.com.

CHAPTER 18

HOW TO AUTHENTICALLY INFLUENCE OTHERS

Example is not the main thing in influencing others. It is the only thing.
—Albert Schweitzer

Have you ever noticed that you're changing faster than the people around you? You're outgrowing some of the things you used to do together? This shows up in many areas of life, but with drinking, we can really see it.

As comedian Jim Gaffigan points out, if you say, "I don't eat mayonnaise," no one questions you. But skip the wine, and suddenly it's *Are you okay?* or *Would you rather I not drink in front of you?* How funny would it be if we did the same thing with mayo? *Excuse me, but I'm going to have some mayo now—is that okay with you? Will it trigger you? Do you need me to step outside to eat my mayo?*

As light as that joke is, reality is tougher: Change—even the good kind—often creates distance in relationships. How do we stay close to others while staying true to ourselves? And what happens when other people's drinking starts to concern us? How do we set boundaries and offer support without enabling or judging?

These are big questions. And the answers begin with one of the most powerful tools in human relationships: differentiation. Understanding differentiation gives you the best chance of influencing others—without losing yourself in the process.

Soon after I stopped drinking, Brian came to me and said, "Not drinking is your thing. I have no intention of stopping." At first I was really upset. I thought my decision might inspire him to stop—or at the very least, that he'd want to support me by drinking less. Isn't that what husbands are supposed to do?

But this wasn't open to negotiation. And while I was disappointed, I can now see the gift. He helped me recognize something vital—where I end and where he begins. His choice wasn't mine to make; it was *his*. And my choice to live alcohol free wasn't about him; it was about *me*. I didn't realize it at the time, but his statement was more than just honest; it was a potent example of differentiation.

What Is Differentiation?

Think of a healthy cell in the human body. It must have a strong, intact membrane that allows it to maintain internal integrity and perform its functions without outside interference. The cellular wall keeps the cell alive. The cell must remain separate to survive. But it cannot be disconnected; if you isolate the cell from the rest of the body, it will die. It must be separate, but it cannot be alone.

A healthy cell must be *both* self-contained *and* remain connected to the larger system. This is also what healthy differentiation looks like. Differentiation means choosing your own path with alcohol—based on your personal values, goals, and needs—while staying connected to people who are making different choices. You don't have to cut yourself off from friends, family, or social situations. You can be independent *and* connected.

Working to maintain this balance between independence and connectivity is incredibly healthy. Neurologically, it lowers anxiety, strengthens identity, and increases self-worth. But here's the catch: It's not easy. Why? Because we're wired—both biologically and culturally—to do the opposite. As we've learned, our nervous system is programmed to equate difference with danger. When we choose something different from what everyone around us is choosing, our body interprets that decision as a threat even before anyone around you reacts. We feel fear—fear of rejection, of rocking the boat. And sometimes before we even try, we give up. We fold and lose track of who we are, just to stay safe.

When we lack differentiation, everyone suffers. Our relationships become strained—not because we're different, but because we don't know how to stay connected *as* different. When we understand and start living as our full selves while in relationships with others, it can change everything about the quality of the relationships we have with the people we care most about.

To understand what differentiation *is*, we will explore what differentiation *is not* and why we so often fall into one of these two reactive patterns, either fusion or cutoff:

- **Fusion:** When we blend with others and lose our sense of self.

- **Cutoff:** When we disconnect from others to preserve ourselves.

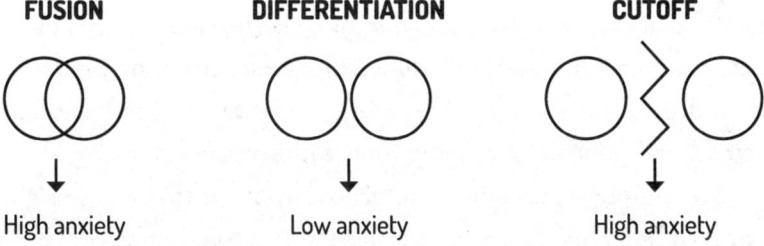

FUSION	DIFFERENTIATION	CUTOFF
High anxiety	Low anxiety	High anxiety

Differentiation Is Not Fusion

Similar to the membrane of a cell breaking and the cell becoming sick, when we're emotionally fused to another person, their moods, words, and actions start to dictate our own. We lose our sense of self. We become like a cell without a wall—vulnerable and reactive.

I remember one night when I was out to dinner with friends and the first person in our group ordered a beer. As the waitress went around the table, no one else ordered alcohol. The woman who'd ordered the beer changed her order. On the surface, it might have looked like she was making a healthy choice. But in reality, her change of heart was a symptom of fusion. Her decision wasn't truly her own; it was a reaction to the group. And what if everyone had ordered a drink? Even if she didn't want one, the internal pressure to fit in would have likely led her to follow along.

Fusion shows up in subtle but powerful ways. If someone I love is in a bad mood, it ruins my mood. If others are hurting, I don't allow myself to be happy. If someone has it worse than I do, I don't allow myself to heal, imagining my pain as something I should be able to handle, because it's not that bad. In fusion, I find myself carrying other people's emotions or behaviors as if they were my own. When we live in fusion, we lose the protective boundary of self. And without that boundary, we also lose the clarity that allows us to make intentional, self-led choices.

In Dr. Roberta M. Gilbert's work on differentiation, fusion is described as a dynamic in which individuals become so emotionally connected that their sense of self is diminished. The emotional boundaries between them blur, making it difficult for each person to think, feel, or act independently. This kind of entanglement can lead to increased reactivity and difficulty managing stress within relationships.

Said simply, we become so influenced by others that we lose sight of our own thoughts, values, or preferences. In a fused state, people tend to react intensely to each other's emotional signals, creating high anxiety. In extreme cases of fusion, you may not feel safe to think your own thoughts or feel your own feelings, or even choose your own behaviors, for fear of rejection or disconnection. This sounds extreme, but shows up all the time—especially when someone decides to live alcohol free. I've heard countless stories from people who felt proud, clear, and empowered . . . until they reunited with old friends and ordered a drink just to fit in. That's fusion.

Our subconscious fear of rejection is primal, powerful. Even if we don't think it should affect us, it does. If we say yes to a drink when we really mean no—just to keep the peace or to avoid disappointing someone—that's fusion. We made our decision based on someone else's comfort rather than our own truth, which often brings anxiety or resentment later. And many of us live like this, across *all* areas of life. We don't know how to say no. We've never felt the permission to choose ourselves first. And, as the airplane safety announcements make crystal clear, we must put on our own oxygen mask before we help others.

Fusion is exhausting. It leads to tension, conflict, anxiety—and often fighting.

At first I wanted to fight with Brian about his drinking. I had all the "proof" that alcohol was bad. I wanted him to quit so that I would feel supported. Even if I had won that fight and he'd stopped drinking, it wouldn't have been a choice that he was making for himself; he would have done it just to please me. Brian wouldn't have been internally aligned with his choice, starting a battle inside him. And that conflict would bubble up over time, threatening resentment and disconnection.

When we're fused, our relationships become filled with stress and often fighting. Eventually we hit a breaking point—and when we do, the most common reaction isn't to heal, it's to swing right past differentiation to the opposite extreme and to *cut off*.

Differentiation Is Not Cutoff

Dr. Murray Bowen describes cutoff as a way we try to reduce emotional tension by pulling away from others. It can look like going "no contact" with family. More often it looks like emotional distance; you build internal walls around your heart so you feel safe. And while this kind of cutoff might bring short-term relief, it also brings something else: loneliness, anxiety, and even more disconnection.

We don't cut off because we've grown beyond a relationship; we cut off because we're emotionally fused and unable to find a peaceful resolution. A version of cutoff becomes our next strategy to manage relational anxiety and discomfort.

Dr. Michael E. Kerr explains that emotional cutoff—where individuals distance themselves from a relationship to relieve tension—may bring short-term relief, but it does not resolve the underlying emotional fusion. Instead, this distancing often leaves the emotional ties intact beneath the surface, allowing unresolved issues to persist or intensify over time. Cutoff may ease the pressure, but without differentiation, the fusion remains—and often grows stronger.

Because it eases the pressure, cutoff can feel like a solution, but it comes at a cost. It's like building a wall to keep yourself safe—only to realize you've locked yourself in. You might feel protected, but you probably also feel stuck and alone.

You can see how this plays out when it comes to alcohol. You try to resist the pressure to drink, but eventually it feels like the only way you can stay true to yourself is by pulling away from your friends, your partner, your parents, your neighbors, or sometimes your entire social circle. In the short term, that kind of reset might be useful, but it's not the same as healing.

Healthy differentiation moves beyond both fusion and cutoff. It is the ability to stay connected while choosing your own path. We will look more closely at what differentiation looks like in a moment. But first we need to discuss a few emotional habits that signal we are not differentiated. These habits are incredibly common, quietly toxic, and often overlooked. Once you see them, you'll spot them everywhere. And that's a good thing; as we now know, awareness is the first step toward change.

Overing

When we aren't differentiated, we fall into two common traps: over-responsibility and over-functioning. These patterns blur the line between what's ours and what's not—what belongs to others and what belongs to us. They create exhaustion, dysfunction, and resentment. They drain our energy and steal our peace.

Over-Responsibility

I first heard the term *over-responsibility* from relationship expert Stacey Martino. My body physically reacted as I recognized this pattern in me, just from the word *over-responsibility*. Until that moment, I didn't know it was possible to be *too* responsible. But I'd been living it since I was four years old.

After one explosive fight, my parents split up. I was a few months away from turning five years old, hiding behind our woodpile as I watched my mom leave. My father didn't cry—not in front of us. He simply picked up the pieces in his quiet, stoic way. And I absorbed one very clear message: Hold it all together, no matter what. From that moment on, I believed it was my job to do just that.

That belief followed me into adulthood. And for a while, it worked. Being the one who could hold it all together made me feel useful, worthy, even safe. But eventually I hit a wall. When I couldn't hold it anymore, everything inside me collapsed. Being responsible for everyone and everything wasn't just a belief; it had become my identity. My worth came from holding things together, so when someone needed help, I felt that it was my job to save them from their pain. Perhaps it was motivated in part by love—I cared and wanted others to be okay—but it was also because I didn't know who I was when I wasn't fixing. I'd built my sense of self around being needed, the one everyone relied on. And when I began to face situations I couldn't fix, it shattered me.

Our culture reinforces the value of over-responsibility. If you're the fixer, the achiever, the dependable one, people bring their problems to you. And they keep coming. Women especially are taught to carry more. Research shows that daughters are expected to take on more chores and responsibility than sons are. We're conditioned to believe that self-care is selfish. We are taught that saying no means we don't care.

Eventually I found alcohol. It seemed to help me survive the crushing pressure.

Learning this concept changed everything. The weight I'd been dragging around for decades finally had a name. Somewhere along the way, I had tied responsibility—specifically over-responsibility—to my worth and how much I cared about other people, how *selfless* I was.

Over-Functioning

Over-functioning is what over-responsibility looks like in action. It happens when you take over someone else's tasks or decisions, when you're constantly picking up after other adults, solving their problems, or doing their work. And it's not just about being "helpful." Over-functioning actually invites others to under-function.

I was frustrated in almost every corporate role I held. No one seemed to pull their weight. I was surrounded by incompetence, and it seemed I was the only one who could make a good decision. I changed teams, countries, geographies, even entire jobs, and the same dynamic followed me. I even had a saying: Everyone is an idiot. (And no, I wasn't always kind during my corporate drinking days.)

I wasn't just frustrated—I was controlling. I was so desperate to hold everything together that I started doing everyone else's job for them. I believed that if I didn't, it would all fall apart.

And then came the hard truth—one that hit like a punch in the gut. I'd created the very problem I was trying to solve. I was the common denominator. I was the over-functioner. I was the drama. In trying to save everything, I had often made things worse. A painful realization, but also the beginning of real change.

I created a dynamic that I took with me, infecting every new team that reported to me. I was *overing*. I was taking responsibility for everything and everyone—so much so that I wouldn't even let anyone else make a decision. I would sweep in with the answers the moment I sensed something was needed. I was holding it all together, for everyone. I thought I was helping. I thought I was keeping everything on track. But there was something I didn't know—over-functioning creates under-functioning. My behavior was creating my team's behavior. It was me, not them.

When we take over too quickly—and solve problems, make decisions, or take on responsibilities that aren't ours—we stunt the growth of those meant to do that work. It's like cracking open a chick's egg too soon. We think we're helping, but we are weakening or even killing what's meant to emerge.

No one wants to be an under-functioner, someone who can't launch out of their parents' household or who can never get ahead financially. But we don't do it on purpose. It is a subconscious reaction to someone like me. As a type A over-functioner, I will rob you of the very lessons you need by doing for you what you can do for yourself. As a result, you become weaker.

Both over-functioning and under-functioning are unintentional. It's just how our brain works. When someone around us is doing the work—even if they're doing it with frustration or resentment—we let them. Our brains are wired to conserve energy. It's subconscious. It just happens.

Dr. John Townsend puts it simply:

When we try to protect people from their own decisions, we make them weak.

When you consistently do for others what they can do for themselves, you weaken them, you exhaust yourself, and you create a dynamic in which nobody wins.

Why do we *over*? Research shows we over because it gives us a false sense of control in an uncertain world. If I do everything, I can be sure it gets done right. I can protect the people I love. I can carry the heavy load so no one else has to struggle.

Emotional fusion drives me to step in, not just out of love, but out of fear—fear that if I'm not holding everything together, it will all fall apart and it won't be okay. But here's the truth: Control is an illusion. Over-functioning doesn't create peace, it creates imbalance. One person does too much, and the other does too little. And that imbalance damages relationships—at work, at home, everywhere.

We can combat this dynamic with awareness. Ask yourself:

- *Where in my life am I being overly responsible—owning things that aren't mine?*

- *Where am I over-functioning—doing things that others should be doing for themselves?*

Notice how it feels to recognize and write your answers. Gently sit with those feelings.

In my experience, just becoming aware of this dynamic is enough to start loosening its grip. When we see the truth clearly, our brains begin to recalibrate. We stop repeating the patterns automatically. While shifting the dynamic can be surprisingly simple, it takes courage. When you start saying no to what isn't yours, a wave of guilt follows, and guilt—because we are communal beings—is incredibly uncomfortable. But guilt, as painful as it is, is far better than resentment.

Guilt Versus Resentment

Guilt isn't a sign you're doing something wrong. It's a sign you're doing something *different*.

Author and researcher Brené Brown draws a powerful distinction between guilt and shame. Brown explains that guilt says, "I did something bad," while shame says, "I am bad." Guilt can motivate positive change because it's tied to behavior. Shame, on the other hand, attacks our sense of self and often leads to silence, hiding, or disconnection. When it comes to relationships, guilt isn't necessarily the enemy. In fact, guilt can actually strengthen your relationships. It's an emotion that helps you reflect, adjust, and stay true to your boundaries.

When you feel guilty, you may . . .

- Think about the impact of your actions.

- Overcompensate with kindness.

- Stay more aligned with your values.

Guilt can strengthen relationships and connection. And even though we don't like the feeling of guilt, a little guilt for saying no is a whole lot better than what's probably been happening in relationships plagued by our overing. When we avoid guilt—by saying yes when we mean no or doing for others what they can do for themselves—another emotion moves in: resentment.

Resentment grows when you override your boundaries. And while it may feel easier in the moment to do what you've always done and avoid guilt, every time you do, more resentment builds. Check in with yourself: How much love or affection can you genuinely feel for someone you've come to resent? Resentment erodes love, making it nearly impossible to stay connected.

Choosing guilt in the short term protects love in the long term. Boundaries may feel uncomfortable at first, but they build a foundation for connection rooted in truth, not resentment.

We over in order to avoid the pain of guilt. We also over when we go beyond helping another person, and when we subconsciously believe our job is to save them.

Helping Versus Saving

Helping is generous. It's grounded in love, not fear. You offer support without strings attached. You do what you can, and then you let go of the outcome. You trust the other person to carry what's theirs. Saving, on the other hand, is rooted in over-responsibility. It comes from fear, not love.

When you're trying to save someone, you're not just offering help; you're trying to protect or control. Saving energy arises when you believe someone else's outcome reflects your worth. You believe it's your job to know what's best for them, to protect them. And if they fail, you feel like you've failed, too.

Author Melody Beattie says it best:

Sometimes the most caring thing you can do is to let people experience the consequences of their choices.

You know you're caught in saving energy when your help feels like it *must* work—and when it doesn't, you're devastated. That's the signal. Because true help empowers; saving suffocates. Learning the difference might be the most loving thing you ever do—for them and for you.

Overing—whether it's over-functioning, over-responsibility, or over-helping—may look like care, but it slowly depletes you. It breeds exhaustion, resentment, and chaos, both in you and in your relationships. When you carry what isn't yours, you strip others of their strength and simultaneously deny yourself of your own. This is because it's a huge energy leak to spend all your time and effort doing things that don't bring you joy—or advance your life.

Letting go isn't easy, but when we let go of something that wasn't really ours to carry, life gets lighter, relationships get healthier, and the pressure that's been simmering, perhaps for years, begins to ease.

The Gift of Differentiation

Differentation is love without controlling, support without rescuing. We stop taking responsibility for things that aren't ours, and in doing so, we put on our oxygen mask first.

When it comes to alcohol, becoming differentiated means I can go to the party and have an iced tea. It means I can connect with people who drink, without judging them or feeling judged. It means I still get invited on the boozy camping trip, even if I decide not to go. Differentiation allows me to show up fully as myself—and let others do the same. It's what lets me leave the party early, guilt-free, curl up with a book, and love every second of it.

Differentiation allows us to belong to ourselves—while still belonging in community.

Differentiation Creates Influence

After I got over my anger about the fact that Brian continued to drink, and accepted that I couldn't change him no matter how much I wanted to, I stopped nagging and pressuring him.

Instead, I prioritized our connection. After all, I was the one who had brought this new thing into our relationship. So I decided it was up to me to reconnect. I would buy him a beer while I got a soda. I stopped at the liquor store for him. I treated him like an adult who had the right to make his own decisions—because he did. And that respect and connection? It changed everything. No matter the situation, when you accept someone exactly as they are, wherever they are in life, you give yourself the best possible chance of influence.

By accepting Brian's drinking, the ideal environment was created for his own transformation. He started to see more clearly what alcohol was costing him. He hated feeling headachy and hungover at 5:45 a.m. when I was getting out of bed with tons of energy. I didn't judge him. I didn't try to fix him. His path wasn't mine to direct. I also stayed anchored in my own journey—while avoiding the trap of seeing my decision as "right" and his as "wrong."

Because he never felt judged, when he was ready to talk about his drinking, he talked to me. About three years after I stopped drinking, Brian took his last drink. Not because I persuaded him. But because I *stopped trying to.*

The Circle of Control

We learn differentiation, in part, by looking honestly at what we can control and what we can't. The best framework I've seen is Stephen Covey's Circle of Control. It is made up of three layers: what you can control, what you can influence, and what you can't control.

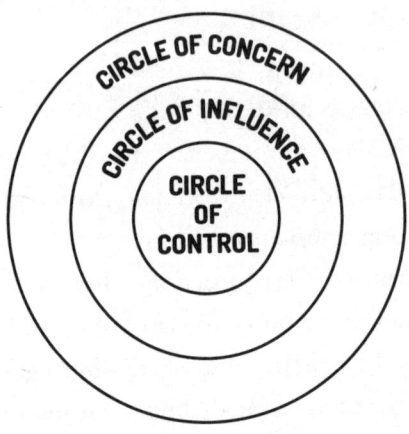

The innermost circle is what we can control—our thoughts, actions, reactions, and choices. That's it. Just us. The next layer is the circle of influence, where our relationships live. We can't control others, but when we are connected, we have a chance of influence through love, consistency, and example. The outermost circle is the circle of concern—all the things we care about but can't control, like the weather, politics, other people, the state of the world, and whether the sun will expand, making life on earth impossible approximately one and a half billion years from now.

Studies show that the more time we spend in the circle of concern, the more anxious and overwhelmed we feel. Peace comes from shifting our energy inward, toward where our true power lives. Power that gets trapped behind subconscious patterns and limiting beliefs. When we focus our attention on what we can actually influence, we begin to create real change.

And when it comes to the people we love most, *the path to influence begins with letting go of control.*

AF Evangelizing

When I took my first alcohol-free trip to Las Vegas, I was thrilled. Energized. Enlightened.

And I did *not* shut up about it.

Not once.

One memory still makes me cringe. I was at breakfast with my friend Kyle. He walked in and slid into the booth across from me, leaving on his dark sunglasses, clearly in the grip of a Vegas hangover. I was annoyingly perky, bright-eyed, and energized about my new alcohol-free lifestyle.

I couldn't help myself. I dove right in and told him alcohol didn't really do anything for him—well, aside from the first twenty minutes. Then I launched into a full-on spiel about how much happier he'd be if he were alcohol free and how much better Vegas was without the hangovers. I meant well, and I believed every word (I was, and remain, a true evangelist of an alcohol-free life), but let's be honest—it was ugly.

Do you think he changed because of that speech? Not a chance.

I was like one of those fire-and-brimstone street preachers I'd pass between Grand Central and Park Avenue on my way to the office—loud, obnoxious, and wholly ineffective.

I had diminished my influence and alienated my friends. In trying to be right, I had cut off connection.

Connection Creates Influence

When we stop trying to change someone, we can shift our energy toward building connection. And connection is where authentic influence begins. People don't change because they're pressured. Or guilted. Or shamed. They don't change because someone gave them a bunch of advice they never asked for. Real, lasting change happens in a space of trust, safety, and love.

Just ask yourself: Who do you, and most adults, actually listen to?

Not the person who judges.

Not the one who lectures or pressures.

Not the one who gives advice that was never asked for.

Studies show that we listen to the people we trust. The ones we feel connected to. The people we respect. The ones who are willing to be honest and vulnerable with us, who speak not from a pedestal, but from the heart.

Somewhere along the way we learned that guilt, shame, pressure, and manipulation were tools for change. They're not. They don't work within us, and they won't work to change the people we love.

Real influence starts with love and without control.

Choose Yourself First

At the heart of differentiation is a revolutionary decision: *to choose yourself first.* It might sound selfish, but it's the opposite. It's oxygen-mask logic—you put on yours first so you can help others. Because the truth is, you can't give what you don't have. You can't pour from an empty cup, and you can't stay connected if you're constantly abandoning yourself.

Differentiation *must* start with being *fully yourself.* Like a healthy cell—intact, whole, and yet part of something greater.

What if we all lived this way? Honoring what is true for us while maintaining deep connections with those around us? This way of living would change everything.

Detangling Self

This journal practice helps you identify what's truly yours—your thoughts, values, beliefs, and feelings—while also supporting you in staying lovingly connected to others. It shows you where you might be tangled up, fused, or emotionally blended with someone else. In just twenty to thirty minutes, this practice can bring clarity, calm, and a deep sense of inner peace.

Step 1: Identify a Situation

Start by identifying an uncomfortable or triggering situation that left you feeling guilty, judged, misunderstood, or responsible for someone else's emotions.

Here are a few examples:

The specific situation causing stress is . . .
. . . my friends brought me a bottle of wine even though they know I no longer drink.

. . . my husband wants to have sex when he is drunk, and I feel pressured.

. . . I'm going on an all-inclusive vacation, and I'm afraid I'll drink.

. . . I went to a party hosted by a supportive friend, but she didn't offer any nonalcoholic options.

These examples relate to living alcohol free, but don't limit this practice to that topic. This works with any situation where you feel emotionally reactive or entangled.

Step 2: Journaling Questions

Relax and answer these questions as honestly as you can. Grab a cup of coffee, open your journal, or record a voice memo—whatever works for you. Take your time. The wisdom is already inside you, waiting to be uncovered. If you give this reflection the time and attention it deserves, your insights can be profound.

1. The specific situation causing issues is . . .
2. My thoughts about this are . . .
3. My feelings about this are . . .
4. My actions about this have been . . .
5. My responsibility in this is . . .
6. This is important to me because . . .
7. I am afraid of . . .
8. I am excited about . . .
9. What I really want is . . .
10. My next steps are . . .

I hope that once you experience how this practice unlocks your internal insight and power, you will use it often. These ten reflections have brought a sense of peace and clarity to my life, in some very difficult moments. It helps me understand where I hold unmet expectations and how to navigate conflict in my marriage. This series of reflections uses the wisdom of ACT (awareness, clarity, and transformation) both to show where we are taking responsibility for things that aren't ours and to understand why. It can help you learn what is truly yours and what never was.

Choosing yourself isn't walking away. It's standing steady. It's saying, "I trust you to carry your load, and I trust myself to carry mine." It's the first brave step toward differentiation—which in turn creates real love, real peace, and real connection.

———

To view the references cited in this chapter, please visit LiveNakedAF.com.

CHAPTER 19

HOW TO GET YOUR POWER BACK

The most common way people give up their power is by thinking they don't have any.
—Alice Walker

My dad always told me I was powerful and that I could do anything I wanted. He taught me that he intentionally chose his life, including his decision to live off the grid for fifty-four years. He made his home in a tiny cabin, eventually raising two kids there—and he did it all as a choice. He taught my brother and me that in our ability to choose for ourselves we hold power, and that in that power we could live life on our own terms, in a way that brought us joy. As a child I found his claims that I could do anything hard to believe. But he was coming from a completely different pyramid of perspective.

My dad was born in the Bronx and raised between New York City and rural Tennessee. He earned a film degree and was interning with a Manhattan media company. Then, at twenty-three years old, he left it all behind and moved to the middle of nowhere, at almost eleven thousand feet in elevation.

His pyramid was built on abundance—he grew up having plenty and never needing to worry. Mine was shaped by wanting what I couldn't have, and the teasing at school whenever a classmate recognized their old clothes on me—clothes they had thrown away and I'd picked up at the thrift store. When my dad told me that I could be anything I wanted, I couldn't imagine being popular, or having people be consistently nice to me, instead of just nice when it worked for them. I couldn't imagine having the right kind of clothes or car or house. I couldn't imagine being able to wash my face with hot water by turning on a faucet rather than starting a fire.

When I was a child, my brain created a false meaning about living in a cabin, so different from my peers. I believed that there was a special place with carpet and the whir of a refrigerator—a magical land that only money could buy—where I would finally feel safe. And if I could become successful, then the lifetime of dread in my stomach would evaporate. That felt impossible because I didn't believe my dad when he told me I could be anything I wanted, even successful.

But he was right, and early in my corporate career—with me working in foreign currency on Wall Street and Brian working on the trading floor of an investment bank—I felt like I had made it. By the time I was thirty-three years old, I had everything I wanted: a wildly successful career, two kids, two dogs, a beautiful home in the mountains of Colorado, and an amazing husband. I had achieved every goal I'd ever had—including the goal I got the most financial motivation from: my lifelong plan to be in a position to take care of my dad when he could no longer haul water and chop wood. There was a room next to our garage that was waiting for him just in case he ever felt he wanted to leave his cabin. I'd done it all.

And none of it, not even the empty room for my dad, made me happy—I didn't want to see him anywhere but at his cabin, looking at the view, living in blissful abundance, deeply fulfilled. Nothing I'd achieved could keep the internal fear away—the gnawing in the pit of my stomach. Achievement was a dead end, and everything I'd ever worked for wasn't going to work to fix the deep sense of dread inside of me. This realization escalated my drinking, and soon I was "enjoying" more than two bottles of wine a night.

I had to learn for myself the principles of intention, choice, and power that my dad taught me his entire life.

He was right: I do have more power than I could have imagined when I was a little girl. While we might not be able to do *anything* we want, I am certain we each have far more power than we realize. So, yes, I can do anything—even become *successful*. But the things I was doing to be successful were not things that brought me true joy. I was fueled by achievement, promotions, and the politics that got me where I wanted to go.

He was also right: True fulfillment is infinitely more valuable than success. I can see, looking at the view he lived within for so long, that true abundance never had anything to do with money. Success and fulfillment are not the same thing. I was outwardly successful and inwardly empty.

But Isn't Power Bad?

One reason we don't fully claim our power is because we've been taught that power corrupts, even viewing power and corruption as synonyms. But as John Steinbeck famously said:

Power does not corrupt. Fear corrupts.

Put simply, power is how fast you can get something done—like how quickly you carry groceries up the stairs. The faster you do the work, the more power you're using. In physics, power is officially defined as *the time-rate of doing work*.

When we gain more power, we get more done. If that work is harmful or corrupt, then yes—power and evil walk hand in hand. But what if the work is good? What if it lifts up rather than tears down? In that case, wouldn't we want *more* power?

I love how Abraham Lincoln put it:

Nearly all men can stand adversity, but if you want to test a man's character, give him power.

Lincoln wasn't saying that power is bad. He was saying that power amplifies—it reveals and magnifies the character that already exists.

Power gives us the energy we need to function in our lives. We need energy to read and apply the tools in this book—energy to get out of bed in the morning. Energy to love and live and build and give and grow. The real question becomes: How do we get more?

Psychotherapist Mira Kirshenbaum has part of the answer. She explains:

Physical energy can supply at most 30 percent of your total energy. The remaining 70 percent of the energy you need must come from your emotional energy.

This means that things like sleep and food supply only 30 percent of our total energy, our total power. If you're dreading the day ahead, you can wake up after a full night's sleep and still feel drained. On the other hand, pull an all-nighter with a new love interest and you'll feel energized and alive first thing in the morning.

That's the power of emotional energy—it shapes how we feel, how we move through the day, and how we experience our lives. I'll illustrate this principle with a story about baseball.

Animating Energy at the Ballpark

My son plays baseball. His coach, a remarkable man, is constantly reminding players to "stay loose and have fun."

Recently, they played a team whose coach had a different approach.

253

Every time one of his kids stepped up to the plate, the coach stood beside them yelling, "Get mad! You want to hit that ball? Then get MAD!!!"

You know who won the game?

The angry team.

Yeah, I know. Bummer. But there is *a lot* of power in anger. If you are hyped up and angry, it seems like you have energy for days. But when you are sad and grieving, even showering can feel impossible. The "get mad" coach was passing along a commonly shared subconscious program about how to get results: Tap into your anger, and ride it to win.

Most of us have been taught that stress, frustration, pushing, and grinding are the most effective ways to get ahead. And we are teaching our children the same lesson. Get mad and win the game.

But at what cost?

After the game, I asked my son how it was and he flopped in the car, saying: "Good. I'm tired, and I wish we would have won, but it was still fun."

Next to us, a car door slammed. One of the players from the winning team sounded really angry and was now was yelling at his mom. Can you blame him? He was told to get mad dozens of times in the last few hours. His mom responded with her own frustration, and soon the little boy in the back was crying. Anger quickly spread through the car. I couldn't help but think about the family members waiting at home. Coach "Get Mad" won the game, but he ruined at least one family's evening.

But we can't blame him too quickly; this is a shared cultural program. If it wasn't, there's no way a grown man could bellow, "Get mad!" at our children dozens of times and it would be acceptable. I'll take that a step further: It is not just acceptable; it's often seen as admirable.

The emotional energy we bring matters. Imagine your mind and body as a delicate futuristic car, designed to run on a unique blend of clean, powerful, renewable energy. I've studied this, and it certainly appears that our minds and bodies are designed to run on clean, pure, sustainable energies—energies like joy, hope, and excitement. But somewhere along the way, many of us started filling our tanks with a harsh, corrosive fuel: anxiety, fear, shame, and relentless striving.

What happens when you put diesel fuel in a gasoline engine? At first the car might sputter along, seemingly functioning, but the wrong fuel causes invisible damage with every mile. Eventually the engine starts to knock and smoke, and finally breaks down. I believe this is a big part of our mental health crisis—we're running our intricate human systems on the wrong energy type. After all, our bodies are made up of fragile materials, and the energy of a bomb will destroy us. But what about the energy when we are excited about something? Or when we fall in love? That's powerful and life-giving, without destruction.

The human system was never designed to sustain certain types of fuel. Sure, in small doses they aren't a big problem, but day after day, year after year, they do significant damage. We are built to run on joy, curiosity, and connection. This is the same pure energy that powers a child's endless play or allows us to get lost in an activity we love or hours of passionate conversation. These renewable energies don't deplete us; they regenerate us. They don't require numbing or escape; they make us feel alive and present.

Just as we can convert a car to run on cleaner, lighter energies, we can retrain our systems to run on better emotional fuel. It's both about removing the toxic stuff and rediscovering the pure, sustainable energies that we've been designed to use. When we do this, we no longer need to escape our lives.

This isn't just feel-good philosophy—it's supported by what we know about human biochemistry. Studies show that these light, positive emotions activate the brain's reward centers, releasing neurotransmitters like serotonin. These neurochemicals not only motivate behavior but also contribute to overall well-being. Science even shows us how lighter animating energies help us live both longer and happier lives. When we experience positive emotions like joy, hope, and connection, our bodies produce natural chemicals that promote healing, reduce inflammation, and enhance mental clarity. Conversely, when we run on stress, fear, and shame, we flood our systems with cortisol and other stress hormones that literally break down our bodies and minds.

But we worry that if we let go of the potent—but toxic—energy sources like anger, fear, and blame, we will lose our edge. These heavy energies in our society can seem like the fuel driving us to succeed. And let's not forget—my son's team lost the game.

But interestingly, the opposite is true. Lighter, cleaner animating energies are significantly more powerful.

I have both a whimsical fable and proven science to illustrate this point.

The Wind and the Sun

The wind believed there was no force stronger than he, not even the sun. To prove it, the wind challenged the sun to a competition to determine who was mightiest.

"Look," said the wind, pointing out a traveler walking along a road. "Whoever can remove his coat is the strongest!"

The sun agreed.

With that, the wind began to blow, almost pushing down the traveler and ripping at his clothing. But the traveler regained his footing, clutched his coat, and resumed walking.

The wind blew harder. The man pulled his jacket tighter and kept going. The harder the wind blew, the tighter the man held his coat. Finally the wind was exhausted and it was the sun's turn. She looked down at the traveler with a gentle smile and began to shine.

The traveler was delighted to feel the sun on his face. And before long, he grew warm, stripping off his coat.

Force was not the mightiest element after all. By simply being her sunniest, most authentic self, and doing what she does best, the sun had won. And so had the traveler, for that matter.

I love this story because it captures the essence of the lighter animating energies. The sun's power is gentle and yet significantly stronger than the wind's. It didn't cost the sun anything to exert this power and she didn't become depleted like the wind did.

Back to the ball field. My son's team lost that game, but he really wants you to know that his team won the entire division that year. At the end of the day, the emotional energies of excitement and fun won it all.

Let's look at the different attributes of heavy versus light animating energy.

Heavy Animating Energy Is ...	Light Animating Energy Is ...
Explosive When we are constantly fueled by things like anger or blame, we snap and find ourselves picking up the pieces.	**Peaceful** Lighter energies bring peace and calm. Instead of boiling over, these energies lighten the load.
Corrosive Heavy emotional energies eat at us from the inside out with stress and self-medication.	**Feel Good** Lighter energies are pleasant and life-giving.
Polluting Heavy energies pollute our bodies and minds, causing both physical and mental health issues.	**Healing** Lighter energies can heal our bodies, our minds, and even our relationships.
Contagious Heavy energies are passed from person to person; if we bring anger, those around us respond with anger.	**Contagious** Lighter energies are also passed from person to person. When you bring hope or excitement, people often respond in kind.

Heavy Animating Energy Is...	Light Animating Energy Is...
Finite We cannot stay stressed or frustrated or angry forever—your body just can't tolerate it—and when we can't tolerate it, we often turn to something like alcohol to try to escape the pain of being fueled by these heavy energies.	**Infinite** When you focus on joy, more joy shows up. Gratitude creates more gratitude. Love creates more love. Laughter, more laughter. You get the point.
Less Powerful Some science shows how these energies have lower vibrational imprints, meaning they have significantly less overall power as fuel sources than lighter animating energies.	**More Powerful** Just like the sun, when we are fueled by joy, excitement, hope, and gratitude, the powerful impact we have in our homes, ourselves, and the entire world cannot be understated.

Heavy Animating Energy Examples	Light Animating Energy Examples
• Anger • Scarcity • Fear • Anxiety • Judgment • Guilt • Resentment • Frustration • Blame • Shame • Regret • Comparison • Proving energy or significance	• Hope • Excitement • Gratitude • Joy • Compassion • Curiosity • Courage • Willingness • Acceptance • Love • Delight • Awe • Peace

Once we recognize that our human system runs largely on the emotions we bring into each day, we can start to examine our emotional fuel. Next, we gently and intentionally shift out of heavy energy into lighter energies. And in this way, little by little, we take back our power.

Imagine a world in which people were powered by love, joy, and excitement. What might we create together?

In the next chapter, I'll share simple ways to help shift your animating energy from heavy to light. We will use the tenets of ACT to transform your animating energy.

———

To view the references cited in this chapter, please visit LiveNakedAF.com.

CHAPTER 20

HOW TO SHIFT YOUR ANIMATING ENERGY

Joy is the most powerful energy we possess—boundless, self-renewing, and immune to circumstance. When we live from joy, we don't burn out—we light up.
—Anonymous

Even before my eldest, Turner, was born, I believed that I was *somehow going to mess him up.* It seemed one wrong move might ruin his future.

To combat this, I read dozens of parenting books, and by the time he arrived, I was completely stressed out. I'd read so much I'd confused myself, trying so hard to get it all *right*, terrified I'd do something *wrong*. I evaluated everything—his sleep, his development, and my reactions—through the exhausting lens of right or wrong. Parenting wasn't joyful. It was a high-stakes pressure cooker. I look back now and wonder how much better off we both would've been if I'd simply let myself be a new mom—flawed, loving, and learning as I went.

Nine years later, at thirty-nine years old, I had my third child. By then, I had more life experience and I'd been AF for years. I was deeply into questioning my thinking, and I became aware that around my children, many of my automatic thoughts were fear-based. When I listened closely, I could hear the old program: *I am probably going to mess them up.*

With clarity, I started to see the cost of that belief by asking myself these clarity-based questions:

- *How does this belief make me feel?*

- *How do I behave in the world, toward myself, and with my kids, when I'm fueled by that feeling?*

I was spending my time with my kids in a state of fear and judgment. I was critical, always on high alert, looking for what I was doing wrong and how I was going to mess them up. As a result, I was stressed and had no energy to play or laugh with them.

Despite seeing the cost, I couldn't let go of this story. I had so much proof for my existing program—it seemed parents mess up their kids all the time.

My internal transformation was finally cemented in during a conversation with my mom. She was sharing regrets—things she thought had messed me up. But I didn't even remember them. And most of the things I *did* remember hurting me? She couldn't recall.

In that moment I saw that the things we think will shape our children often don't. And the things that *do* shape them . . . we may not even notice. I realized that my mom was only one part of the ecosystem of my childhood. Friends, teachers, siblings, even strangers—they all played a role. And through my unique set of experiences, I became who I am, and today, I wouldn't trade that for anything.

I choose to believe that I can't mess up my kids—*without proof.* And even though I can't prove it, I still think it's the right belief to choose and practice because of how it changed my parenting. Living with the idea that I could mess up my kids was stealing my joy. I felt anxious. I overthought everything. I spent more time reading about parenting than I spent actually parenting. I was uptight, controlling, and hard on myself. I missed so many sweet, spontaneous moments because I was obsessing with trying to *do it right*.

On the other hand, when I believed I couldn't mess them up, I was *present*. I took things lightly. I laughed more. I felt gratitude instead of fear. Parenting became filled with joy and connection, not perfectionism and pressure. So yes, even without proof this is what I choose to believe.

A Higher Standard Than True

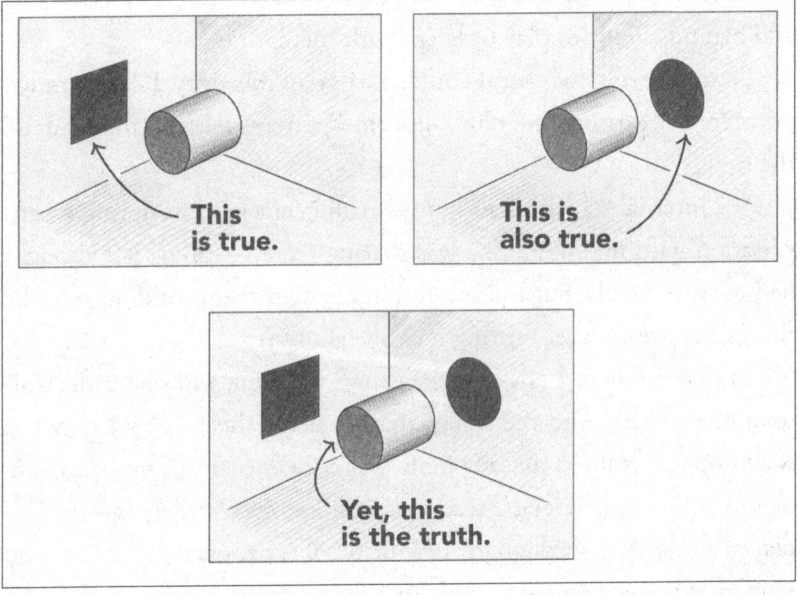

This image can be confusing at first. It visually represents a core idea of this book: What we see as *true* depends on our perspective. Imagine you could see only the shadow of what looks like a square. You'd never guess the shape casting it was actually spherical. Both are technically true, but beyond both, there is a deeper, more universal truth. When we see more, we understand more.

And the truth is, your body runs better when it's fueled with cleaner, healthier power. Fear-based programs fuel our days with fear, anger, hopelessness, and a desire to numb and escape. Joy-based programs fuel our days with gratitude and excitement for the future. When I chose to let go of the fear that I could mess up my kids, I also chose to savor every moment.

And in my life, even if it's not technically *true*, the *truth* of this belief transformed my parenting. I love being a mom more than anything. And my kids feel it every day. Just recently, I dropped off my son Turner at high school and we had this exchange:

Me: *"Bye, Turner! Have a great day—I love you so much."*
Turner: *"Thanks, Mom. I love you so much, too, and me, I love me so much."*

A teenage boy who can say out loud, "I love me so much"—and mean it?

That's not a kid I need to worry about.

ACTing on Animating Energy

Using the principles of ACT, you can change the programming that fuels your days and shift your energy source. Some programs may be deeply buried in the subconscious and require the help of a certified ACTing coach, while others may shift as easily as a single thought or journal entry. In the rest of this chapter, I'll share a few energy shifts that can help right now with changing your fuel source.

The most powerful way to shift your fuel source might be the simplest practice. And yes, you've probably heard of it. Since the American Psychological Association proved we know what to do and we just don't do it, you will probably groan when I tell you what it is. So before I tell you, I want to lower your subconscious resistance by first explaining why it works.

Your Reticular Activating System

Take a look around. Notice what you see, smell, taste, hear, and are touching. In every moment, your senses take in billions of bits of information while your conscious mind can only process mere hundreds. It's staggering.

How does the brain decide which sensory input matters? It uses a predictive encoding system called the reticular activating system (RAS). Think of the RAS as the smallest funnel in the world—its job is to protect you from sensory overload by constantly filtering out information. The RAS is a network of neurons that acts like your brain's gatekeeper. It sorts through sensory data and prioritizes what it believes is important. When you buy a new car, you suddenly start seeing that same model everywhere. That's your RAS at work.

But here's the problem: As we've discussed, our filters are often set incorrectly—we are funneling *out* the right things and, even more concerning, funneling *in* the wrong things.

And most of us have, through habit and conditioning, unintentionally trained our RAS to look for the negative. We filter out the good and hyper-focus on what's missing, broken, or threatening. Complaining feels natural, while gratitude can feel awkward or forced.

Research shows that two people in the exact same situation can have radically different emotional responses, simply because their reticular activating systems are focused on different things.

Your Primary Question

What if our RAS is looking for the wrong things? Asking the wrong question?

Tony Robbins teaches that we all have a primary question—a core, often-unconscious question that our brain is constantly trying to answer. This question shapes our focus, fuels our emotions, and filters our reality.

What do you think you're constantly, unknowingly, automatically asking yourself? Here's what is fascinating about brains: They work a lot like a search engine, and they are super fast. For example, if I ask you, "What room are you in right now?" Boom—your brain has already answered it—automatically. Maybe even before you finished reading the sentence.

What if you are constantly, unconsciously, asking yourself, *What's wrong with me?* Your brain will answer, and the answers will be guesses, spoken with so much authority and repetition that the answers to the toxic question—*What's wrong with me?*—will get written into the mind.

If you shift the question to *What am I grateful for?* your brain automatically answers.

This is why shifting your focus and practicing a new question is so powerful. Because our brains are wired to automatically answer questions, even a small shift can radically change your animating energy. You don't even have to know what question you've been asking (although doing that work is incredibly valuable). You can begin right now by asking a more useful, empowering question. Which brings us to one of the simplest and most transformative sources of animating energy we have: gratitude.

Gratitude

I know, cue another eye roll. But stay with me. Because gratitude isn't just a nice idea; it's a powerful, scientifically proven tool.

Research shows how gratitude . . .

- Increases your energy levels.

- Boosts your ability to forgive yourself and others.

- Strengthens resilience in the face of adversity.

- Improves your coping strategies during tough times.

- Raises your emotional intelligence.

- Reduces your risk of anxiety, loneliness, and depression.

Gratitude works in part because of a neurological concept called predictive encoding. When you consistently prime your brain to focus on favorable outcomes, your RAS begins to look for the good *automatically*. In this way, gratitude can *actually rewire the way you see the world*.

Good is always available. The problem is that, over time, most of us have trained our brains to mark good things as spam. Imagine your brain as if it were an email inbox. Negative messages are flagged as urgent and the good stuff—connection, joy, progress—are sent straight to junk mail. RAS deletes the joy and keeps the fear.

That's why we have to change the rules by changing the program. We can retrain the brain, retrain our RAS, to notice what's working, what's beautiful, and what's worth holding on to.

When we train our brains for gratitude, we increase the number of positive experiences we perceive. This happens because our new RAS enhances our awareness of the good things we otherwise overlook.

A Simple Gratitude Practice

Gratitude is a powerful animating energy. It's contagious, and it creates more of itself. So what's the simplest way to practice gratitude? To ensure it's something you'll actually stick to? Here's how I do it. And by the way, if I could choose only one practice from this book to carry into my alcohol-free life, it would be this one.

Each evening, take just one minute and list five things you're grateful for from the past twenty-four hours. They don't need to be big or dramatic. They can be small, quiet, ordinary things. The breeze on your face, the sound of laughter, a hot cup of tea, or the peaceful stillness after everyone else is asleep.

It's actually not about *what* you list. It's about training the brain, using the RAS encoding system, to start to notice what is right with the world instead of what is wrong with it.

You can do this in your head.

You can write it down.

You can send yourself a voice memo.

This is how you reprogram your subconscious through predictive encoding. When you review your day and intentionally look for what felt good and what brought lightness, joy, or calm, you're creating a powerful shift. You are literally training your RAS to find more of those things. Once that neural pattern is established, your brain begins to *automatically* focus on the things you are grateful for rather than the negative things it habitually looked for.

My favorite way to practice gratitude is around the dinner table. It's a small ritual with a big impact—a new, healthy program to install in my kids, one that trains their minds to intentionally seek out goodness and joy.

Gratitude helps us unhook from the default negativity of our culture. When you reflect on the past twenty-four hours and recall even one positive moment, your brain starts to change. Your overall mood improves. Your default filter begins to prioritize happiness and optimism.

When you begin to intentionally shift the energy you bring to your life, something incredible happens. You don't just change your mood;

you also change your reality. And the more consistently you make these shifts, the more fully you step into your power. In this way we build a life we never need—or want—to escape.

But you might be thinking, *Annie—look around. What is there to be grateful for?* The world feels heavy with fear and tension. Or maybe you're going through a season of life characterized by pain or grief, when gratitude feels out of reach.

I want to offer a different program, one you can hold on to even when gratitude feels impossible. It's the ALP theory: across the arc.

Across the Arc

What if we are collectively headed somewhere where tomorrow is better than today? That across the entire arc of human history, things are getting better. This can be hard to see from our perspective and individual life experiences. But what if, from across a high-enough vantage point, we are moving forward? I like how Martin Luther King Jr. put it:

> *We must accept finite disappointment, but never lose infinite hope.*

I was curious if there was proof for this perspective. Turns out countless studies track human progress over time, and the findings are surprisingly consistent: Life is, on the whole, getting better. Statistically and historically, we're living longer, experiencing less disease, enjoying more freedom, and developing greater self-awareness. We have access to more education, medicine, and personal choice than it seems we ever have had.

That doesn't mean there aren't major problems—there are. But there's also another side to the story, one that often gets overlooked amid the noise of fear, pain, and despair.

Take life expectancy, for example. For most of history, the average person lived just thirty years. By 2023, global life expectancy reached seventy-one.

In 1970, 35 percent of the world's population suffered from malnutrition. By 2015, that number had dropped to just 12 percent. Although 12 percent is still far too high—any hunger in today's world feels like too much—the progress is undeniable.

There have also been powerful cultural shifts. Homosexuality, once criminalized in most countries, has been decriminalized across much of the world. Laws have changed, and with them, public attitudes are beginning to shift toward greater inclusion and human dignity.

Child labor, another long-standing global issue, has also seen dramatic change. In 1950, nearly 30 percent of children under the age of ten in Europe were part of the workforce—and in many regions, the rate was even higher. Today, the global rate of child labor has fallen to around 10 percent.

And then there's literacy. In 1750, only six girls for every ten boys could read and write. Today, gender parity in literacy has been achieved in most of the world. Even in places like Pakistan and Afghanistan, where progress has been slow and hard-won, female literacy continues to rise.

The list goes on: Violent crime is declining. Leisure time has increased. Global IQ scores have continued to rise.

Are you surprised? I was, too.

There's evidence for hope—but what if there wasn't? Even without proof, would choosing hope be the right choice? If your goal is shifting your animating energy and reclaiming your power, then yes—hope is an excellent choice. It's a powerful, action-oriented energy. Hope sparks anticipation, and anticipation has tons of energy. Just think of kids the night before Christmas or a birthday. Anticipation energy is so potent for my children that they usually can't sleep.

Studies confirm that hope isn't just an emotional comfort; it's a psychological and biological necessity. One study found that people with higher levels of hope experienced less depression and anxiety and demonstrated stronger problem-solving skills. Another linked hope with greater life satisfaction, self-esteem, and a deeper sense of joy.

A comprehensive meta-analysis went even further, connecting hope to a wide range of positive outcomes: academic achievement, athletic performance, physical health, emotional regulation, and progress in therapy. One study even found that higher levels of hope correlated with better physical health and less pain among patients living with chronic illness.

So yes, your brain, your biology, and your psychology—every system in your body—seem to benefit from hope. But the most important research is your own experience.

How do you feel when you're hopeful?

Doesn't it feel better to believe that things are improving, even if we can't see it in the day-to-day? Doesn't it feel good to believe that life isn't just something we survive, but something we can shape? To believe that human progress is real—and that we are part of it? And that maybe we are leaving the world better than we found it?

To believe that we are each doing our part both internally and externally so that some of the shame, guilt, and unworthiness we carried as kids won't be passed down in the same way? To hope the subconscious cycles that imprison us break a little more with each generation?

I choose to believe that most people—especially the quiet ones who never make headlines—are doing their best. I choose to believe kindness is important. That small, positive actions ripple outward. That our lives matter.

I choose to believe this even when I can't see the results. Even when all the progress we've made still doesn't feel like enough—I choose to still believe it's all getting better because that belief gives me the power I need to keep turning my mess into my message.

The experiences with alcohol that allowed me to write this book were some of the most monstrous and painful of my life. I lost control of who I was. I didn't understand what was happening. I was in a free fall—frantic, confused, and afraid.

But now I am free. And this work—the work of personal freedom—is a battle I want limitless power to keep fighting.

———

To view the references cited in this chapter, please visit LiveNakedAF.com.

CHAPTER 21

GRACE FIRST:
A NEW ORDER OF OPERATIONS

*I do not at all understand the mystery of grace—only that it
meets us where we are but does not leave us where it found us.*
—Anne Lamott

When we first started dating, I found out Brian loves musical theater,
and his favorite Broadway show was *Les Misérables*. I got us tickets, and
although our hotel had the big, scary union rat staged out front and the
entire staff was on strike (no wonder I got such a good deal), we had a
magical trip. The highlight was the show.

Les Mis is a story of redemption, a story that shows us how grace has
the power to change us in ways that shame and punishment cannot.
Jean Valjean has just been released after nineteen brutal years in prison—
five for stealing a loaf of bread to feed his starving nephew and fourteen
more for trying to escape. He walks out with nothing but a yellow pass-
port branding him a criminal.

With nowhere to go, Valjean is repeatedly turned away until Bishop
Myriel invites him in for food and warmth. In response to this kindness, Valjean wakes in the middle of the night and betrays the bishop,
stealing his silver.

Caught with no way out, Valjean will end up back in prison for the
rest of his life.

But then—grace.

Before Valjean can admit to his crime, the bishop says, "Oh, Valjean. I'm so glad you came back. You forgot the best part." And then the bishop gives Valjean the rest of his silver and the candlesticks.

In this moment the bishop gives Valjean more than candlesticks: He gives the undeserved gift of freedom to a condemned man. Valjean's heart changes; he builds a new life, becoming an honest businessman, a protector, a father figure, and a servant of the people. He was able to change because the bishop saw his humanity when he no longer could. Grace didn't excuse his past. It transformed his future.

This story is fiction, but it's also deeply true. We don't change because we're shamed. We change because we're seen—completely naked and exposed—and accepted anyway.

Grace says: "I see who you really are, even when you've forgotten."

Grace Is Surprisingly Hard

If you ask my daughter, Demi Lovato said it best: "I'm a black belt when I'm beating up on myself." With our current programming, this is true for most of us. We attack ourselves with blame, judgment, condemnation, and punishment—it's wired into our brains. But something inside us also knows this isn't how it's supposed to be. When we hear stories of a baby learning to walk we see the truth of unlimited chances—knowing that with grace, we are always safe to make mistakes, learn from them, turn from them, and try again.

But grace can be hard for our brains to understand. Even when we know—at least on some level—that grace heals, a part of the brain resists, clinging to the familiar weapons of shame and blame. Our society's default mode is punishing ourselves into submission and using our will to overpower ourselves. It is passed down from authority figures and reinforced by the behavior we see all around us.

The reality—that grace works better than shame, blame, or regret—is the most important lesson in this entire book.

Within ALP, we use systems science to better identify the patterns happening within us. In systems science, a leverage point is a point in the system where a small shift creates massive change. It was Archimedes who said, "Give me a lever long enough and I can move the world." That's the power of leverage—and it applies within us, too.

Grace over shame is one of the most powerful leverage points for lasting change.

But rewriting our shame-based programming is surprisingly hard, so I'm bringing in a secret weapon: high school math—and the logic of the order of operations.

How can high school math be my secret weapon? Because the brain sees what's logical and mathematically sound as irrefutable. Math and logic offer a powerful kind of authority; the brain can recognize and understand the truth, step by step, rule by rule. And once something makes logical sense to the conscious mind, we no longer have to rely on someone else's perspective or opinion; we're able to think it through and prove it to ourselves.

Order of Operations

I have two teenage boys at home, and our kitchen table is covered with homework, laptops, and lots of math problems. I am hopeless when it comes to high school math. Thankfully, Brian is always ready to step in. A few weeks ago, the three of them were discussing the order of operations. Learning the concept through the acronym PEMDAS:

P = Parentheses

E = Exponents

M = Multiplication

D = Division

A = Addition

S = Subtraction

When solving an equation, you must first solve inside the parentheses, then the exponents, followed by the multiplication and division, and finally the addition and subtraction. The order in which you perform these steps matters. If you add before you multiply, you'll get the wrong answer. This is true even if every other part of the problem is correct. Your calculations can be flawless, but if you do them in the wrong order, the final answer will be wrong.

In the United States, the addiction rehab industry generates revenues in excess of $5.2 billion annually. Yet from 2012 to 2022, alcohol-related deaths rose by 70 percent.

It's safe to say we're getting the wrong answer.

We aren't getting the wrong answer because of any single approach, group, meeting, tactic, or technique—but because our *order of operations* is wrong. What if we've simply put the wrong thing first? I think that's what happened; we put behavior first, above emotion, compassion, curiosity, and ultimately, healing.

It seems this is our current order of operations: BJNE.

B = Behavior first

J = Judgment

NE = Negative emotion

For six years, BJNE was my order of operations. I wanted to stop drinking; my health and my marriage were in danger. I wasn't the mom I wanted to be, the one my boys deserved. I was closer to giving up than I was willing to admit. My drinking was out of control, and the more I tried to control it, the worse it got.

This is how the BJNE order of operations worked in my journey: I would put my behavior first—prioritizing the goal of not drinking. Inevitably I would mess up and judge myself harshly. At the end, I was drinking more than I ever had. I was consuming more calories in wine than in food. I was emotionally unraveling. I couldn't even meet my own eyes in the mirror because of the hate and distrust I felt. I began to believe I deserved to feel this way—because I couldn't get my *behavior* under control.

When I focused on my behavior, the next step was always judgment, and the shame was overwhelming. It seemed I had no choice but to come down hard on myself—to beat myself up.

When my behavior was wrong, I judged myself as weak, lacking willpower, and fundamentally broken. And inevitably, that judgment pulled me deeper into a cycle of negative emotion—fear, blame, guilt, and crushing shame. This order—BJNE, with behavior first, judgment second, negative emotion third—was destroying me. This is what logically happens when our order of operations is BJNE:

- We judge ourselves based on our behavior as worthy or unworthy.

- An unworthy judgment leads to pain and internal conflict.

- Since our brains have been neurochemically programmed to crave a drink when we are in pain, the more pain we feel, the more cravings we have.

- The more cravings we have, the more we drink.

- The more we drink, the higher the shame.

- The more shame, the more worthless we feel.

- The more worthless we feel, the more likely we are to drink ourselves to death.

Graphically represented, the shame spiral that BJNE causes looks like this:

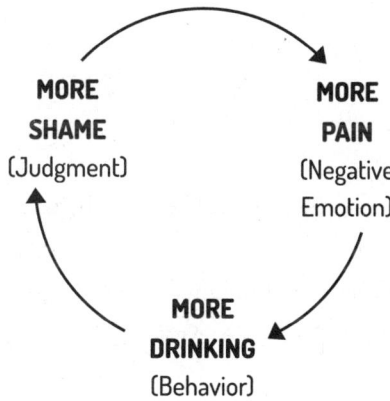

A New Order of Operations

Awareness came at one of my lowest moments, the first time I'd drunk vodka at six in the morning. I had been trying so hard for so long—and exhausting myself in the process. I was terrified and didn't know what else to do. I just knew that vodka first thing in the morning was one of the last checkpoints before the end of the road. The shame, despair, and pain were overwhelming. I felt like a failure, someone who was only worthy when I wasn't drinking. And I *was*. I couldn't do that *one thing*, and I didn't understand why.

You know how my story goes: A different voice—only audible in the stillness and peace that came after my tears—whispered to me. This voice was gentle and soothing. It said, *Stop, baby girl. Just stop. Take a breath. Take a break. It's okay. You are okay. You are more than your behavior.*

With grace first, the first step isn't quitting drinking. It's quitting the fight. Letting myself off the hook. Giving myself *grace*.

But I was terrified of grace, so I resisted. I told the voice I couldn't afford to keep drinking, that I had to fix this now, that it was *dangerous*. I believed that if I stopped trying, I would lose everything—my family, my health, maybe even my life.

But the voice was calm and logical—it even quoted Albert Einstein:

Insanity is doing the same thing over and over again and expecting different results.

All those years of judging myself for my behavior blocked the one thing I needed most to break the cycle: curiosity. I needed to get curious enough to notice something didn't make sense. Curious enough to find out *why*. That question changed everything—and my curiosity became insatiable:

- Why do we follow the worse, even when we know better?

- Why was I able to get other things under control, but drinking remained the exception?

- Why was it that the harder I tried to cut back, the more I found myself drinking?

You cannot be both curious and judgmental at the same time. It doesn't work. Judgment shuts down curiosity—it literally blocks the door, keeping curiosity outside of your experience. And without curiosity, there is no investigation, no understanding, and no answers. And curiosity is *only* available to us on the other side of grace.

Slowly, a new order of operations began to emerge: GCPEB.

G = *Grace first*

C = *Curiosity*

PE = *Positive emotion*

B = *Behavior*

And as I leaned into curiosity, asking better questions and showing myself compassion, a suffocating weight lifted from my chest. I began to experience what we now know is essential for lasting change: positive emotion. Then, surprisingly, almost effortlessly, my behavior began to change. My eyes looked clearer. I could meet my own gaze in the mirror.

Eventually—by putting grace first—I was able to walk away from alcohol completely. Not through pain, shame, rules, or willpower, but with joy. Excitement.

I like what Jeff Buckley says about grace:

Grace is what matters, in anything . . . It keeps you from reaching out for the gun too quickly . . . It keeps you alive.

When we start with grace, we calm the chaos in our minds. We put down the weapons we've wielded against ourselves. We wave the white flag. We loosen the noose around our neck.

We create the space to slow down and think clearly. We begin to ask questions gently—not to criticize, but to understand.

This type of curiosity naturally leads to compassion. We start to notice not just what we've done, but why. And when we can truly see ourselves and our intentions, we begin to soften. Research confirms what we feel in our bones: Self-compassion is one of the most effective tools for lasting behavior change. Because instead of attacking ourselves, we begin to care for ourselves.

That care fuels discovery. We build a new pyramid of perspective—a reorganization of the stories we've been telling ourselves. Old programs lose their grip.

And through compassionate inquiry, we recognize that we've always wanted the best for ourselves. We see how even the drinking, the numbing, the escapes were never about failure or weakness but acts of self-protection, coping, and even survival.

We come to not only believe but *know* that alcohol is not right for us. That it may, in fact, be one of the worst tools for healing. And as recognition and acceptance bloom, something powerful happens—positive emotions arise.

Joy. Relief. Hope.

I wasn't the problem—my order of operations was. Wrong order, wrong answer. Getting the order right opened the door for healing.

I am certain this isn't the *right* answer—because that's not how science works. My hope is just that it bring us one step closer to freeing ourselves, and those we love, from the darkness of addiction.

Grace for the Day

My given name is Annie Grace. *Annie*, interestingly, also means "grace." When I was little, my mom used to call me Gracelet. Eventually—don't ask me how—it evolved into Goosiegracelet, and that nickname stuck. But that's a story for another time. Let's go back to when the nickname was cute, before the goose got involved—just Gracelet.

When you add -*let* to a word, it means "small." So *Gracelet* means "a little bit of grace." I've always loved the idea of a gracelet. Maybe that's all we need, to know we don't have to get it right all at once. A gracelet encourages you to be just a little bit more gentle with yourself today than you were yesterday. And that changes everything. A little more grace, a little more curiosity, and a little less judgment.

And since the only way to lose an infinite game is to stop playing, grace is *the* key to this journey of change. As long as we have a little bit of grace—grace for the day—we can stay in the game.

I witnessed the power of grace firsthand at a Byron Katie event. A heartbroken father stood up, his voice shaking as he spoke about his thirty-year-old son who was drinking heavily—dangerously. The father tried everything—rules, punishments, consequences, even an intervention—but nothing worked. He didn't know what else to try.

At this point, Katie's daughter, Roxann, stood up to share her story. As a teenager, Roxann drank dangerously. She described how I also felt during my darkest days—hopeless, worthless, and broken. Despite facing some of the most terrifying moments a mother can face, Katie never saw her daughter as bad or wrong. And she made sure Roxann knew that.

Katie never confused her daughter's worthiness with her behavior. She loved Roxann without expectation, unconditionally. Katie saw Roxann as whole, perfect, holding Roxann with grace, through everything—even the darkest parts of her addiction.

At this point in the story, Roxann turned to her mother with tears in her eyes and said:

You saw me as good, so I knew I must be good. And that is when I started to get sober. That was how I healed.

We cannot break ourselves whole.

The last thing we need is more blame, more judgment, or more shame.

I know it can feel impossible to extend grace to yourself. I think that's because each of us has a front-row seat to our own darkness and shadow. We see the worst—up close. We ruthlessly compare the *inside of us* to the *outside of everyone else*. Yet learning to forgive ourselves is the most important work we can do—as we put down our internal weapons, we also put down the weapons we use against the world.

It is often said that we teach what we most need to learn. And this is what I am still learning:

We must love ourselves whole.

There is no other way.

Love,
Annie Grace

———

To view the references cited in this chapter, please visit LiveNakedAF.com.

AFFECTIVE LIMINAL PSYCHOLOGY

Affective refers to emotion, and decades of research confirm what many of us already know intuitively: When we feel different, we act different. And yet our traditional change models tend to treat behavior as purely rational—just a matter of logic or willpower. ALP bridges this gap; it doesn't bypass emotion. It works with it—directly and compassionately—as the most powerful force in transformation.

Liminal means "in between." In ALP, the liminal space is the subconscious—the bridge between the unconscious (our automatic programming shaped by biology, chemistry, and past experiences) and the conscious mind (our present awareness and intention).

The subconscious is powerful. It's where we have the ability to create or rewrite the programs that structure our perception and therefore the quality of our lives. It's where we can explore our inner world and update the patterns we didn't choose—programs that influence our thoughts, emotions, and behaviors.

ALP and System Dynamics

Affective Liminal Psychology borrows wisdom and decades of research from systems dynamics. Viewing ourselves as a system offers a powerful, evidence-based way to understand and change human behavior.

Through system dynamics we learn that if we want different outputs, we have to examine our inputs—emotional, mental, and biological. ALP considers system-wide elements like fuel sources (your animating energy), bottlenecks (the areas your system gets stuck in blame or shame), and leverage points (the aspects of your system where a tiny shift can create gigantic change). This also allows ALP practitioners to see the broader internal, familial, and cultural systems that shape our behavior.

We recognize that we are not just a series of random actions or isolated behaviors. We are complex, interconnected beings. Our habits, emotions, biology, environment, and history all work together as part of a larger system—the *Self*.

The Science of the System (of Self)

A systems view allows us to stop asking *What's wrong with me?* and start asking *What's going on within me?* We stop blaming ourselves and begin to investigate.

Many psychological models support a systems view. Internal Family Systems teaches that we are made up of many parts. Jung identified twelve archetypes. Freud described the mind as a balance of id, ego, and superego. These models reflect the same truth: We are a system made in part of many selves. And when we work with the system as a whole, rather than forcing isolated change, we stop fighting against ourselves.

You're not broken. You're complex. And that's not something to fix—it is something to understand.

The Five Principles of ALP

ALP Principle 1: You Have More Power Than You Realize

Our will, conscious choices, and ability to direct our thoughts and behaviors give us tremendous strength. Yet we often feel powerless—

failing to realize how much power we have because of unseen forces that quietly sabotage our freedom. These forces work slowly and subtly, forming the hypnotic rhythm of what Carl Jung called the collective unconscious.

It's not a lack of power within us. It's a lack of understanding about how to break free of the collective unconscious in order to access our power. When we understand the system and work within it, we are able to intentionally shape our lives. We remove the foggy, distorting lenses that block us from seeing truth.

The programs keeping you stuck or holding you back aren't external. They were created, live, and run inside *you*. We give our power away by blaming things outside ourselves—people, circumstances, or external events—for what's happening within. We take our power back when we realize that change is always an inside job—when you recognize the full extent of your strength and trust yourself to use it, shifting the system from the inside out.

ALP Principle 2: Your System Runs on the Fuel of Animating Energy

Scientists now confirm that everything is energy. Even matter, at its smallest and most basic level, is made up of energy. As Einstein put it:

Everything is energy and that is all there is to it.

But not all energy is created equal, especially when it comes to the energy we use to fuel our lives—the *type* of energy matters.

Animating energy fuels our system, and it comes in two types: heavy and light. Heavy animating energies pack a punch, but their power is short-lived. Anger and fear can be strong motivators, but you risk burnout, fatigue, adrenal issues, and even addiction. Light animating energies are healing, endlessly renewable, and far more powerful. No matter what kind of energy you're running on, you can switch. And when you do, the power within you—and your ability to transform the system of self—grows exponentially.

ALP Principle 3: The System Is Biological

We are biological. We are chemical. We are fragile. And we are wired to protect our biology through ancient yet powerful parts of the brain that prioritize survival and safety. The instinctual brain misinterprets modern "threats"—like a missed deadline or criticism—as physically threatening, and reacts accordingly. Unless we become aware of the physical, chemical processes happening inside us, we misjudge our behavior as wrong, weak, or broken.

ALP teaches us to get curious about our system and how it works. We learn how habits and substances can chemically hijack us, and over time even override our ability to choose.

This isn't weakness or a lack of willpower. It's *biology.* When a substance or behavior lights up the brain's reward system, it creates strong neural patterns—pathways that pull us toward short-term relief, at the cost of long-term well-being.

This doesn't excuse our behavior—it explains it. When we recognize the role biology plays, we can start working *with* our system instead of against it. Real change begins when we stop seeing ourselves as broken—and start seeing ourselves as human.

ALP Principle 4: Your System Exists Within Systems

We are shaped by social and structural systems. They influence, guide, and often limit how we live. You live within a family system. That family system exists within a cultural system, a political system, an educational system—and so on.

Many of humanity's challenges are systemic. Embedded in the structures that surround us. Transforming our internal programming requires recognition of the external forces that shape us. Understanding the influence of our family systems, religious systems, school systems, educational systems, and governmental systems removes distorted lenses. It gives us the wisdom and insight needed to reshape even the most deeply rooted—and most harmful—sociocultural systems.

ALP Principle 5: The System Is Intelligently Designed

Science supports what many ancient traditions have long taught: We live in a quantum, energetic universe where everything is connected. We're all made of the same essential matter, part of a greater, unseen— yet deeply felt—whole. Our conscious existence defies easy explanation. Maybe we spontaneously erupted from stardust. Maybe, at the most fundamental level, energy itself is intelligent and conscious. Maybe it's all a simulation. Maybe we were created by God. One way or another, we find ourselves here—part of something bigger and full of mystery. And because we have intelligence, it's reasonable to assume that whatever created us—whether divine or evolutionary—was also intelligent.

And if it turns out that it was accidental and nothing intelligently created human beings and the earth we call home, then I'll borrow the words of my friend Pete Holmes, who said:

> *If your nothing somehow spontaneously erupts into everything,*
> *that's a pretty g*dd*** magical, f***ing nothing.*

I'm not here to convince you that the system is intelligently designed—maybe that's for the next book. The point is this: To truly change ourselves, we need to understand the systems we're part of— both the ones within us and the ones we navigate every day.

The Liminal Process

While ALP includes many different processes, the one most relevant to this book is ALP's primary change model: the Liminal Process.

The Liminal Process follows four steps, each of which should feel familiar—we've explored them, and even internalized them, throughout this book.

Change is a nonlinear process, rarely unfolding in a straight line. It loops, overlaps, and even moves backward. And with the steps of the Liminal Process, you might go out of order, revisit steps, or go through them all at once.

The Liminal Process looks different for everyone because your system, your story, and your healing are as unique as you are.

The Liminal Process Step 1: End Cognitive Dissonance

When conflict erupts, our inner world becomes loud, chaotic, and feels deeply unsafe. With cognitive dissonance—or internal conflict—the danger comes from within. When we are embroiled in cognitive dissonance, we can't explore or reflect—we can only attack and defend. To change the system, we have to call a ceasefire. We must choose grace over judgment. Compassion over criticism. Forcing behavior change without grace is like charging onto the battlefield, launching more attacks, and wondering why peace never comes.

The Constitution was written after the Revolutionary War was won—*four years later*. It wasn't drafted in the chaos of combat but in the stillness that followed. It came from reflection, which was only possible after the guns had gone silent. When an ALP practitioner works with someone who's made countless attempts to stop drinking, the first thing we ask them to do is *Stop trying to stop*. We call it the "Pause."

The Pause is an internal ceasefire. The time for reflection. Without conflict, we can put down force and fear, and pick up understanding and alignment. We stop wasting energy fighting ourselves. That energy becomes available for curiosity, clarity, and compassion. In the Pause, we begin to ask new questions. The questions that heal—and in the Pause we get on the path to wholeness.

Healing comes when we stop making any part of ourselves an enemy.

The Liminal Process Step 2: Rewrite Subconscious Programming

Our perspective isn't reality—it's built on layers of perception unique to each of us. This structure is called the pyramid of perspective.

At the base is our environment—everything from geography to culture. The next layer is made up of our experiences, and both of these shape the final layer: the meanings we create.

The experiences and observations most influenced by ERA (emotion, repetition, and authority) determine what encodes into our subconscious. We have the power to rewrite this code. One of the ways is with ACT, a simple yet profound process. ACT allows us to recognize the internal programs we can't see, and gently rewrite them to reflect a version of the world that's more accurate, grounded, and true.

The result of rewiring the subconscious mind is that we move beyond willpower. When we rewrite the underlying programming, we don't have to fight the urge to drink—we eliminate it. And without desire, there's no temptation.

The Liminal Process Step 3: Play the Infinite Game

An infinite game means infinite chances. Instead of viewing setbacks as signs of defeat, we begin to see them as data points—valuable learning that helps us grow. Failure becomes feedback. Loss becomes opportunity. And the game of change becomes one we can actually win.

The Liminal Process Step 4: Build a Life You Don't Want to Escape

Life hurts—sometimes a lot. When it does, we face a choice: We can numb ourselves, or we can do the inner work to build a life we no longer want to escape.

This doesn't mean striving for constant happiness. It means facing our struggles and embracing all of what life is—with its ups and downs, joys and pains, triumphs and failures. Recognizing, often after the fact, that even the hardest and most regrettable moments move us forward.

ALP allows us to see why lasting change doesn't happen by force, willpower, or shame. It happens by going within—by understanding your internal programming and rewriting the stories that no longer serve you.

In the end, ALP is about coming home to yourself.

ALP gives you the tools to shift your subconscious, end internal battles, and move toward lasting transformation—not by becoming someone else, but by finally becoming fully yourself. You can learn to listen to the most profound source of wisdom you have—*the wisdom found within*.

It's about understanding that you are not broken—you are a system. A system shaped by biology, emotion, experience, culture, and the subconscious patterns that run beneath your awareness.

The work we do to free ourselves from the habits and behaviors that keep us stuck is brave and selfless work. Discovering the hidden patterns in our subconscious—like we've done with alcohol in this book—matters because beliefs behave like viruses. When you break free from them, you stop passing them on.

Viral beliefs spread through repetition, reinforced by the crowd. The more we hear them, the more normal they sound, and the safer they feel. The chains quietly close around us. Whether it's the stigma of not drinking, the pressure to fit in, or the discomfort of saying no, the result is the same: We lose sight of the prison we're trapped in.

We become the captives in Plato's cave—trapped in shadow play, believing it is real.

Your freedom breaks generational curses, changing the lives of your family, friends, children, and future generations. Change starts with you, but it doesn't end there, because when you change your life, you create belief and authority for others to do the same. A small ripple of just one person can create a giant wave. It is the smallest spark of truth that can start the bonfire of personal revolution. It's about more than personal freedom; it's about becoming so free that your very existence becomes a powerful force for good in our world.

I began this book with a quote, and maybe now, at the end, as you read it with a new—improved—pyramid of perspective, it resonates more deeply:

> *The only way to deal with an unfree world is to become so*
> *absolutely free that your very existence is an act of rebellion.*
> —Albert Camus

Welcome to the rebellion.

FILTERS FOR TRUTH

Reality is ultimately unknowable. We are each seeing our own version of what we believe is true through the lenses of our pyramids, rather than objective truth. That's why in order to minimize the impact of my pyramid of perspective, these filters guide what I choose to write and to teach. They ensure that what I present is not only helpful, but also responsible, thoughtful, and closer to truth.

Filter 1: Grace

I believe grace is essential. I ask: Does this information help us extend grace to ourselves and others? Or does it promote judgment, fear, shame, or condemnation? If it doesn't support compassion and compassion-based change, it doesn't pass this test.

Filter 2: Science

I look for evidence across as many disciplines as possible—biology, psychology, neuroscience, and even physics. If something is backed by credible research, I feel good about applying it to my own life and sharing it with you.

Filter 3: Ancient Wisdom

Do these ideas align with wisdom that has been passed down through generations, across continents, cultures, and languages, standing the test of time? If people have carried a teaching forward for thousands of years, and it fits within the paradigm of grace and the logic of science, it passes my personal filters for truth.

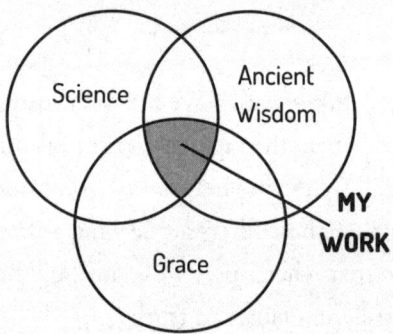

ACT QUESTIONS

These questions allow you to rewrite the subconscious programs in your mind. For more detailed guidance on how to use the ACT process, refer to chapter 7. Make this practice your own and add questions to this list as your ACTing practice deepens.

Start with one or two questions from each section. If you're not experiencing a shift, ask additional questions in order to dig deeper.

Questions for awareness:

- Is this belief true?

- Can you absolutely know it's true?

- How do you know it's true?

- Has this belief always been true?

Questions for clarity:

- How do you feel when you believe this?

- How does this thought make you act?

- How have you acted in the past when believing this?

- What images of the future come to mind when you believe this?

- How do you treat yourself when you believe this?

- How do you treat others when you believe this?

- What has this belief cost you?

- What truths are you unable to see when you believe this?

- How has this belief kept you safe?

- What other benefits have you gotten from believing this?

- When did you decide to believe this?

- What are you afraid might happen if you let go of this belief?

- What would be great about letting go of this belief?

- What positive feelings might you experience if you let this go?

- Without this belief, would you treat yourself better?

- Without this belief, would you be more connected to others?

- Will this always be true?

Questions for transformation:

- What is the opposite of this belief?

- How might the opposite be true?

- What is a slightly different version of this thought that you could believe instead?

- Does this new belief help you feel better?

- Will this new belief help you act in ways that are better for you and for those you love?

ACKNOWLEDGMENTS

To my dad. I feel your guidance as I learn how to be in relationship with you now that your body has again become dust in the wind. And in that wind I am reminded of just how close you still are, even in death. And for the profound and unique life you lived, which continues to inspire and shape me and my writing. Thank you.

To Lucia and the entire team at Avery—wow. You moved mountains and broke the practical laws of publishing to accommodate my many—*almost complete*—rewrites, which created more work for everyone and pushed us well past deadlines. But I hope we all agree—what we've created in these pages is well worth the pain. Thank you.

To my team, coaches, and mentors, and especially the crew at *This Naked Chat*—this book was never mine, it's belonged to all of us since the beginning. I am surrounded by a community that shows up with love, radical authenticity, deep skill, and steady belief in this work. Thank you.

To Russell and Eileen—never have two people been a better sounding board for all my crazy. You spoke life into this book, both in faith and in friendship. Thank you.

To all my friends. You are a vital part of my healing, medicine for my continued mental health and wholeness. I hope I am the same for you. You are also the most hilarious group of human beings I've ever met. Even, and perhaps especially, when we are more mild than wild. Here's to many more completely alcohol-free living room conversations—where the laughter reaches such heights that a few of us ladies have to sneak off and change our underwear. Thank you.

To Ladies. Every day. Every. Single. Freaking. Day. In the biggest things and the most mundane. I love us. GGM forever. And for being the first to call me out on the original version of the sex chapter, encouraging me to tone it down; you were right—the world is not yet ready for *below the belt*. Thank you.

To Turner, who gives the best pep talks when I've been at the dining room table for ten hours, surrounded by empty cacao mugs and sparkling-water cans, convinced I'll never get it right. When I'm worn down, you meet me there and help me keep going. You've had deep wisdom and knowing from day one, and I am so thankful when you share them with me. You live in kindness and radical acceptance of everyone around you, showing me how much better I can be; in fact, I believe you are as kind and accepting as anyone I've ever known. I bet you learned that from my dad, your grandpa Jordan. Thank you.

To Trace, who shares my drive for excellence and precision, and who, in the eleventh hour, took on the exhausting task of transferring my endless red-pen edits into the manuscript. You live with intense passion and relentless drive—achieving seemingly impossible results. And even as a teenager, you're not afraid to wrap your arms around me and just hold me—wordlessly—as I've cried endless tears over the loss of my dad. I delight in seeing how much of him lives in you, and how through you, his namesake, he remains deeply present in our lives. Thank you.

To Daelyn. I named you Daelyn so I could call you Dae—a daily reminder to rejoice in *this* day. The only place joy can be found. And you embody joy, moving through the world with wonder, energy, and a wholehearted yes to life. You've been both surprisingly patient—and at times hilariously impatient—through the countless nights of sharing bedtime with me and my computer. We listened to audiobooks instead of reading together and that is more sacrifice than I wanted you to have to make for this book. Still, I hope someday you'll remember falling asleep to the glow of my screen, watching me chase a dream. I remember the first time you saw your reflection in the mirror—you reached out, giggling, completely captivated by the little creature staring back. In that moment I realized that delighting in ourselves is natural— maybe the truest part of who we are, even if we forget. And what I'm most grateful for is this: As I learn to delight in myself again, you are my best teacher. Thank you.

To Brian. Your opinion is the one I seek first and trust most—even when I pretend otherwise. Thank you. You're still my favorite person. We won.

INDEX

Note: Italicized page numbers indicate material in photographs or illustrations.

A

abandonment fears, 168
Acamprosate, 208
acceptance, 39, 182
adaptogens, 207
addiction
  addictive behaviors, 8
  and alcohol use disorder, 79–81
  brain physiology of, 76
  chemical addiction/dependency,
    145–48, 204, 210
  and chemical impact of alcohol, 16–17
  diagnostic criteria, 76, 79
  experiential element of, 53
  and habits, 63
  impact of addictive substances, 63–64
  and marketing of alcohol, 112
  and profitability of alcohol, 114–15
  psilocybin as treatment for, 206
  and "responsible drinking," 111
  true chemical addiction, 145–48
Addictive Behaviors Research Center, 142
adrenaline, 61
advertising, 117. See also marketing of
  alcohol
Affective Liminal Psychology (ALP)
  and ACT process, 89
  and Awake to Alive framework, 19
  five principles of, 284–87
  focus on biology, 229–30

and the liminal process, 287–91
and principle of firsts, 102
and scope of text, xvi, 11
and systems science, 274, 283–84
"alcoholic" label, 74–81
Alcoholics Anonymous (AA), x, 38, 73,
  75, 77–78, 152, 193–94
alcohol poisoning, 107
alcohol use disorder, 79–80. See also
  addiction
alive phase. See Awake to Alive framework
Allegory of the Cave, 12–13, 290
alpha brain waves, 227
alternatives to alcohol, 121–22
American Psychological Association
  (APA), 8, 31, 32, 202, 263
amygdala, 176
ancient wisdom, 294
anger, 253–56
animal experimentation, 147, 151, 186
animating energies, 253–56, 257–58,
  260–71, 285–86
anthropological view of alcohol use,
  132–38
anxiety
  and alcohol-free firsts, 98
  and alcohol's impact on sex, 167–68
  and animating energies, 255
  and approaches to going alcohol free, 7
  author's struggle with, ix

anxiety (*cont.*)
  and benefits of music, 228, 229
  and benefits of time in nature, 227
  and the Circle of Control, 245
  and differentiation vs. fusion, 232–235
  and meditation, 219, 221–22
  and parenting pressures, 261
  and personal costs of alcohol, 134
appreciation, 161
archetypes, 284
Archimedes, 274
Aristotle, 82
artificial intelligence (AI), 136–37
associations, 62
Atomic Habits (Clear), 220
attention, 181, 214. *See also* mindfulness
attention deficit hyperactivity disorder
  (ADHD), 17
audience for book, xv
authentic social connection, 152–53
authority, 66–69, 213
autonomic nervous system, 225
awake phase. *See* Awake to Alive
  framework
Awake to Alive framework, 19–29, 41–43
awareness, clarity, and transformation
  (ACT) process
  and Affective Liminal Psychology, 289
  and "alcoholic" label, 78–79
  and animating energies, 263–64
  applied to alcohol, 89–95
  and author's alcohol experiment, 69–70
  awareness element of, 19–20, 83–84
  and barriers to social connection, 163
  and benefits of journaling, 249
  clarity element of, 84–85
  compassion experiment, 190–91
  and deference to authority, 68
  and expectations, 157–61
  finding joy, 181
  and personal choice, 118
  and principle of firsts, 105
  questions used in, 295–97
  scope of applications, 81
  and switches, 211–12
  transformation element of, 85–89

  and tyranny of "normal," 73
  and urge surfing, 143

B

Barrett, Lisa Feldman, 60
basal ganglia, 140
Beattie, Melody, 242
beer, 115
behavioral change, 273–77
behaviorism, 112
belief system
  and ladder thinking, 85–89, *87*
  and parents' influence, 58
  and pyramid of perspective, 51–53
  and repetition, 64
  See also cultural beliefs and pressures
Bell, Rob, 130, 202
Ben-Shahar, Tal, 156
bias, 48, 63
The Big Book (Alcoholics Anonymous), 73
biological effects of alcohol, 133
biological systems, 286
blackouts, 1–2, 108, 168
blind-men parable, 55–56
blood pressure, 134
body image, 167, 168
boredom, 210
boundaries, 120–21, 124–25
Bowen, Murray, 235
brain physiology and function
  and addictive nature of alcohol, 76
  and alcohol-free firsts, 99
  alcohol's effect on brain, xiv
  and Awake to Alive framework, 42–43
  and chemical impact of alcohol, 16–17
  and cravings, 138
  default mode, 44–57
  and emotion, 59
  instinctual brain, 47–49, 78, 84, 146
  and limits of brain power, 57
  and neurochemistry of alcohol cravings,
    139–40
  and personal costs of alcohol, 136
  and repetition, 64–66
  and reticular activating system, 264,
    266–67

and subconscious programming, 14–15
and willpower, 32
See also neurochemistry; subconscious
programming; *specific brain areas*
breathing and breathwork, 219, 220–21,
224–26
Brooks, Garth, 30
Brown, Brené, 241
Buckley, Jeff, 279
Buddhism, 174, 201
Burch, Noel, 19

C
Camus, Albert, ix, 291
cancer, 110, 116–17, 118, 136
cannabidiol, 208
cannabis, 209–10
Carnegie, Dale, 153
Carrey, Jim, 215, 229
Castillo, Brooke, 68, 87, 159
CBD, 208, 210
Centers for Disease Control and
Prevention (CDC), 76, 145
central nervous system, 165. *See also* brain
physiology and function
chemical addiction/dependency, 145–48,
204, 210
chemical effects of alcohol, 16–17, 18, 26.
See also neurochemistry
children
childhood trauma, 58–59
and marketing of alcohol, 116
and societal costs of alcohol use, 134
See also parents and parenting
choice, 41, 117–20
Circle of Control, *244*, 244–45
clarity. *See* awareness, clarity, and
transformation (ACT) process
Clear, James, 220
coffee, 121, 204, 207, 212, 215, 248
cognitive dissonance, 30, 219, 288
collective unconscious, 52, 205–6, 285.
See also cultural beliefs and pressures;
social settings and pressures
communication, 159, 160, 171
compassion, 189, 190–91, 210

conditioning, 42–43. *See also* cultural
beliefs and pressures
confidence, 150–51
conflict avoidance, 128
conformity pressure, 109, 125–27. *See also*
social settings and pressures
consciousness and conscious effort
and Awake to Alive framework,
20–21
beliefs about substance, society, and
self, 15–16
and emotion-based change, 27–28
and expectations, 158
and limits of brain power, 57
and neurochemistry of alcohol
cravings, 140
and urge surfing, 144
and willpower, 21, 28, 31–43,
141–42, 197
conversational skills, 150–51
coping strategies, 8
cortisol, 5, 61, 256
Covey, Stephen, 244
COVID-19 pandemic, 185–86
cravings
and addiction criteria, 200
anthropological view of, 132–38
and chemical addiction, 145–48
and cultural pressure, 131–32
described, 137–38
and habit of living alcohol free, 18–19
and limits of willpower, 141–42
neurochemistry of, 138–41
overcoming, 131–48
and saying no, 129, 130
and urge surfing, 142–45
criminalization of drugs, 205
cultural beliefs and pressures
and "alcoholic" label, 78–79
and alcohol's association with events,
105–6
and animating energies, 254–55, 266
and authority figures, 66–67
and cravings, 131–32
and dopamine, 113–15
and individual choice, 117–20

cravings (*cont.*)
  and marketing of alcohol, 112–13, 116–19
  and over-responsibility, 237–38
  and parenting, 107–9
  and pyramid of perspective, 51–52
  and "responsible drinking," 108–12
  and saying no to alcohol, 120, 125–28
  See also social settings and pressures
curiosity, 99, 103, 144, 153, 278–79

D
dance, 227–29
data points, 185–87, 193–95, 289
Dax, 45
"Dear Alcohol" (Dax), 45
death, 201, 213
deception, 123–24
decision fatigue, 196, 238
decision-making center/process, 197
decriminalization of drugs, 151–52, 207
default mode of the brain, 44–57
dehydration, 197
dementia, 134
dendrites, 42
denial, 77, 198
dependency, 134, 206
depressant effect of alcohol, 67, 165
depression, 219, 221–22, 228, 229
detoxification, 147
The Diagnostic and Statistical Manual of Mental Disorders, 199
DiClemente, Anthony, 225–26
differentiation, 231–36, *233*, 243–45, 247
divorce, 134
domestic violence, 134
dopamine, 62, 63, 113–15, 138–39, 207
drugs, 79–81
"duck mode," 129
dynorphin, 177

E
ego, 284
Einstein, Albert, 278, 285
Emerson, Ralph Waldo, 149

emotion, repetition, and authority (ERA) system, 57, 59, 67–68, 69, 70, 89, 289
emotions
  and Awake to Alive framework, 23–25
  and chemical impact of addictive substances, 17, 63
  construction of, 60–61
  emotional energy, 253
  emotional well-being, 174
  emotion-based change, 25–29
  feelings contrasted with, 60–61
  and ladder thinking, 88
  and learning process, 58
  and meaning, 61–64
  and memory formation, 59
  paradox of, 60, 63
  and repetition, 64–66
  and transformation, 69–70
empathy, 188. *See also* compassion
endorphins, 62, 205
energy conservation, 47, 48–49, 84
environment, 51–53, 140
evangelizing, 245–46
evolution, 67, 286
exercise, 216, 221
expectations, 156–60, 161–62
experience, 51, 53, 54–57, 63, 67
explicit bias, 48–49

F
familiarity, 65–66
fear, 59, 78, 141, 255
feedback, 192, 225
feelings, 60–61. *See also* emotions
fentanyl, 204
fight-or-flight response, 47–48, 61
filtering, 50–51, 56, 57, 264–65, 267, 293–94
financial burden of alcohol use, 135
finite games, 191
firsts (alcohol-free), 97–106
focus, 51, 172, 219, 265. *See also* attention; mindfulness
Fogg, BJ, 23–24
forecasting tactic, 98

foreplay, 171
Frankl, Viktor, E., 148
Fredrickson, Barbara, 178
"Funeral for Your Partner" exercise,
    161–62
fusion, *233*, 233–35, 240

G
Gaffigan, Jim, 231
gamma-aminobutyric acid (GABA),
    139, 206
gateway drugs, 208
Gilbert, Roberta M., 234
Goldhamer, Alan, 47
Gottfried, Sara, 113
grace, 272–82, 293
gratitude, 162, 265–68
Gray, Dave, 56
guilt, 141, 240–42
gummies, 207, 210, 212

H
habits
    and Awake to Alive framework, 42–43
    and chemical impact of addictive
        substances, 63
    and differentiation vs. fusion, 236
    and dopamine, 113–15
    and emotional reprogramming,
        23–25
    living alcohol free, 18–22
    and meditation, 220
    and neurochemistry of alcohol
        cravings, 140
    and paradox of willpower, 41–42
    and repetition, 64
    and subconscious programming, 14–15
hangovers, 1–2, 100, 244, 245
Hạnh, Thích Nhất, 183
happiness
    and effects of alcohol, 176–78
    finding joy, 181–83
    Happiness Equation, 156–57
    measuring, 178–80
    misconceptions about, 173–75
    and pain suppression, 175–76

Hari, Johann, 107
Harris, Russ, 173
Hay, Louise, 189
Hebb's law, 65, 97, 140
helping vs. saving, 242–43
herbal remedies, 207, 208
Holland, Tom, 131
Holmes, Pete, 287
hope, 256, 269–70
hormones, 165
How Emotions Are Made (Barrett), 60

I
id, 284
identity, 74–81
imagination, 182–83
implicit bias, 48–49
impulsiveness, 32
The Infinite Game (Sinek), 191–92
infinite games, 191–92, 281, 289–91
inflammation, 227, 256
influence
    and differentiation vs. fusion, 231–36,
        243–45
    and evangelizing, 245–46
    and guilt vs. resentment, 240–42
    helping vs. saving, 242–43
    and overing, 237–40
    and self-care, 247–49
    and social connection, 246
instinctual brain, 47–49, 78,
    84, 146
intelligent design, 287
intentionality, 31, 33–36, 38, 210,
    225, 252
internal conflict
    and Awake to Alive framework,
        42–43
    and emotion-based change,
        26, 28
    length of battle, 40–41
    and pain of conflict, 31–38
    and paradox of willpower, 41–42
    and subconscious beliefs, 38–39
    and subconscious programming,
        17–18

Internal Family Systems, 39, 68, 284
International Agency for Research on
    Cancer (IARC), 134
International Journal of
    Environmental Research and
    Public Health, 11

J

journaling, 248
joy and joyfulness
    alcohol's impact on, 176–78
    and animating energies, 256, 260–62,
        266–68, 270
    and benefits of alcohol
        free life, xi
    and benefits of exercise, 222
    finding, 181–83
    and social connection, 153
    and switches, 201–14
judgment, 127, 275–77, *277*
Jung, Carl, 12, 52, 284, 285

K

Katie, Byron, 68, 156, 281
kava, 208
Kerr, Michael E., 236
kindness, 270
King, Martin Luther, Jr., 268
Kirshenbaum, Mira, 253

L

ladder thinking, 85–89, *87*
Lamott, Anne, 272
Leaf, Caroline, 64, 85
learned helplessness, 192
learning process, 187–89, *188*
Les Misérables, 272–73
The Let Them Theory (Robbins), 130
libido, 165
life expectancy, 268–69
limbic system, 141
liminality, 281, 287–91. *See also* Affective
    Liminal Psychology (ALP)
Lincoln, Abraham, 253
Lisle, Douglas, 47
listening skills, 154

liver damage, 134, 208
long-term switches, 209–10
Lovato, Demi, 273

M

Manson, Mark, 175
mantras, 86. *See also* meditation
Marcus Aurelius, Emperor of
    Rome, 50
marketing of alcohol, 111–13, 116–17
marriage dynamics
    and author's history with alcohol, x
    and expectations, 158, 159, 161–62
    and need to be right, 155–56
    and personal costs of alcohol, 134
Martino, Stacey, 160, 237
McGonigal, Kelly, 217, 221
meaning, 54–57, 61–62, 63–64
medical detoxification, 147
meditation, 216, 217–21
memory, 59, 140
Meninger, Karl, 154
microcommitments, 223
mimicry, 66
mindfulness, 143, 171, 181. *See also*
    attention
minibars, 44–45
mirror neurons, 66
Moderate Alcohol and Cardiovascular
    Health (MACH) trial, 117
moderation, 193–200
motivation, 33–34, 47
music, 227–29

N

Naltrexone, 208
National Institute on Alcohol Abuse and
    Alcoholism, 29
National Institutes of Health (NIH), 117
National Library of Medicine, 32
National Survey on Drug Use and Health
    (NSDUH), 146
nature, 226–27
negativity, 266
neural pathways, 42
neural toxicity, 64

neurochemistry
  alcohol's impact on joy, 176–78
  and animating energies, 255
  of cravings, 138–41
  neurogenesis, 59
  neurotoxicity, 110, 118
  neurotransmitters, 63, 113, 139, 206
  and switches, 204–7, 211–13
  See also brain physiology and function
nicotine, 142–43
No Bad Parts (Schwartz), 39
nonalcoholic beverages, 122, 208
nootropics, 207
Notion AI, 137
nucleus accumbens, 139, 176
numbing effect of alcohol
  and Affective Liminal Psychology, 289
  and alcohol's impact on sex, 166–67,
    169, 171
  and animating energies, 255, 263
  and author's history with alcohol, 45
  and decision to live alcohol free, xii
  and emotional well-being, 174
  and the instinctual brain, 48
  and internal conflict, 34
  and neurochemistry of switches, 207
  and pain suppression, 175–76
  and personal costs of alcohol,
    135–36
  and potential for relapses, 38
  and subconscious programming, 16–17

O

objective reality, 50–57
observation, 61
opiates, 204
order of operations, 274–77
Osbourne, Kelly, 184–86
outdoor time, 226–27
overing, 237–40, 242
Ovid, 1, 8

P

pain
  avoidance and suppression of, 47–48,
    175–76

childhood trauma, 58–59
  and coping with death, 201
  and instinctual brain, 84
  and order of operations for change,
    276, *277*
  and pyramid of perspective, 53
parents and parenting, 58, 66, 107–8,
    109, 201, 213, 260–62
Pathak, Jay, 161
Paul (biblical), 9
The Pause, 288
perception, 12–13, 49–57,
    262, 266
performance anxiety, 167, 168
personal power, 250–59, 284–85
perspective, 44–46, 49–57
pharmaceuticals, 204, 208
physical effects of alcohol, xii–xiii, 26. *See
    also* neurochemistry
physical violence, 134
physiological effects of alcohol, 130, 133
Plato, 12–13, 58, 290
pleasure-seeking, 47, 84, 176–77
Portugal, 151
The Power of Now (Tolle), 218
predictive encoding, 266
prefrontal cortex (PFC), 99, 139–41, 197,
    218–19, 222
premature death risk, 136
prescription painkillers, 204
presentness, 262. *See also* mindfulness
pride in alcohol-free firsts, 102
privacy, 71–72
problem-solving, 239
profitability of alcohol, 112–15, 118–19
psilocybin, 206
psychology
  and ACT process, 89
  and barriers to moderation, 197
  and internal conflict, 39
  and Internal Family Systems, 284
  and marketing of alcohol, 112
  psychological effects of alcohol, 133
  and saying no to alcohol, 120
  See also Affective Liminal
    Psychology (ALP)

pyramid of perspective, 49–57,
    164–65, 280

R

Rat Park experiments, 151, 186
Rayleigh scattering, 49
reasons for drinking, 4–5
recordkeeping, 224
Red Table Talk, 184–85
rehabilitation industry, 9, 275–76
rejection, 168, 235
relapses
    and "alcoholic" label, 78
    as data points, 185–87, 193–95
    and infinite game perspective, 191–92
    and learning process, 187–89
    and neurochemistry of repetition, 64–65
    rate of, 9
    science on, 189–91, 195–200
relationships
    and addiction criteria, 200
    alcohol's impact on social skills, 150–51
    and authentic connection, 152–53
    and healing addiction, 151–52
    and personal costs of alcohol, 134
    roadblocks to connection, 155–63
    social value of curiosity, 153–55
    value of appreciation, 161
relaxation, 67, 69, 164
repetition, 64–66, 95–96, 219, 290
resentment, 240–42
"responsible drinking," 108–12
reticular activating system (RAS), 264,
    266–67
Revolutionary War, 288
Ricard, Matthieu, 174
Robbins, Mel, 130
Robbins, Tony, 264
Rogers, Carl, 184
Roosevelt, Eleanor, 97
rules for alcohol use, 199. *See also*
    moderation

S

Saturday Night Live, 205
saying no to drinks, 120–30, 148

Scazzero, Geri, 157
Scazzero, Pete, 157
Schedule 1 drugs, 205
Schumann resonance, 227
Schwartz, Richard, 39, 68
Schweitzer, Albert, 231
sedative effect of alcohol, 67
seeds
    author's, 214
    breathwork, 224–26
    meditation, 217–21
    movement and exercise, 221–24
    music and dance, 227–29
    outdoor time, 226–27
    switches contrasted with, 202–3
    value of, 215–17, 229–30
self, beliefs about, 16, 46, 63
self-awareness, 213
self-care, 247–49
self-compassion/self-love, 189, 280
Seneca, 8
serotonin, 226–27
sex, x, 5, 102, 164–72, 204, 248
shame
    and "alcoholic" label, 78
    and animating energies, 255
    and author's history with alcohol, 128
    and challenges of grace, 273
    and internal conflict, 33, 35, 37, 40–41
    and neurochemistry of alcohol
        cravings, 141
    and pyramid of perspective, 54
    and relapses as data points, 188
    sexual, 166
Sharma, Robin, 95
Shaw, George Bernard, 71
sleep, 227
Smith, Jada Pinkett, 184–85
smoking, 77, 114–15, 142–43
social connection, 246, 256
social media, 73, 112, 114, 204, 215
social settings and pressures
    and alcohol-free firsts, 97–100, 102
    and deference to authority, 67
    and pressures to drink, xi
    and relapses as data points, 186

and "responsible drinking," 108
and social skills, 149–51
and tyranny of "normal," 72
See also cultural beliefs and pressures
societal costs of alcohol use, 134
society, beliefs about, 16, 46, 63
sports, 222
Steinbeck, John, 252
stimulants, 204
Stoicism, 50, 105
stress
  and ACT process, 85, 93–95
  and animating energies, 254, 256,
    257–58, 260–61
  and approaches to going alcohol free, 7
  and attitudes toward coping
    mechanisms, 205
  and benefits of journaling, 247
  and benefits of outdoor time, 227
  and brain's default mode, 46
  and differentiation vs. fusion, 234–35
  and effects of conflict, 31–32
  emotional well-being, 174
  and exercise, 221
  and feelings vs. emotions, 61
  and habit of living alcohol-free, 20
  and the instinctual brain, 48
  and internal conflict, 36
  and ladder thinking, 88
  and meaning-feeling spiral, 62–63
  and neurochemistry of alcohol cravings,
    139, 141
  and neurochemistry of switches,
    207, 208
  and physical effects of alcohol, 5
  and potential for relapses, 38
  and saying no to alcohol, 120
  stress hormones, 256
subconscious programming
  and Affective Liminal Psychology,
    289, 290
  and alcohol's association with
    happiness, 176
  and animating energies, 263,
    267, 270
  and Awake to Alive framework, 22–23

and barriers to social connection,
  162, 163
and biases, 48–49
and brain's default mode, 45–46, 57
and chemical effects of alcohol, 16–17
described, 14–15
and effects of pain, 58–59
and emotion, 23–29, 174
and expectations, 159
and habit formation, 42
and habit of alcohol-free living,
  18–22
and instinctual brain, 48–49
and internal conflict, 17–18,
  38–39, 42
and marketing of alcohol, 112
and overcoming cravings, 132
and Plato's cave allegory, 12–13
and pyramid of perspective, 49–50,
  52–55, 57
and repetition, 65
and social connection, 154, 155
and social pressure to drink, 125–27
substance, society, self framework,
  15–16
and tyranny of "normal," 73
substances, beliefs about, 15–16,
  45–46, 63
sugar, 202, 204, 207, 212, 215
suicide risk, 134
superego, 284
survival instinct, 47, 67
switches
  and ACT process, 211–12
  author's, 212–14
  and collective unconscious, 205–6
  and joyfulness, 201–14
  neurochemistry of, 204–5, 206–7
  problems associated with, 210–11
  seeds contrasted with, 202–3, 215
  short-term, 207–9
systems science, 274, 281–84, 286–87

T
Talmud, 45
temptation bundling, 224

THC gummies, 210
This Naked Mind (Grace), xv, xvii, 6–7, 77, 209
This Naked Mind Institute, 102, 116, 169–7, 186, 209, 223
tobacco industry, 114–15
Tolle, Eckhart, 217
touch, sense of, 169
Townsend, John, 239
transformation. *See* awareness, clarity, and transformation (ACT) process
trauma, 17, 58, 166–67
Twelve Steps, 193
Twelve Traditions, 193

U
unconditional love, 281
University of New Hampshire, xii
University of North Carolina, 59
urge surfing, 142–45
US Constitution, 288

V
vacations, 100–102, 248
valerian root, 208
ventral tegmental area (VTA), 176
video games, 210
Vietnam War, 151
violence associated with alcohol, 108, 134
viral beliefs, 290
Voltaire, 131

W
Walker, Alice, 250
Warren, Lee, xiv
weddings, 97–100
well-being, 134
willpower, 21, 28, 31–43, 141–42, 197
withdrawal, 196, 199
The Work (process of self-inquiry), 68
World Health Organization (WHO), 118, 136
worldview, 51–53. *See also* cultural beliefs and pressures